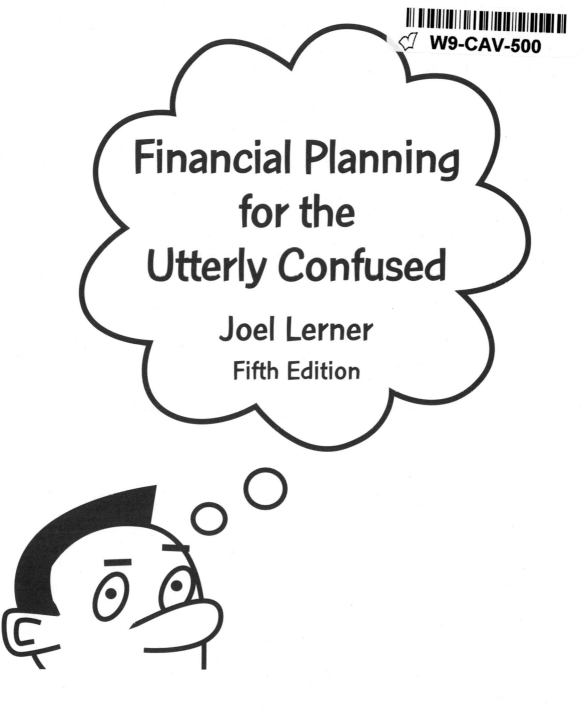

# Financial Planning
# for the
# Utterly Confused

## Joel Lerner

### Fifth Edition

**McGraw-Hill**

New York   San Francisco   Washington, D.C.   Auckland   Bogotá
Caracas   Lisbon   London   Madrid   Mexico City   Milan
Montreal   New Delhi   San Juan   Singapore
Sydney   Tokyo   Toronto

**Library of Congress Cataloging-in-Publication Data**

Lerner, Joel J.
    Financial planning for the utterly confused / Joel Lerner. — 5th ed.
        p.    cm.
    ISBN 0-07-038164-X (alk. paper)
    1. Finance, Personal—United States.    2. Investments—United States.
I. Title.
HG179.L45    1998
332.024—dc21                                                97-43777
                                                              CIP

*McGraw-Hill*

*A Division of The McGraw·Hill Companies*

    2   3   4   5   6   7   8   9   0      DOC/DOC      9   0   2   1   0   9   8

ISBN 0-07-038164-X

The sponsoring editor for this book was Mary Glenn, the editing supervisor was
Wayne Coleson, and the production supervisor was Claire Stanley. It was set in
Times Ten by North Market Street Graphics.

Printed and bound by R. R. Donnelley & Sons Company.

McGraw-Hill books are available at special quantity discounts to use as
premiums and sales promotions, or for use in corporate training programs.
For more information, please write to the Director of Special Sales, McGraw-
Hill, 11 West 19th Street, New York, NY 10011. Or contact your local bookstore.

# Contents

Preface                                                      vii

Introduction to Financial Planning                           ix

PART I      Investment Instruments: Corporate

CHAPTER 1   Annuities for Today's Living                      3

CHAPTER 2   Certificates of Deposit—Old Faithful            15

CHAPTER 3   Corporate Bond Market—For the Future            25

CHAPTER 4   Gold, Silver, and Diamonds—
            Investment or Enjoyment?                         37

CHAPTER 5   Money Market Accounts—The Parking Lot           49

CHAPTER 6   Mutual Funds—The Basics                         57

CHAPTER 7  Mutual Funds—Spreading the Risk                    69

CHAPTER 8  Stock Market—Bulls, Bears, and Pigs               81

CHAPTER 9  Stock Market Information—Where to Get It          93

CHAPTER 10  Zero Investment                                  105

PART II  Investment Instruments: Government

CHAPTER 11  Ginnie Mae—The Misunderstood
            Instrument                                        119

CHAPTER 12  Ginnie Mae Alternatives                          129

CHAPTER 13  Municipal Bonds—The Tax-Free Choice             139

CHAPTER 14  Municipal Trusts and Funds—
            Tax-Free Alternatives                            149

CHAPTER 15  Treasuries Are a Treasure                        157

CHAPTER 16  U.S. Savings Bonds—Safety First                 173

PART III  Other Financial Considerations

CHAPTER 17  Life Insurance—The Risk Protector               187

CHAPTER 18 **Real Estate as Security and Investment** 199

CHAPTER 19 **Condominiums and Co-ops—
A Living Investment** 207

CHAPTER 20 **Mortgages—The Finances
of Home Ownership** 217

CHAPTER 21 **Mortgages—In Reverse** 229

PART IV **Financial Planning for the Future**

CHAPTER 22 **Planning Your Retirement—An Overview** 243

CHAPTER 23 **The IRA** 249

CHAPTER 24 **The 401(k), the SEP, and the Keogh Plan** 265

CHAPTER 25 **Social Security** 277

CHAPTER 26 **Will It?** 287

CHAPTER 27 **Trust Me** 299

PART V **Financial Planning for Women**

CHAPTER 28 **For Women Only: An Introduction** 313

CHAPTER 29 **Prenuptials and the Marriage Vow**                        327

CHAPTER 30 **Unpleasant but Necessary:**
           **Health Care Issues for Seniors**                          337

**Epilogue**                                                           347

**Index**                                                              349

# Preface

I am a teacher, not a stockbroker, bank executive, or insurance salesperson. My specialty isn't fancy jargon, hucksterism, or statistics. Rather, it's explaining financial and economic matters to ordinary people in plain English. That's what *Financial Planning for the Utterly Confused* is all about.

There used to be a time when most of us thought that investing was something only for the rich and that very few people could afford to take on any apparent risk. But, of course, times have changed as we have become a nation of investors who realizes that we cannot achieve financial freedom from Social Security and company-based pension plans. And just as we, as potential investors, have increased in number, so too have the various types of investment choices. There were at one time stocks or bonds, but now the possibilities are vast, including Annuities, CD's, Ginnie Maes, Money Markets, Mutual Funds, Treasury Obligations, Zero Coupons—the list goes on and on. As you are aware, everyone wants choice but too many alternatives can be confusing. This book attempts to narrow down those choices and explain each financial instrument for the layperson. You won't find tips on high-flying stocks that promise to help you double your money overnight. As you already know, no one can make such promises with any certainty. What you will find here is an honest appraisal of the advantages, disadvantages, costs, and benefits of each type of financial instrument—an appraisal based on current tax laws and their effects upon you, the investor.

A glossary of common financial terms is provided to serve as a handy reference tool as you read the money-managing columns in your daily newspaper or your favorite magazine. It should help you penetrate some of the verbal fog generated by brokers, bankers, salespeople, and especially government agencies that enforce the many financial policies of the current administration. I wish to thank Donna Zebro Esq., Francesca Johnson and Stuart R. Miller, Financial Network, for their valuable assistance.

My hope is that *Financial Planning for the Utterly Confused* will be a valuable tool for the millions of Americans who need help in managing their small- to medium-sized investment plans. The information in this book can be the first building block in the creation of a secure and comfortable financial future that only you can initiate. There is a saying that sums up financial planning in 10 two-letter words:

> *If it is to be,*
> *It is up to me.*

JOEL LERNER

# Introduction to Financial Planning

*Money never changes, only pockets.*

**Do I Need to Read This Chapter?**

→ Do I know something about my finances—but not enough?

→ Am I making the mistake of expecting others to do my work for me?

→ Have I identified and prioritized my financial goals?

→ Am I where I should be, given my age and family situation?

→ Does risk scare me?

→ Do I know the "hidden" factors that might be eating away at my nest egg right now?

→ Am I keeping the right records?

The best investment you can make is in yourself. Financially you must have some knowledge about your own affairs because you cannot hand over everything to some financial adviser or broker and expect that person to do it all. Each month you no doubt receive a monthly statement of your financial position, but do you really have any idea what those figures mean? If you will take the time to learn about money matters, you will receive a rich reward—dividends in understanding that in the long run will improve your financial position.

# How Do You Begin a Financial Plan?

To begin a financially secured plan, your personal and family financial goals must be identified. Goals are based on what is most important to you. Short-term goals (up to a year) are things you desire soon (household appliances), while long-term goals are items you want later on in life (a home, education for your children, sufficient retirement income). Take these short- and long-term goals and put them into an order of priority, making sure you have an emergency fund as the first item. Then estimate the cost of each goal and set a target date to reach the goal (Table 1).

You are all aware of the changing life cycle. Your goals must be updated as your needs and circumstances change. In your early years, short-term goals may include adequate insurance, establishing good credit, and just getting under way. During your middle years, the goals shift from immediate personal spending to education for children and planning for retirement. In your latter years, travel may become a primary goal.

Also, when planning for your future, consider age as a vital factor.

## Quick Tips

Inflation hasn't run rampant for a while. But it may be a sleeping giant. If it awakens, don't get crushed. Be sure to consider the cost of inflation (see Table 2), because it most certainly will affect your long-term goals.

**TABLE 1**   Interest Tables to Meet Your Goals

| | 5 YEARS | 10 YEARS | 15 YEARS | 20 YEARS | 25 YEARS | 30 YEARS |
|---|---|---|---|---|---|---|
| **1. $10,000 LUMP SUM** | | | | | | |
| 5% | $12,763 | $16,289 | $20,789 | $ 26,533 | $ 33,864 | $ 43,219 |
| 6% | 13,382 | 17,908 | 23,966 | 32,071 | 42,919 | 57,435 |
| 7% | 14,026 | 19,672 | 27,590 | 38,697 | 54,274 | 76,123 |
| 8% | 14,693 | 21,589 | 31,722 | 46,610 | 68,485 | 100,627 |
| 9% | 15,386 | 23,674 | 36,425 | 56,044 | 86,231 | 132,677 |
| 10% | 16,105 | 25,937 | 41,772 | 67,275 | 108,347 | 174,494 |
| 11% | 16,851 | 28,394 | 47,846 | 80,623 | 135,855 | 228,923 |
| 12% | 17,623 | 31,058 | 54,736 | 96,463 | 170,001 | 299,599 |
| 13% | 18,424 | 33,946 | 62,543 | 115,231 | 212,305 | 391,159 |
| 14% | 19,254 | 37,072 | 71,379 | 137,435 | 264,619 | 509,502 |
| 15% | 20,114 | 40,456 | 81,371 | 163,665 | 329,190 | 662,118 |

| | 5 YEARS | 10 YEARS | 15 YEARS | 20 YEARS | 25 YEARS | 30 YEARS |
|---|---|---|---|---|---|---|
| **2. $100 PER MONTH INVESTMENT** | | | | | | |
| 5% | $6,801 | $15,528 | $26,729 | $ 41,103 | $ 59,551 | $ 83,226 |
| 6% | 6,977 | 16,388 | 29,082 | 46,204 | 69,299 | 100,452 |
| 7% | 7,159 | 17,308 | 31,696 | 52,093 | 81,007 | 121,997 |
| 8% | 7,348 | 18,295 | 34,604 | 58,902 | 95,103 | 149,035 |
| 9% | 7,542 | 19,351 | 37,841 | 66,789 | 112,112 | 183,074 |
| 10% | 7,744 | 20,484 | 41,447 | 75,937 | 132,683 | 226,049 |
| 11% | 7,952 | 21,700 | 45,469 | 86,564 | 157,613 | 280,452 |
| 12% | 8,167 | 23,004 | 49,958 | 98,926 | 187,885 | 349,496 |
| 13% | 8,389 | 24,404 | 54,973 | 113,324 | 224,709 | 437,327 |
| 14% | 8,620 | 25,907 | 60,579 | 130,117 | 264,583 | 549,297 |
| 15% | 8,857 | 27,522 | 66,851 | 149,724 | 324,353 | 692,328 |

**TABLE 1**   (Continued)

| 3. ANNUAL INVESTMENT REQUIRED TO REACH $100,000 | | | | | |
| 5 YEARS | 10 YEARS | 15 YEARS | 20 YEARS | 25 YEARS | 30 YEARS |
|---|---|---|---|---|---|
| **5%** $17,236 | $7,572 | $4,414 | $2,880 | $1,966 | $1,433 |
| **6%** 16,736 | 7,157 | 4,053 | 2,565 | 1,720 | 1,193 |
| **7%** 16,254 | 6,764 | 3,719 | 2,280 | 1,478 | 989 |
| **8%** 15,783 | 6,392 | 3,410 | 2,024 | 1,267 | 817 |
| **9%** 15,332 | 6,039 | 3,124 | 1,793 | 1,083 | 673 |
| **10%** 14,890 | 5,704 | 2,861 | 1,587 | 924 | 552 |
| **11%** 14,467 | 5,388 | 2,618 | 1,403 | 787 | 452 |
| **12%** 14,055 | 5,088 | 2,395 | 1,239 | 669 | 369 |
| **13%** 13,658 | 4,805 | 2,190 | 1,070 | 568 | 301 |
| **14%** 13,270 | 4,536 | 2,001 | 963 | 482 | 245 |
| **15%** 12,898 | 4,283 | 1,828 | 848 | 408 | 200 |

Notes: 1. Amounts to nearest dollar.
2. Rates compounded annually.
3. These are year-end values.

# Get Started

Although every financial plan will be different, each should meet certain criteria:

1. An emergency fund equal to 3 months of net income (after taxes)

2. Specific amounts for investments set aside on a regular basis

3. Adequate insurance

# How Does Age Enter into Financial Planning?

Here are some guidelines to use depending on your present age:

*Age 20 to 40:* When you are young, growth should be your primary goal; a relatively high degree of risk is tolerable. Suggestion: invest in a diversified portfolio of common stocks or in a mutual fund managed for growth of assets, not income. Speculation (real estate, coins, metals, etc.) is acceptable.

*Age 40 to 50:* Stocks are still an attractive choice, but now you need a more balanced approach. Begin to invest in fixed-rate instruments (bonds) and look into ones that arc tax-free (municipals).

*Age 50 to 60:* At this point, growth is less important, risk less acceptable. Move most of your investments out of stocks and into bonds, in order to minimize risk and increase your current flow of income.

*Age 60 and over:* By now, the majority of your funds should be in income-producing investments to provide safety and maximum current interest.

There is a rule of thumb that may be appropriate here. It is based on the concept that the percentage of your portfolio in bonds should approximate your age, the balance going into equities. For example at age 40, you would keep 40 percent in bonds and a 60 percent stock (and/or other) position. At age 60, the reverse would be appropriate: 60 percent bonds and 40 percent equities. Of course, this is a very general idea.

When you plan investments for your age bracket, consider the following:

1. *Security of principal:* This refers to the preservation of your original capital. Treasury bills are guaranteed by the government while stocks fluctuate greatly.

2. *Return:*  This means the money you earn on your investment (interest, dividends, profit).
3. *Liquidity:*  This deals with the ease of converting your investment into cash.
4. *Convenience:*  This refers to the time and energy you are willing to expend on your investment.
5. *Tax status:*  Depending on your tax bracket, each investment will bear heavily on your personal situation. Municipal bonds are tax-free while CDs are fully taxable.
6. *Your personal circumstances:*  Included under this category would be your age, your income, your health, your individual circumstances, and your ability to tolerate risk.

# How Should You Deal with Financial Risk in Planning for the Future?

As you'll learn, the single most important factor in deciding on the best investments for you is the level of risk you can afford to take. Thus, the first step in formulating your investment plan is a careful self-examination. How much money do you have to invest? How great will your financial needs be for the foreseeable future? How much of your capital can you realistically afford to risk losing? And how great a degree of risk can you and your family handle psychologically? Each of these factors will have a bearing on the degree of risk you can tolerate in your investment decisions.

The trade-off is simple: To get larger rewards you have to take greater risks.

You can achieve a balance by investing in a pyramid fashion: begin with conservative (safe) investments at the foundation (Treasury obligations, insured money markets, CDs) and then gradually build up, accepting a bit more risk at each step. At the very top, you may have high-risk investments (coins, gold, real estate), but because of the pyramid, the investment will be small compared with the rest

---

**Don't Forget**

Every investor must find a comfort-zone balance of security and risk. This is one of the cardinal rules of financial planning. Ironically, the goal is to live in comfort, but the key is not to get too "comfortable." You don't want to miss out on profitable opportunities.

---

of your holdings. Also, to minimize loss, you should have at least two different types of investments that perform differently during a specific period of time. For example, when interest rates are low, stocks usually gain while money markets do poorly. Diversify!

# How Can You Overcome Obstacles to Your Financial Plan?

Regardless of how well you plan financially, certain obstacles will always arise. Four factors that could have a major impact on your investment objectives are as follows:

1. *Inflation:* It is obvious that if you are to plan financially for your future, you must receive a return that is high enough to outpace any long-term effects of inflation. If, for example, you kept retirement money in a savings account paying 3.5 percent per year and over the same period of time the inflation rate averaged 5 percent per year, your investment would have less purchasing power at retirement than it did when it was started. Table 2 is designed to illustrate the effect of the inflation rate on the cost of living for future years. Look down the column to the number of years until you retire and read across to the column under the estimated inflation rate. Multiply your plan or budget by that number to adjust for future costs. For example, if you are planning to retire in 10 years and the inflation rate is 4 percent, multiply your cost of investment or budget by 1.480 in order to reflect inflated adjusted costs. Ten

## Get Started

Here's a series of guidelines for handling risk. They should make you more "comfortable"—in both senses of the word.

1. Don't invest in any instrument in which you can lose more than you can potentially gain. This factor is sometimes referred to as *risk-reward balance.*

2. Diversify your holdings. Spread your investment dollars among a variety of instruments, thereby minimizing the risk potential.

3. When investments fail to perform up to your expectations (the period to hold them is based upon your objectives), sell them. "Cutting your losses" is the only sure way to prevent minor setbacks from turning into financial nightmares. A rule of thumb is to sell when the value declines by 10 percent of your original cost.

4. Did you ever hear of a "stop order"? Most small market investors have not, yet it can "cut your losses" automatically. When you purchase a stock, you give your broker instructions to sell that stock if it should decline by, say, 10 percent of its original purchase price. The moment the predetermined level is reached, your stock will be sold.

5. Don't discount risk altogether. The rewards may justify "taking a chance." Remember the turtle. It makes progress only when it sticks its neck out.

years from now it would cost you $59,200 to buy the same items you could have bought today for $40,000 ($40,000 × 1.480 = $59,200).

2. *Interest rate risk:* A change in interest rates will cause the price of fixed-rate instruments (bonds) to move in the opposite direction of interest rates. If interest rates go down, the value of bonds goes up, and, conversely, if interest rates go up, the value of the bonds goes down. You have interest rate risk with all types of bonds. The longer the maturity of the bond, the greater the interest rate risk, so if you are concerned about this risk, stay short-term.

**TABLE 2**   Effect of Inflation Rate on Cost of Living in Future Years

| YEARS TO RETIREMENT | INFLATION RATE | | | | | | | |
|---|---|---|---|---|---|---|---|---|
| | 3% | 4% | 5% | 6% | 7% | 8% | 9% | 10% |
| 1 | 1.030 | 1.040 | 1.050 | 1.060 | 1.070 | 1.080 | 1.090 | 1.100 |
| 2 | 1.061 | 1.082 | 1.103 | 1.124 | 1.145 | 1.166 | 1.188 | 1.210 |
| 3 | 1.093 | 1.125 | 1.158 | 1.191 | 1.225 | 1.260 | 1.285 | 1.331 |
| 4 | 1.126 | 1.170 | 1.216 | 1.262 | 1.311 | 1.360 | 1.412 | 1.464 |
| 5 | 1.159 | 1.217 | 1.276 | 1.338 | 1.403 | 1.469 | 1.539 | 1.611 |
| 6 | 1.194 | 1.265 | 1.340 | 1.419 | 1.501 | 1.587 | 1.677 | 1.772 |
| 7 | 1.230 | 1.316 | 1.407 | 1.504 | 1.606 | 1.714 | 1.828 | 1.949 |
| 8 | 1.267 | 1.369 | 1.477 | 1.594 | 1.718 | 1.851 | 1.993 | 2.144 |
| 9 | 1.305 | 1.423 | 1.551 | 1.689 | 1.838 | 1.999 | 2.172 | 2.358 |
| 10 | 1.344 | 1.480 | 1.629 | 1.791 | 1.967 | 2.159 | 2.367 | 2.594 |
| 11 | 1.384 | 1.539 | 1.710 | 1.898 | 2.105 | 2.332 | 2.580 | 2.853 |
| 12 | 1.426 | 1.601 | 1.796 | 2.012 | 2.252 | 2.518 | 2.813 | 3.138 |
| 13 | 1.469 | 1.665 | 1.886 | 2.133 | 2.410 | 2.720 | 3.066 | 3.452 |
| 14 | 1.513 | 1.732 | 1.980 | 2.261 | 2.579 | 3.937 | 3.342 | 3.797 |
| 15 | 1.558 | 1.801 | 2.079 | 2.397 | 2.759 | 3.172 | 3.642 | 4.177 |
| 16 | 1.605 | 1.873 | 2.183 | 2.540 | 2.952 | 3.426 | 3.970 | 4.595 |
| 17 | 1.653 | 1.948 | 2.292 | 2.693 | 3.159 | 3.700 | 4.328 | 5.054 |
| 18 | 1.702 | 2.026 | 2.407 | 2.854 | 3.380 | 3.996 | 4.717 | 5.560 |
| 19 | 1.754 | 2.107 | 2.527 | 3.026 | 3.617 | 4.316 | 5.142 | 6.116 |
| 20 | 1.806 | 2.191 | 2.653 | 3.207 | 3.870 | 4.661 | 5.604 | 6.727 |
| 25 | 2.094 | 2.666 | 3.386 | 4.292 | 5.427 | 6.848 | 8.623 | 10.835 |
| 30 | 2.427 | 3.243 | 4.322 | 5.743 | 7.612 | 10.063 | 13.268 | 17.449 |

3. *Taxation:* Determining to what extent any tax-advantaged investment would help you is a serious consideration. You must therefore take into account your tax bracket (presently up to a maximum whopping 39.6 percent), present income, future income, and investment holdings before you do financial planning.

4. *Procrastination:* This is an obstacle that depends solely on you. Don't imitate the person who says, "Someday I'm going to stop procrastinating." Regardless of how well a financial plan is structured, if you don't follow it through, it will be doomed before it begins.

Do you realize that even small amounts of money increase rapidly over a period of years? If you would put aside a dollar a day, that $30 per month invested in a tax-sheltered plan would grow to over $40,000 in 25 years at 10 percent. And that 10 percent is not an overstatement as it is the long-term historical return from large company stocks. Therefore, discipline yourself by continuing regular investing. Remember, it wasn't raining when Noah built his ark. Don't wait.

## Quick Tips

Interested in calculating your investment strategy? Here's the first step the experts advise. Apply the simple formula called the "Rule of 72." It will help you figure out how long it will take, or what interest rate you will need, to double your money.

For example: If you invested $10,000 at 6 percent, it would take you 12 years to have $20,000 (72 ÷ 6). You simply divide the number "72" by the interest. Another approach might occur if you knew how long a specific period of time your money was invested and you needed to know at what rate of interest you would "double" at the end of the time period. For example: If I were 56 years old and I wanted to retire at age 65, 9 years from now, I would need 8 percent interest each year to double my money (72 ÷ 9). You would divide "72" by the number of years which would result in the required interest. As a sidelight, if you were interested in tripling your money, use the number "115" instead of "72" and then continue with your calculations.

Now that your goals have been defined and the areas of risks and rewards examined, the next step is getting all the "paper" together.

# What Financial Records Should You Keep?

Start by developing a "road map" so that you or your heirs (in case of disability or death) will know where documents are. Records that should be kept available are:

1. Professional numbers: Telephone numbers of your lawyer, doctor, accountant, insurance company, business associates, and financial adviser or broker.
2. Account numbers: Brokerage, bank, credit cards, insurance policies (and beneficiaries), and safe deposit box (keys and authorized deputies).
3. All business records (tax returns, company books, payroll data, etc.).
4. An updated will and trust agreements, if any.
5. Retirement benefits: Social security, Keogh plans, simplified employee pensions plans (SEPs), 401(k)s, and the like.
6. Burial arrangements: cemetery plot, deeds.
7. Any outstanding liabilities.

# How Can Computers Help You with Financial Planning?

Financial planning and computers are an ideal match. You put in the information; the computer crunches the numbers, makes the projections, and helps keep you on track.

There's plenty of software out there designed especially for personal financial planning and investment. Some popular choices

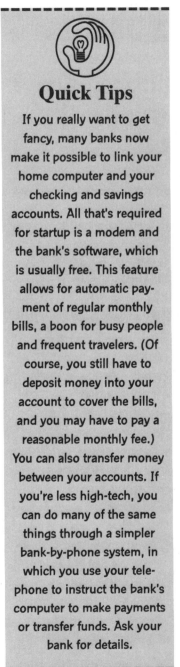

### Quick Tips

If you really want to get fancy, many banks now make it possible to link your home computer and your checking and savings accounts. All that's required for startup is a modem and the bank's software, which is usually free. This feature allows for automatic payment of regular monthly bills, a boon for busy people and frequent travelers. (Of course, you still have to deposit money into your account to cover the bills, and you may have to pay a reasonable monthly fee.) You can also transfer money between your accounts. If you're less high-tech, you can do many of the same things through a simpler bank-by-phone system, in which you use your telephone to instruct the bank's computer to make payments or transfer funds. Ask your bank for details.

include Quicken, Microsoft Money, Managing Your Money, and Financial Tools. Your computer may even have one of these programs preinstalled. Whichever program you choose, it's hard to go wrong—just about all of them are fast and easy to use.

These programs can help you devise a household budget, monitor your expenditures in numerous categories, keep meticulous records, and plan for the future. Some programs allow you to make year-by-year projections of your income, expenses, and retirement benefits from now to age 125! And virtually all the programs let you import pertinent data into tax preparation software. Whether you prepare your own tax returns or have them done by a professional, having good records is a real boon when that April 15 deadline starts looming.

If you're into visual data, these programs will delight you by producing spreadsheets, charts, and graphs galore. Most programs can even print out your checks for you, if you so choose.

Computer programs make it especially easy to track your investments. You can enter as many accounts and portfolios as you wish, including your stocks, mutual funds, bonds, IRAs, and so on. With a link to the Internet, these programs allow you to calculate your current net worth with the touch of a key.

## What Are Some On-Line Financial Planning Resources?

The major on-line services are packed with financial information. You can research the invest-

## Get Started

1. If you're not already on-line, an easy way to start is to call the major services for free trial subscription software: America Online, 1-800-827-6364; CompuServe, 1-800-848-8199; Microsoft Network (MSN), 1-800-386-5550; and Prodigy, 1-800-776-3449.

2. Use your 5 to 50 free startup hours to explore the offerings and determine which service you like best.

3. Alternatively, you can sign up with an Internet service provider (ISP). They're listed under that heading in the Yellow Pages. You can choose from national providers, such as AT&T (1-800-967-5363), Netcom (1-800-353-6600), or Pipeline USA (1-800-827-7482), as well as a host of local providers. ISPs typically give you e-mail capability and other features, as well as Web access.

ments that interest you, "chat" with other financially savvy people, and use these services as gateways to the World Wide Web.

The World Wide Web is a happy hunting ground for those seeking help with financial planning. Go to one of the major search engines, like www.yahoo.com or www.altavista.com; enter a key word or phrase like "stocks" or "retirement planning"; then sit back and select from among the hundreds of sites that present themselves.

## Are There Special Resources for Retirement Planning?

Retirees and future retirees are big business. Lots of specialized software and Web sites cater to them. If you already have retirement funds invested with one of the fund families, call the company's investor service line and ask what programs they have to offer. (Two examples are "Vanguard Retirement Manager" from

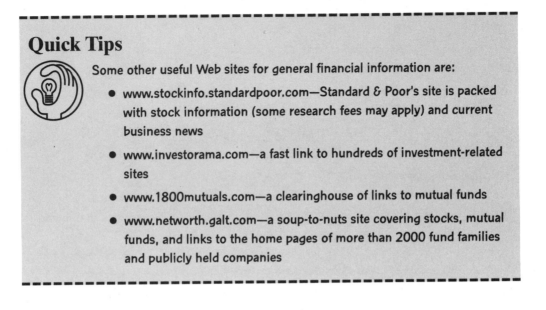

**Quick Tips**

Some other useful Web sites for general financial information are:

- www.stockinfo.standardpoor.com—Standard & Poor's site is packed with stock information (some research fees may apply) and current business news

- www.investorama.com—a fast link to hundreds of investment-related sites

- www.1800mutuals.com—a clearinghouse of links to mutual funds

- www.networth.galt.com—a soup-to-nuts site covering stocks, mutual funds, and links to the home pages of more than 2000 fund families and publicly held companies

the Vanguard Group, 1-800-999-1529, and "Retire Secure" from Price Waterhouse, 1-800-422-5579. These programs, like dozens of similar ones, are nominally priced at $20 to $50.)

The Web site of the American Association of Retired Persons (www.aarp.org) was recently cited in *BusinessWeek* as one of the "best sources for general information on retirement planning. . . . It offers tips on financing your retirement and lists other nonprofit groups that serve seniors." Also recommended is the Social Security Administration's site—www.ssa.gov—which provides access to more than 600 documents.

This introduction to financial planning lays the foundation for all the topics in the forthcoming pages of this book. You owe it to yourself to read (newspapers, magazines, annual reports), learn (seminars, courses), ask (brokers, financial planners), and make certain that you can apply the knowledge gained from reading the following chapters so that when opportunity does knock, you are not in the backyard looking for four-leaf clovers.

# PART I

# Investment Instruments: Corporate

# CHAPTER 1

# Annuities for Today's Living

*Forever is a long time,*
*but not as long as it was yesterday.*

**Do I Need to Read This Chapter?**

➜ Am I worried about retirement?

➜ Do I run the risk of outliving my money?

➜ Have I considered annuities?

➜ Am I choosing the right type of annuity?

➜ Do I realize that insurers that sell annuities can go bankrupt?

➜ How can I make sure my annuity investment is safe?

➜ What do all those safety rankings, like "Aa2," really mean?

➜ I'm middle-class. Will annuities have special tax benefits for me?

➜ Do annuities compare favorably to mutual funds?

Today, either tax-free municipal bonds (see Chap. 13) or tax-deferred annuities seem to be at the center of many investment portfolios. The insurance industry's offering of the annuity has become a serious alternative for investors who wish to look for deferred income, possible tax deduction, and safety of investment.

# How Does an Annuity Work?

When you retire, you will want to be able to live comfortably for life on the income from your investments. However, because of modern medicine, many people run the risk of outliving their investment income. To avoid this problem the purchasing of an annuity could be the possible solution. An annuity may be considered the opposite of a traditional life insurance policy. When you buy insurance, you agree to pay annual premiums to an insurance company. In return, the company will pay, according to your instructions, the face value of the policy in a lump sum to your beneficiaries when you die. By contrast, when you buy an annuity, you pay the company a sum of money and, in return, receive a monthly income for as long as you live. Naturally, the longer you survive, the more money you'll receive. Therefore, you can never outlive your return regardless of how old you become. It thus can be stated that life insurance protects against financial loss as a result of dying too soon, while an annuity protects you against financial loss as a result of living too long.

# What Are the Different Characteristics of Annuities?

There are several different types of annuities. They can be categorized according to three main characteristics:

1. *Premiums:*  The cost of the annuity will depend on many factors:

- How much you will contribute to your account
- The rate of return earned by the fund
- The length of time the money is left in the fund
- The procedure for distribution of the funds to beneficiaries (note that options can raise or lower your monthly annuity return)

## Quick Tips

When evaluating annuities, pay attention to four details: minimum initial investments; maximum age for starting to receive payouts; terms for switching among funds; and rules for partial withdrawals. These details can be found in each contract's prospectus.

An annuity may be purchased either through a single lump-sum premium or through annual premium payments. If you happen to have a large sum of money to invest at one time—for example, from an inheritance or from a pension fund—you may want to purchase an annuity with a lump-sum payment. This is known as a single-premium deferred annuity (SPDA). Once you have made the initial investment, no further contribution is required. An SPDA is a basic annuity which works in the following way: you buy a contract and pay a lump sum ($2500–$500,000) up front, which guarantees future payments. If you die before you begin to receive withdrawals, the policy will pay the estate the contract's face value plus interest. If you live past age 59½, you may begin your withdrawal program or you may cash in the policy and receive your principal plus all interest earned on it tax-deferred. This is similar to a nondeductible IRA, since the income earned stays tax-deferred in the annuity until it is withdrawn, yet it is better because you are not limited to a $2000 maximum deposit.

Annuity income depends on life expectancy and is thus classified as life insurance. This is important for you to understand, because the classification allows the annuity's investment earnings to be treated as tax-deferred, with no tax on its accumulation until the money is withdrawn. This is surprising, since well over 95 percent of the annuity is investment while only a very small balance is for insurance.

## Don't Forget

This is easy to remember. It's *good* news. With annuities, you'll find that your assets accumulate more quickly than occurs with most other investments, because the interest you earn is not subject to income tax until you begin to withdraw it. In other words, you can save in three ways:

- Your principal earns interest.
- That interest earns interest.
- You earn interest on the money you save in current taxes.

But watch out if you withdraw before age 59½. Except in certain cases (see page 253), a premature withdrawal will cost you an IRS penalty of 10 percent. There is also an insurance company surrender penalty (in some cases) of 7 percent of your investment if you withdraw it during the first year; 6 percent during the second year; 5 percent during the third year and so on. From the eighth year on, no penalty is charged. Make sure you find out about surrender charges before deciding on where to invest in an annuity, and be sure to ask your agent or broker about sales charges (if there are any) before you buy. These charges could affect your total yield and future income. Most companies charge annual administrative fees which further reduce your income. These fees vary, but they average 1.5 percent of the amount invested. Find out the amount of the fee before you invest, and compare the rates charged by several companies. These fees are important in determining the annuity to be chosen because they directly affect its yield. The Securities and Exchange Commission (SEC) has issued rules that now require the annuity companies to show their charges in a standardized table located near the beginning of the information booklet (prospectus).

These charges could include:

- Front-end sales commissions
- Annual maintenance costs

- Annual mortality and expense charges
- Annual investment advisory fees
- Surrender charges

2. *Payment return:* An annuity may provide for either *immediate* return to the investor or *deferred* return. An *immediate* annuity is purchased at the time you want to start receiving income, and requires a single lump-sum premium. The insurance company begins sending you monthly checks right away. One of the most important advantages of a fixed-rate immediate annuity is that it allows you to lock in an interest rate for the rest of your life when rates are high. You always know exactly how much you will receive. However, bear in mind that once the rate is set, it can never change. If current rates drop you know you did the right thing, but if they should rise, there isn't a thing you can do about it but feel bad. Also, that fixed amount today may seem high but diminishes as time goes by because of inflation. A *deferred* annuity, on the other hand, is purchased prior to the time when the income is needed (deferred period). During this period, which may be very short or may last as long as 40 years, your investment earns interest tax-free. If you should decide to cancel your annuity before withdrawal time, you may have to pay a surrender charge which will vary from company to company.

3. *Return on investment:* Annuities may be classified as either *fixed-dollar* or *variable. Fixed-dollar* annuities guarantee you a certain minimum interest rate. The actual rate you'll receive is fixed for only a few months or years, but there is a minimum rate below which your return cannot drop. Insurance companies usually invest fixed-dollar annuity funds in highly secured investments, such as government bonds. With a fixed-dollar annuity, you'll know that your principal is secure and that you'll receive at least a specified minimum income. Some companies will offer what is known as a "bail-out" provision in their annuity contract, which states that if the annuity fails to earn a specified interest rate, the holder can withdraw his or her money without penalty. *Variable annuities,* on the other hand, are usually invested in more risky, but potentially more lucrative instru-

ments. The amount of interest your money earns, and therefore the size of the payment you'll receive, will vary according to the success of the insurance company's investments. However, your principal is not untouchable. For example, a market disaster could wipe out part of your investment. There were major negative impacts on the values of annuities immediately after the October 1987 and 1989 stock market crashes and after the invasion of Kuwait. Also look what happened with the 554 point drop in October 1997. Therefore you may earn more with a variable annuity but the risk you take is greater. Variable annuities are best for those individuals who start their retirement programs late in life, as it is a fast (though risky) way to "catch up."

## Quick Tips

If you're interested in annuities, probably you're also interested in mutual funds. And you're wondering how these two types of investments stack up against each other.

On one side of the coin, annuities have a major advantage over funds. Here's why. The earnings of annuities housed inside the instrument cannot be taxed. Thus your money builds up tax-deferred (until withdrawn) just as it would as a nondeductible IRA. This occurs, as stated before, because there is life insurance that covers the annuity. This insurance assures your heirs that if you die before beginning any withdrawal, they will receive at least the amount of the investment.

But look at the other side of the coin. Variable annuities have an annual fee of about 2 percent, whereas mutual funds run almost half that amount. Also, most of the gain from stock mutual funds is considered a capital gain, while all of the earnings from an annuity are taxed as ordinary income.

Whichever type of annuity you choose, your ability to tolerate risk should be the deciding factor. Younger people may move toward the variable annuity because they may feel that there will be enough time to recoup any possible losses, whereas older people may choose fixed-rate annuities because of the guaranteed yield. Regardless of which type you choose, insurance products are still among the safest savings plans around.

# What Are the Different Repayment Options Offered?

As I've explained, with an annuity, the longer you live the greater the return you can expect to earn. This means, of course, that if you die early you may never recoup the amount you originally paid for the annuity. Because of the different needs of investors, there are several repayment options from which to choose:

1. *Individual life annuity:* Here, payments (which are the highest of any option) are continued throughout your life with no further payment made after you die (even if you should die only a year or two after payments begin). This plan is designed only for a person who wants the highest amount of regular income and has no spouse or other dependents who might need financial support after the annuitant dies. If you are married, federal law requires you to obtain a notarized waiver of benefits from your spouse.

2. *Joint-survivor annuity:* This plan provides monthly payments for as long as either you or your spouse lives. In other words, at your demise, your spouse would continue receiving payments until he or she died. It is obvious that the payouts each month will be smaller than the individual life annuity because the payments extend to two lives and therefore will have to stretch over a longer period.

3. *Guaranteed-minimum annuity:* Under the terms of this annuity, there is a minimum payout period established. In the event that the annuity holder dies shortly after the payouts begin, more pay-

ments will be made to the beneficiaries for a specified period of time. For example, an investor might buy this type of policy in order to receive payments for the rest of his or her life but wants to make certain that the insurance company will make payments for, say, at least 10 years. This is known as a "10-year certain contract." If the investor dies after receiving 2 years of payouts, he or she will be assured that whoever is designated as the beneficiary will receive money for the next 8 years. For this privilege, the investor will receive a smaller payback (about 6 percent less than from the other previously mentioned options). Also, if the investor should die before distribution begins, the named beneficiaries can receive the full value of the annuity which will bypass probate and its time and cost procedures.

# What Are the Risks Associated with Annuities?

Regardless of where you purchase an annuity, even at a bank, the insurance company and not the bank stands behind the policy. Although banks are federally insured, insurance companies are not. If the insurance company should fail, your deposits can be frozen for years. If you will do a bit of homework and learn about your company and your annuity, your fears may be for nothing.

1. *Credit rating:*   There are three companies that will rate the ability of the insurers to meet their financial obligations. Examine the chart following and if you find that your company has a quality rating lower than line 3 of this chart, it could indicate a problem.

2. *Junk-bond holdings:*   Any company's strength can be determined by the quality of its investments. The ratio of junk bonds (bonds rated BB or lower) to total assets has an industry average of 6 to 8 percent. If your company has a ratio between 10 and 15 per-

| RATING | BEST COMPANY | S&P | MOODY'S |
|:---:|:---|:---:|:---:|
| 1 | A+ | AAA | Aaa |
| 2 | Contingent A+ | AA+ | Aa1 |
| 3 | A and Contingent A | AA | Aa2 |
| 4 | A− | AA− | Aa3 |
| 5 | Contingent A− | A+ | AA1 |
| 6 | B+ | A | A2 |
| 7 | Contingent B+ | A− | A3 |
| 8 | B | BBB+ | Baa1 |
| 9 | Contingent B | BBB | Baa2 |
| 10 | B− | BBB− | Baa3 |

cent, you should be a bit concerned and if over that rate, be greatly concerned.

3. *Reserves:* Your company must have at least 5 percent of its total assets put aside in investment reserves and surplus in order to meet any immediate financial obligation and investment losses. Between 2 and 4 percent of reserves held back is a concern, but less than 2 percent should produce some serious thoughts about how your company is run and its potential to meet its obligations when they come due. It is better to be safe today than sorry later when you are ready to retire.

4. *Dividend payments:* Your company should pay its dividends on a continuous basis. If it does not, this may indicate that the company needs cash, and withholding dividend payments becomes an easy first choice. Therefore, if there has been either a reduced or a curtailed dividend recently, a major cash flow problem could be developing. Be forewarned!

### Get Started

Of course it's easy for me to explain to you what to look out for when assessing a company's solvency. But how do you go about securing the information I have mentioned?

1. Your insurer will supply you with reports on its fiscal condition. The company's address and telephone number appears on your policy.

2. Find out what your coverage limits are under your state's Life Insurance Guaranty Fund. Each state has set up a fund for your protection. The limits vary state by state, with New York having one of the best coverages available.

3. Call Standard & Poor's (S&P) at 212-208-1527 for an evaluation of its rating for your specific company.

# What Are the Tax Consequences of Annuities?

A large portion of what you receive in each payment will be a tax-free return on the money you invest as long as the annuity you bought was not funded from an IRA or a company retirement plan. Only the amount that represents earnings is taxed. If however, the money comes from an IRA or tax-deferred plan, most likely it will be fully taxable. This occurs because the money used to buy the annuity was untaxed originally. If you are fortunate to outlive your life expectancy, all of the payments you receive from that point are taxable because you have recovered your initial immediate investment. If, however, you should die prior to recovering all your investment, your estate can claim a deduction on your final tax return of the balance you did not receive.

Annuities have certain other distinct advantages. The most important benefit lies in the fact that annuity income is guaranteed

## Quick Tips

In the middle class? Feeling squeezed? It's a pretty rare investment that offers special tax benefits to folks like you, but I believe that annuities qualify. With annuities, you'll find that your assets accumulate more quickly than occurs with most other investments because the interest you earn is not subject to income tax until you begin to withdraw it. As stated before, you can save in three ways:

1. Your principal earns interest.

2. That interest earns interest.

3. You earn interest on the money you save in current taxes.

for life, no matter how long you live. It's pretty comforting to retire with an income that you know will always be there. Also, when death does occur, regardless of the payout plan you choose, the annuity is free from probate because an annuity is an insurance product having a named beneficiary with the proceeds going directly to the designated heirs, by-passing court costs, legal fees, and long delays. And on the topic of life and death, never worry about life being short, because life is too short for that.

It's a Wrap

✔ Annuities are a form of insurance in which the policy-holder pays a specified premium and, in return, receives regular payments for the rest of his or her life.

✔ The several different types of annuities are classified according to premiums (lump-sum or annual), payment return (immediate or deferred), and return on investment (fixed-dollar or variable).

✔ Annuities have a tax advantage over mutual funds, but they also tend to have higher annual fees.

✔ Annuities offer several different repayment options: individual life, joint-survivor, and guaranteed-minimum.

✔ You must carefully evaluate the credit rating of any insurer that sells annuities. That's because insurers, unlike banks, are not federally insured—and if they default, your funds may be frozen for years.

✔ Annuities provide certain income tax benefits that are of special advantage to middle-class investors.

*Never worry about life being short,*
*because life is too short for that.*

# CHAPTER 2

# Certificates of Deposit—Old Faithful

*It may not seem as exciting as trading in pork bellies, but it always brings home the bacon.*

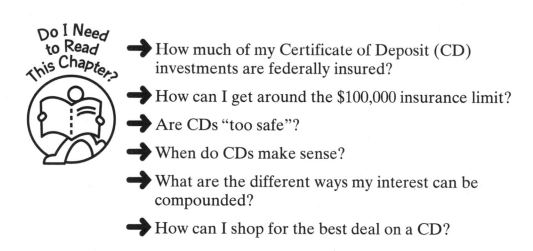

**Do I Need to Read This Chapter?**

➡ How much of my Certificate of Deposit (CD) investments are federally insured?

➡ How can I get around the $100,000 insurance limit?

➡ Are CDs "too safe"?

➡ When do CDs make sense?

➡ What are the different ways my interest can be compounded?

➡ How can I shop for the best deal on a CD?

At one time, you needed $100,000 or more to invest in a bank *certificate of deposit*. This restriction had been established by the Federal Reserve Board in order to protect savings banks, savings and loan institutions, and credit unions from competition with commercial banks. The fear was that if commercial banks could issue high-yielding certificates of deposit in small denominations, small savers would withdraw their funds from low-yielding passbook savings accounts in order to buy the certificates. This, in turn, would adversely affect the savings banks, most of whose holdings were tied up in low-yielding, long-term mortgages. In effect, the Federal Reserve sought to protect the banks at the expense of small savers.

All this changed over 25 years ago when the first money market mutual fund offered its shares for sale for as little as $1000. Money market funds, which paid rates comparable to those offered on bank certificates, quickly became a favorite investment for small savers. The savings banks began to lose customers. As a result, the banks themselves demanded that the rules be changed so as to allow them to compete with the money market funds. Thus was born the certificate of deposit (CD) for the small investor.

Today, most federal restrictions governing insured time deposits in banks have been lifted, since banks are free to compete with one another in setting terms for their own CDs. You can now buy a CD from a savings and loan institution, a savings bank, a credit union, a commercial bank, or a broker.

## Quick Tips

Do you pine for the "good old days," not so long ago, when CDs paid double-digit interest?

Sad to say, most likely they won't be back. That's because competition among the aforementioned CD suppliers tended to keep rates high, and for the small saver, the revolution of the 1970s and early 1980s was certainly beneficial. Now however, the rates are low as compared to other investments.

# How Does the Certificate of Deposit Work?

The concept of the CD is simple. It is a savings instrument issued by a financial institution which pays you interest at a guaranteed rate for a specified term. When the CD reaches maturity, you will receive your principal and all interest earned. Unlike bond interest (paid periodically) the interest from a CD usually compounds, which means you will be earning interest on your interest. The amount you invest in a CD is insured by the federal government for up to $100,000. However, it is not wise to put the entire $100,000 in one account, since the federal insurance ceiling applies to both principal and interest. I suggest that you have no more than $85,000 to $90,000 in any single certificate, because any interest you earn on the CD could increase your balance, surpassing the maximum insured sum and thereby not being automatically protected if the bank should fail.

## Don't Forget

Bear in mind the following points when determining how to "spread around" your CD investments:

1. When a bank has several branches, the main office and all branch offices are considered one bank.

2. Individual retirement accounts (IRAs) and Keogh Plan funds held in trust, or in a custodial capacity by a bank, are insured separately from any other deposits owned by the same investor—to a maximum of $100,000.

3. Actual title to each insured account must be in the name of the account holder designated.

4. Each co-owner of a joint account must have equal withdrawal rights and must personally sign a signature card.

5. "Your money is safe, so do not fret. Backed by government trillions in debt."

# Who Should Purchase CDs?

Generally, I do not believe in certificates of deposit in an investment portfolio because there are so many better alternatives. Many millions of people own them because of their safety, convenience, and general familiarity with their bank, yet investors lose because they deny themselves the chance for higher yields which come with accepting more risk. However, there are certain times when CDs do make sense.

1. *Emergency savings:*   As stated, you need an emergency fund (after taxes) equal to at least three months of your salary. Short-term CDs are excellent for this as they can be very liquid.

2. *Short-term goals:*   Savings for a house in two or three years make a good justification for CDs.

3. *Completing a long-term goal:*   For sixteen years, since the birth of your child, you have invested in stocks in a mutual fund. Now, as college looms in two years, you want to safeguard those funds. In steps the CD.

4. *The parking lot theory:*   An inheritance, switching jobs, any windfall may give you a large sum of money. However, you may need a little time to decide where to invest. CDs make a fine short-term parking lot for those funds.

# What Plans Should You Make When Purchasing a CD?

There are two primary considerations in planning for your investment in a CD:

1. *Term:*   The most popular type of CD is the 6-month certificate, but CDs are available with maturities ranging from 7 days to 10 years. During the term of your CD, the money you've invested is

relatively costly to liquidate (illiquid). If an emergency arises which requires you to withdraw your money before maturity, you'll be penalized for it. This penalty is known as *EWP* (*early withdrawal penalty*) and will vary from bank to bank. Thus you'll want to consider carefully when you're likely to need the money before you invest in a CD. If a college tuition bill is due to be paid in 1 year and 3 months, you know that you'll want a certificate which matures at that time. It may pay for you to buy CDs in smaller denominations instead of purchasing one large certificate. Remember, you never know what the future holds, and at some time you may need to withdraw a portion of the funds. For example, if you were to buy a $50,000 1-year CD and 8 months later you needed $10,000, some banks would charge you a penalty on the entire $50,000, since you would have to cash in the full CD. You would have been wiser to have purchased five $10,000 CDs, thus having to break only one of them, leaving the other four intact. And the interest rate is usually the same on five smaller certificates ($10,000 each) as it is on one larger one ($50,000).

2. *Rate of return:* The interest paid on a CD will vary not only according to the term of the certificate but also from time to time (as interest rates fluctuate) as well as from bank to bank. Don't buy your CD at the first bank you visit; the competing bank across the street may well be offering half a point more. Shop around! In these times of low interest yields, you have no other choice. Ask about how the bank credits the interest earned to your account. The more frequently interest is credited, the better for you, since each time your account grows through an interest payment, the amount of money you have working for you grows as well.

As an example, a CD paying 4 percent for 1 year will produce interest of 4.06 percent if compounded quarterly, 4.07 percent if compounded monthly, and 4.08 percent on a daily compounding basis.

For long-term, a $10,000, 6 percent, 10-year certificate would pay at maturity the following various amounts:

- Simple interest, no compounding: the money grows only to $16,000 because interest is paid only on the original principal.

- Interest compounded quarterly: the money grows to $18,140.

- Interest compounded monthly: you end up with $18,194.

- Interest compounded daily: the original $10,000 grows to $18,220.

Thus, it pays to investigate these various bank policies. If you find a bank that compounds your interest on a daily basis, you may want to make a switch and do your investing there.

How many times have you seen two rates offered by banks in their advertisements? Banks will sometimes reflect their compounding policies by listing a true rate of return (known as the *effective annual yield*) along with the no-compounding nominal rate (known as the *interest rate*) for a given CD. Thus a CD with an interest rate of 6.05 percent may pay an effective annual yield of 6.32 percent. Use the effective rate, if available, for comparison.

Also, for comparison purposes, look at this scenario. An investment company proudly states that its instrument has had an average annual return of 20 percent a year for the last 10 years. Sounds great? Not necessarily. The investment increased 200 percent

## Quick Tips

If you want to compare simple and compound rates of return on CDs, but don't have a compound-interest table, try this formula (it's easier than it looks!):

$$A = P(1 + r)t$$

where: $A$ = amount of money you'll have at the end of a specific period of time
$P$ = principal
$r$ = rate of interest
$t$ = time period

(20% × 10 years) over the decade, based upon simple interest. But this 20 percent earns only 11.6 percent compounded interest.

For example, a $1000 investment that yields 5 percent in 3 years compounded annually would produce $1160:

$$A = 1000(1 + .05)^3$$
$$A = 1000(1.05)^3$$
$$A = 1000(1.05 \times 1.05 \times 1.05)$$
$$A = 1160$$

# What Else Should You Know When Comparing CDs with Other Instruments?

Here are some other points to consider when shopping for the best deal on a CD:

- Ask about variable-rate CDs. These rates are usually based on the current rates on Treasury bills issued by the federal government. They may be higher or lower than the rates paid on fixed-rate CDs, depending on financial conditions. These variable rates are designed for people who believe that interest rates will rise. If the ups and downs of these variable rates concern you, stagger your maturity dates. In this way, as you receive your principal back, you will be able to reinvest it in higher-yielding CDs if rates have gone up or in another investment if rates have fallen.

- Ask whether you can increase the size of your investment after the original purchase of your CD has been made. This can be advantageous if you expect more funds to be available shortly (and if you expect interest rates to decline in the future).

- Don't forget that since 1982 brokers have also been able to offer CDs. The certificates sold by brokers are units, usually in denominations of $1000 or more, of larger certificates issued by savings institutions. Although these CDs are liquid, there may be a fee imposed for selling them before maturity. Also, brokered CDs may not carry compound interest (which would lower their effective yield), so ask questions of your broker before committing any funds.

- Inquire about some hybrid types of bank CDs. For example:

  1. *Odd terms:*  This type offers unusual lengths of time until maturity (7 months, 13 months, etc.), which, by the way, makes it very difficult to compare yields with those of other instruments.

  2. *No early withdrawal penalty:*  Although most banks still charge an early withdrawal penalty (EWP), some are now offering a "no penalty" CD. However, these "no penalties" may pay a lower interest rate than the traditional CDs; so compare both yields to determine if the "no penalty" clause is worth the difference.

  3. *Step-ups:*  This type of CD pays a rising rate of interest periodically (usually every 6 months) if interest rates rise. *Warning:* Watch out when you see advertisements about these "step-ups," because the banks usually quote only the last (and highest) rate, which does not represent all the earlier interest rates that were received by one holding on to these CDs.

In addition, when considering buying CDs, compare them with such similar investment instruments as Treasury notes. (See Chap. 15.) On the one hand, a Treasury note pays interest which is free of state and local taxes, whereas earnings on a CD are fully taxable. On the other hand, the market value of a long-term Treasury note can decline drastically if interest rates rise. With a CD, a sharp increase in interest rates can be much less painful. The worst that can happen is a partial loss of interest, in the event you decide to withdraw your investment before maturity in order to take advantage of the new higher rates available. The more lucrative invest-

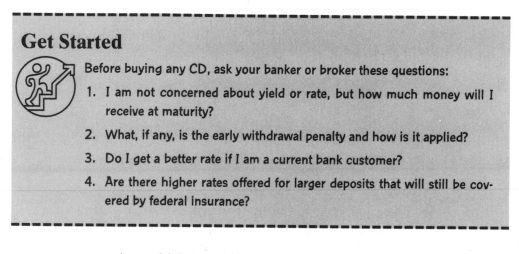

## Get Started

Before buying any CD, ask your banker or broker these questions:

1. I am not concerned about yield or rate, but how much money will I receive at maturity?

2. What, if any, is the early withdrawal penalty and how is it applied?

3. Do I get a better rate if I am a current bank customer?

4. Are there higher rates offered for larger deposits that will still be covered by federal insurance?

ment into which you shift your funds will probably more than make up for that loss. So look carefully at your alternatives before making a decision.

Although CDs generate low yields, and the general investing public is "crying" about its returns, they are still being sold in huge amounts. Thus, it seems safe to say that the bank certificate—with its high degree of safety and flexibility as to maturity—will remain a popular investment choice for people. And on the topic of choice, it may be true that there are two sides to every question, but it is also true that there are two sides to a sheet of flypaper, and it makes a big difference to the fly which side it chooses.

✔ Certificates of Deposit (CDs) are savings instruments issued by banks or brokers that pay interest at a guaranteed rate for a specified term.

✔ CDs are federally insured to a maximum of $100,000 *per certificate.*

✔ You can circumvent the insurance limit by having certificates from different issuers—which is to say, putting your eggs in more than one corporate basket.

✔ The upside of CDs is safety, liquidity, and convenience. The downside is lower yields.

✔ CDs make sense as emergency funds, savings for short-term goals, a way to complete a long-term goal, and a place to "park" money while you study more lucrative investments.

✔ CDs should be evaluated by length until maturity ("term") and rate of return.

✔ You can shop for better deals on CDs by asking about variable-rate CDs, "step-ups" that pay escalating interest, and other hybrid CD products.

✔ When you consider a CD, compare it to a similar investment instrument known as a Treasury note (described in Chap. 15).

*It may be true that there are two sides to every question, but it is also true that there are two sides to a sheet of flypaper, and it makes a big difference to the fly which side it chooses.*

# CHAPTER 3

# Corporate Bond Market—For the Future

*If a company can't pay as it goes, it may be going too fast.*

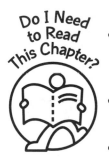

**Do I Need to Read This Chapter?**

➔ I've heard that corporate bonds are a good investment, but I don't really understand what they are or how they work.

➔ What's the difference between a primary and a secondary bond market, and how does it affect me?

➔ What happens to corporate bonds when interest rates rise or fall?

➔ Can corporate bonds be recalled?

➔ What are the various types of yields I can expect?

➔ How can I identify and assess the risks involved in buying corporate bonds?

➔ How do I decipher those fine-print bond listings in the financial pages of the newspaper?

Although bonds have become popular with many investors, they are still widely misunderstood. There are many kinds of bonds, and investing in them wisely can be a complex, challenging task. However, the rewards are often great, and bonds are an option well worth investigating for the middle-income investor.

# How Do Corporate Bonds Work?

A *bond* is a form of debt issued by a government or a corporation. In exchange for a sum of money lent by the buyer of the bond, the issuer of the bond promises to pay a specific amount of interest at stated intervals for a specific period of time. At the end of the repayment period (that is, at maturity), the issuer repays the amount of money borrowed. You can read about the bonds issued by local, state, and federal governments elsewhere in this book (Chaps. 11 to 14).

In this section we'll discuss the special characteristics of corporate bonds—those issued by corporations.

Newly issued corporate bonds are usually sold by a brokerage firm, which acts as underwriter of the issue. The underwriter receives the bonds from the issuing corporation and guarantees the corporation a specified level of sales, and then sells the bonds to the public. This is known as the *primary* bond market.

There is also a *secondary* bond market operated through brokerage firms. The secondary market deals in previously issued bonds, which, as you'll see, may have either increased or decreased in value since their initial offering.

# What Are the Characteristics of Bonds?

Some bonds are issued with property (such as land, buildings, machinery, or other equipment) as collateral against the loan, just

---

## Quick Tips

It's important to understand the differences between corporate bond-holders and corporate stockholders. Here's a brief explanation. The holder of a corporate bond is a creditor of the corporation which issues the bond, not a part owner like a stockholder. Therefore, if the corporation's profits increase during the term of the bond, the bondholder will not benefit; the amount of interest he or she receives is fixed at the time the bond is purchased. On the other hand, the bondholder's investment is safer than that of the stockholder. Interest on bonds is paid out before dividends are distributed to stockholders. Furthermore, if the corporation goes bankrupt, the claims of bondholders take precedence over those of stockholders.

---

as you might offer collateral to a bank in exchange for a personal loan. These bonds are known as *secured bonds.* Bonds not secured by collateral are called *debentures.* The value of a debenture is guaranteed by the good faith of the corporation, and if issued by a strong corporation, the debenture can be a highly secure investment.

All bonds bear both a face value and a maturity date. The *face value* is the amount you will receive when the bond reaches its maturity date. The *maturity date* is when the face value of the bond must be repaid. Thus a 20-year bond issued in 1998 must be repaid in full by the year 2018.

Interest on corporate bonds is usually paid in one of two ways. *Coupon bonds,* also called *bearer bonds,* have interest coupons attached to them. You clip the coupons as they become due and present them for payment of interest. Your name usually doesn't appear on a coupon bond; it is a negotiable instrument, and anyone who clips the coupons can claim the interest due. However, this type of bond is no longer issued, but it may be available in the secondary marketplace. By contrast, a *registered bond* bears its owner's name and can be transferred from one owner to another only by the endorsement of the registered owner. Interest on a registered bond is paid through the mail by check.

Corporate bonds are usually issued in denominations of $1000. After issue, however, their prices vary. A bond's *par value* is $1000, and its value at any given time is quoted as a percentage of par. Thus a bond quoted at 100 is selling at 100 percent of par, or $1000. If the price is quoted at 95, it is selling at 95 percent of par; you could buy such a bond for $950. This is known as a *discounted bond*. A *premium bond* is one which sells at a price higher than par. A bond with a quoted price of 102, for example, will cost $1020, which is 102 percent of par. When fractions occur, an eighth of a point equals $1.25. Thus, a bond at 94⅛ would sell for $941.25 (.94125 × $1000).

## Don't Forget

Bonds and interest rates are like certain married couples: they can't get along with *or* without each other. To put it another way, they share an inverse relationship: When interest rates rise, bonds you currently hold become less valuable; when interest rates fall, bonds become more attractive. Why? Let's look at an example: say a new bond floated by Uncle Sam offers a 6.5 percent rate, competitive with current interest rates (the prime rate, mortgage rates, personal loan rates, etc.). Now two years later the prevailing interest rate has fallen to 5.5 percent. Since new bonds are then issued at that rate, your bond becomes more valuable and could sell at a profit in the secondary bond market. In the opposite scenario, if interest rates rise to 7.5 percent, the value of your bond falls because it returns less than new bonds being issued at the higher rate. To sell it, you would have to offer it at a discount to what you originally paid.

# What Are the Different Types of Bonds?

There are many variations in the types of bonds issued by corporations. You should understand some of the most important ones.

A bond may be issued with a *callability* clause. A callable bond may be redeemed by the issuing corporation prior to the maturity date; that is, the corporation may, at its option, call in the bonds early and repay them at that time (though usually at a premium over the face value). The corporation is likely to exercise this option when market interest rates have fallen below those in effect at the time the bond was issued. If new market conditions call for interest rates of 7 percent, why should a corporation continue to pay 9 percent on its previously issued bonds? As you can see, callability is a drawback for investors, since it prevents them from locking in the high interest rates till maturity. For this reason, callable bonds usually pay a higher interest rate than comparable noncallable bonds. Most bonds issued today are callable.

## Quick Tips

Today some corporations have begun to offer protection for a specified period against the possibility of a bond being called. The "call protection" usually runs 5 to 10 years and guarantees the bondholders a specific interest rate for at least a minimum number of years. Always check the call provision in any bond contract you are considering.

All bonds issued since July 1983 must be registered. This means that the issuer of the bonds records the purchase and sends out the interest checks. If the bonds are registered in your name, the issuer will notify you of the call. If the bonds are registered in the street-name account held by your broker, the broker will be notified of the call and in turn will notify you. For bonds issued before July 1983 that were not registered (coupon bonds), it is the bondholder's responsibility to find out about the call.

Corporations may also issue bonds with a *convertibility* feature. These bonds may be exchanged for shares of the corporation's common stock at the option of the bondholder. This can allow you to participate in a greater-than-expected growth in the profits and value of the corporation. Convertible bonds thus combine the stability and safety of bonds with the growth opportunity of common stock. If you believe a company will move upward but you are concerned about the ups and downs over the short term, the convertible bond would be a good investment for you. If the common-stock value goes down, the convertible bond keeps its fixed yield. But when the common stock rises, you might want to sell the bond and take advantage of the gain. For example, a company with common-stock trading at $20 per share might issue a $1000 convertible bond that pays 7 percent interest and is exchangeable for 40 shares of common stock ($25 per share). The bondholder would not convert at the present time to shares because he or she would be able to buy those same 40 shares at $800 ($20 × 40 shares) in the current market. But if the shares increased in value to more than $25 per share, he or she could convert the bonds to shares, sell the shares, and make a profit. Until a decision is made to convert, the bond will pay $70 per year ($1000 × 7%) in interest. As usual, however, there's no free ride: You must ordinarily sacrifice about 1 percentage point in interest yield in exchange for the convertibility feature. The important feature is that there is a limited downside risk but virtually a limitless upside potential.

# What Factors Should You Consider When Purchasing Bonds?

## What Is Yield as Applied to Bonds?

With regard to bonds, the very term *yield* can be confusing. There are several types of yields associated with bonds.

## Get Started

When considering the purchase of any particular corporate bond, you must weigh two principal factors:

1. The yield offered by the bond

2. The safety of the investment

Unfortunately, these factors aren't as simple as they appear. So let's examine them in greater detail.

The *coupon yield,* or *coupon rate,* is the interest rate stated on the bond itself. A $1000 bond with a coupon yield of 7 percent will pay $70 in interest each year.

The *actual yield* is the rate of return that the coupon yield actually produces when the cost of the bond is taken into account. If you purchase the bond above par, the actual yield is lower than the coupon yield; if you purchase the bond below par, the actual yield is higher. For example, a $1000 bond with a 7 percent coupon rate bought at 82 (for a cost of $820) would produce an actual yield of 8.5 percent (7 percent of $1000 = $70 ÷ $820). The same bond bought at 104 (for a cost of $1040) would actually yield only 6.7 percent ($70 ÷ $1040).

The *current yield* is the actual yield based on the closing price of the bond on the bond market for a given day. When the price of the bond declines, the current yield increases; when the price of the bond increases, the current yield declines. For example, suppose a $1000 bond with a 7 percent coupon rate closed on the trading market on Friday at $910. The current yield for the bond on Friday would be 7.7 percent ($70 ÷ $910).

Finally, *yield to maturity (YTM)* represents the total rate of return if the bond is held to maturity, taking into consideration the purchase price of the bond, the interest paid, and the redemption price. Any broker can refer to a standard reference book which contains yield-to-maturity figures for almost any conceivable bond. The YTM is important because current yield does not reflect any difference between the current purchase price and the value at maturity. If you purchased a bond for $850 and held it to its maturity, you would receive the bond's face of $1000—in other words, a capital appreciation of $150 in addition to the annual interest. The YTM takes all this information into consideration as part of its calculation. The rate plus prorated discount (or subtracting prorated premium) is divided by the average of the total of the face plus purchase price. For example, the YTM of a 7 percent, $1000 bond sold for $850 with 10 years to maturity would be calculated as follows:

$$YTM = \frac{\text{coupon} + \text{prorated discount}}{(\text{face value} + \text{purchase price}) \div 2}$$

$$= \frac{\$70 \ (\text{rate}) + \$15 \ (\$150 \div 10 \ \text{years})}{\$1000 \ (\text{face}) + \$850 \ (\text{purchase price}) \div 2}$$

$$= \frac{\$85}{\$925}$$

$$= 9.2\%$$

Naturally, all things being equal, the higher the yield on a particular bond, the better buy that bond is likely to be. But all things are not always equal. Bonds also differ in their degree of safety. That brings us to the second dominant consideration in choosing a bond for purchase.

## How Is Safety Applied to Bonds?

The degree of risk associated with the purchase of a particular bond depends on the strength of the issuing corporation. Of course, it's not easy for the average middle-income investor to analyze the performance of all the many bond-issuing corporations. For a full examination, it would be necessary to study the company's financial statements, its earnings projections, the track record of management, prospects for the industry, and many other factors.

Fortunately, you don't need to do all this research yourself. There are special advisory services which have assumed the task of analyzing and rating the safety of corporate bonds. These ratings can be obtained from reference books you can readily find at your public library or request from any brokerage house.

The two best-known rating services are Moody's and Standard & Poor's (S&P). They rate bonds according to two slightly differing scales. Starting with the highest-rated bonds, the two scales are as follows:

Moody's: Aaa, Aa, A, Baa, Ba, B, Caa, Ca, C
S&P: AAA, AA, A, BBB, BB, B, CCC, CC, C

The most risk-free bonds—those issued by large, stable corporations showing excellent future earnings projections—are rated Aaa or AAA. Bonds rated AA or A are issued by firms whose ability to pay interest and principal is quite strong, but the safety of these bonds is somewhat more vulnerable to changes in economic conditions.

As you move toward the lower end of the rating scale, yields are likely to be higher; the lower-rated firms must offer higher interest rates to induce investors to accept the greater degree of risk.

Most brokers will quote the standard bond ratings along with prices and yields when you inquire about possible investments. For maximum safety, you'll probably want to stick to bonds rated A and higher. However, even though a bond may have an AA rating when you purchase it, that rating is always subject to change, upward or downward. The only exception would be if you want to choose a low-rated, high yielding bond on a speculative basis. If you do, make sure that the amount you risk in this way is no greater than the

## Quick Tips

You're probably wondering where "junk bonds" fit into the bond picture. In my opinion, they're not unlike junk food. Allow me to explain.

Junk bonds are those on the lowest rungs of the ladder. These bonds have ratings of BB or lower and usually pay yields about 3 percentage points higher than A-rated bonds. They received their disparaging nickname in the late 1920s and early 1930s, when the Great Depression led to numerous defaults by bond issuers, and are today considered one of the major factors in the inadequate financing of major mergers and acquisitions.

Junk bonds offer neither the security of bonds nor the growth of stocks. Yet there are those who will argue that junk bonds have done well in the past. Perhaps a statement I heard about them will suffice. If you ask a drunk at 11 P.M. how he feels, the answer is "fine." The big question is, how will the drunk feel in the morning?

amount you can afford to lose. Greed—especially for the ill-informed investor—can lead to devastating mistakes.

# How Do You Learn About Bonds?

If you're interested in getting into the bond market, you should know how to read the bond quotations which appear on the business page of your daily newspaper. These are a good basic source of information about currently available bonds. Figure 3.1 provides a sample bond listing as it might appear in the newspaper. You'll find an explanation of the information each column provides below the sample listing.

Bonds make an excellent choice for many middle-income investors, especially those whose primary need is for income rather than

| ISSUE | DESCRIPTION | CURRENT YIELD | VOLUME | HIGH | LOW | LAST | CHANGE |
|---|---|---|---|---|---|---|---|
| J&J | 6¾  0.8 | 7.6 | 28 | 90 | 88½ | 89 | +2 |

**Issue:** The abbreviated name of the corporation issuing the bond.

**Description:** A description of the bond. This bond has a coupon yield of 6¾ and matures in 2008.

**Current yield:** The annual interest on a $1000 bond divided by today's closing price for the bond. In this case, 6¾ percent of $1000 ($67.50) divided by $890 = 7.6 percent.

**Volume:** The number of $1000 bonds traded that day.

**High:** The highest price of the day; in this case, 90 percent of par, or $900 for a $1000 bond.

**Low:** The lowest price of the day; in this case, 88½ percent of par, or $885 for a $1000 bond.

**Last:** The day's closing price; in this case, 89 percent of par, or $890 for a $1000 bond.

**Change:** The difference between today's closing price and yesterday's. Since today's closing price of $890 is 2 points higher than the previous day, yesterday's closing price must have been 87, or $870.

**Figure 3.1**  Sample corporate bond listing.

growth. Older people looking toward retirement, for example, are likely to find bonds a particularly attractive investment. However, since bonds are available in so many different forms, be careful in your selections. Remember the importance of safety, and use the standard ratings as your guide. Also be sure you understand the details of the particular bond issue you are considering before you buy. The informed investor can do very well in today's corporate bond market. And on the topic of information, education is what you get when you read the fine print; experience is what you get when you don't.

*It's a Wrap*

 Bonds are forms of debt issued by a government or corporation.

 In general, corporate bondholders enjoy more safety than corporate stockholders. On the other hand, stockholders may share in unlimited potential profits while the bondholder's return (interest rate) is fixed.

 When interest rates rise, bonds lose value; when interest rates fall, bonds become more attractive.

 Most bonds issued today are "callable." That means corporations can recall them if interest rates rise. However, it's sometimes possible to purchase "call protection" as insurance against this.

 Bonds offer several types of yields—coupon rate, actual yield, current yield, and yield to maturity—which you should study before purchase.

 Ratings issued by Standard & Poor's, Moody's, and other advisory services can help you analyze the safety of corporate bonds.

*Education is what you get when you read the fine print; experience is what you get when you don't.*

# CHAPTER 4

# Gold, Silver, and Diamonds—Investment or Enjoyment?

*The golden rule: whoever has the gold rules.*

Do I Need to Read This Chapter?

➡ Am I looking to introduce an entirely different type of asset into my portfolio?

➡ Does my portfolio include foreign holdings that could be balanced by investment in precious metals and jewels?

➡ Will gold really shield me in times of upheaval?

➡ Do I understand the risks involved in buying and holding this type of investment?

➡ What types of gold investments are available?

➡ How about silver and diamonds as investment performers?

*G*old has been used as money since biblical times. It has several characteristics that have made it desirable as a medium of exchange. Gold is scarce. It is durable. More than 95 percent of all the gold ever mined during the past 5000 years is still in circulation. And it is inherently valuable because of its beauty and its usefulness in industrial and decorative applications.

The traditional portfolio is invested primarily in traditional financial assets—stocks, bonds, mutual funds, and the like. Adding gold to a portfolio introduces an entirely different type of asset. The point of diversification is to protect the total portfolio against fluctuations in the value of any one particular class of asset. Gold does exactly that. With more American investors seeking opportunities in foreign markets, this form of diversification is particularly applicable. Indeed, gold is an excellent hedge against foreign exchange volatility.

The economic forces that determine the price of gold are different from, and in many cases opposite to, the forces that determine the prices of currencies. The value of an equity depends on the earnings and growth potential of the company it represents. The value of the debt security depends on safety, yield, and the yields of competing fixed-income investments.

## Quick Tips

Remember that phrase by Thoreau about "marching to a different drummer"? Gold is like that. It doesn't conform to the more predictable patterns of mainstream financial instruments. Investors must be prepared for this.

In short, the value of gold depends on a wide variety of factors: worldwide supply, fabrication demand, central bank sales/purchases, currency movements, political turmoil, and inflationary expectations. The effects of all these factors are somewhat complex and variable. But the important point to remember is simply that they cause the price of gold for the most part to move independently of the prices of financial assets, including stocks and bonds.

# Why Is Gold Considered an Investment?

Gold has long been referred to as the "doomsday metal" because of its traditional role as a bulwark against economic, social, and political upheaval and the resulting loss of confidence in other investments, even those guaranteed by national governments. Yet this may not be true, as was seen during the stock market crash of 1987, the terrible stock downturn in 1989 and 1997, when the price of gold was expected to soar. As you may be aware, nothing occurred to its price, although the volume of sales of American Eagles in 1989 (1-ounce gold coins) increased 300 percent in a single month. When Iraq invaded Kuwait on August 2, 1990, the price of gold went up only 2 percent while crude oil leaped by 27 percent. Also, look at what happened when gold hit an all-time high of $825 on January 21, 1980, and then fell only 5 days later to $634 per ounce when people realized that the world wasn't coming to an end.

Let me illustrate. It was wise in the 1970s to hold gold because high interest rates coupled with a high inflation rate could not provide a real rate of return. It is obvious that if you received an interest rate of 17 percent with an inflation rate of 16 percent, your true return would be only 1 percent. Therefore, gold became an investment as a store of value. But as the inflation rate dropped over the years, gold lost much of its appeal.

## Don't Forget

Gold is not for the faint of heart or for people who love predictability. Its value can fluctuate daily, owing to economic and political conditions. When interest rates in the United States fall, the dollar grows weaker in relation to other currencies. As a result, foreign businesspeople find U.S. investment less attractive, and some of them turn to gold instead. This forces the price of gold higher. When interest rates in the United States rise, the reverse occurs.

# Why Is *Gold* Considered Risky?

The value of gold is volatile. Investing in gold carries with it a definite degree of risk. Any number of events which investors cannot control can influence the price of gold. Many government actions, such as a decision by the U.S. Treasury to sell some of its vast gold holdings, can cause a sharp drop in the price of gold. Even a soaring gold price can carry risks for the investor. If the price of gold becomes prohibitively high, industrial users of the metal may turn to substitutes. This could quickly increase the supply of gold relative to demand and so force the price down. On the other hand, gold could rise because of a sudden demand. For example, if a country has "too many dollars," it may in the near future become an active participant in buying gold.

There's one more drawback to investing in gold. Gold is a non-income-producing asset. That is, it earns profits only when it is sold for a price greater than its purchase price. Gold earns no interest while it sits in your vault.

## Get Started

Should you go for gold, or rule it out of your portfolio altogether? If you can answer "yes" to each of these questions, gold may be right for you:

1. Do I have no need of current income?

2. Do I have the time and interest to watch the market and sell my gold at an advantage?

3. Am I prepared to trade off short-term income from other assets in exchange for gold's long-term, but not guaranteed, profit potential? (This is what is known as *opportunity cost.*)

Another sensible test is to look at how you feel about investing in real estate. Gold is a similar investment—it's easy to get into but difficult to leave.

I personally feel that it takes a lot of "brass" to speculate in gold today. It is not all glitter because its opportunity cost can be high. If you are more concerned with current income than with future gain, then gold is definitely not the investment for you.

Despite these drawbacks, gold can be considered a good investment for some. During its strong periods, gold has been known to increase in value many times over a short span of weeks or months. And, of course, gold has a strong aesthetic and emotional appeal. Unlike most other investments, gold can serve not only as a source of security for the future, but also as an ornament to be worn today.

## What Do the Numbers Mean?

**Quick Tips**

Here's an eye-opening little fact that most jewelers don't reveal. 14K jewelry is only 58 percent gold!

Pure gold is known as *24-karat* (24K) gold. In this form, it is too soft to be made into jewelry. Therefore, it is generally mixed with other metals, such as zinc, copper, nickel, and silver, for additional strength. The number of karats marked on an item of jewelry indicates the ratio of gold to other metals contained in the piece; the higher the karat rating, the more gold the item contains (and the higher its price is likely to be). For example, using 24K as pure gold, 18K gold contains 18 parts gold, 6 parts other metals; 14K gold contains 14 parts gold, 10 parts other metals.

## What Are the Options for Investing in Gold?

See Table 4.1 for an overview of the types of gold investments in the following discussion.

**TABLE 4.1**  Types of Gold Investments

| | BULLION | COINS | SHARES AND FUNDS | CERTIFICATES |
|---|---|---|---|---|
| Who should invest? | Conservative investors prepared to hold large amounts of gold for years | Conservative investors who wish to own small amounts of gold | Aggressive investors | Conservative investors, particularly those interested in buying at regular intervals |
| Where to purchase? | Large banks, coin dealers, stockbrokers | Most banks, stockbrokers, coin dealers | Stockbrokers, financial planners, by mail from no-load and low-load funds | Brokers, large banks, and Deak International |
| What is the smallest investment? | Tiny bars weighing 1 gram (0.032 ounce); more typically, 1 ounce, 10 ounces, and 1 kilogram (32.15 ounces) | 0.1-ounce coin, more typically 1-ounce | The price of one share of an individual company; usually $250 in a mutual fund | $250 in systematic buying programs that let you subsequently invest as little as $100 a month |
| Advantages | Low markup on large bars (2 to 3 percent) | Ease of buying and selling; portability | Maximum gains when gold prices rise; possible dividend income; no storage costs; diversification and professional management in funds; ease of buying and selling | Low dealer markup (3 to 3.5 percent) |
| Disadvantages | Cost of storage (usually in a bank vault) and insurance; cost of selling | Higher markup than on bars based on minting charges; cost of storage and insurance (about $7 a year for each coin) | Maximum losses when gold prices fall; risk of loss if a mine becomes unprofitable or because of political unrest (South Africa) | Annual storage fee |

*Gold bullion:* When you buy gold bullion (that from Engelhard and from Johnson-Matthey is the most widely traded), you are buying gold in the form of bars that are 99.9 percent pure gold. You can actually take physical possession of the gold bars, or you can buy gold through a bank or broker that stores the gold in its own secure facilities. Although you can buy as little as an ounce of gold bullion, a minimum of 10 ounces is usually required, with a kilo bar (32.15 ounces) being the standard. When you buy gold bullion from metal brokers, you must pay certain charges (2 to 4 percent over the spot price) apart from the ounce-for-ounce value of the gold. In addition, some banks may charge a storage fee as high as 1 percent of its value per month for holding your gold.

## Don't Forget

You may choose to have gold bullion stored by a bank or broker. Nothing wrong with that, but you must make certain that it is in a totally "nonfungible" storage program. This means that your gold is not combined with the assets of others but rather held separately and labeled with your name. Under such an arrangement, you have legal title to the gold, and it cannot be considered part of the assets of the bank or dealer which could be tied up by creditors in case of a liquidation.

*Gold coins:* Coins are a popular form for the purchase of gold. They are not only valuable but attractive, and since they are small and portable, they can be kept in a safe in your home or in any bank vault. Most gold coins are minted to weigh 1 ounce, but some weighing as little as 0.1 ounce are available. Expect to pay between 4 and 17 percent beyond the value of the gold to cover the expense of minting and retail costs.

*Gold stocks:* These are shares in companies whose business is gold mining. The purchase of gold stocks is a way of betting on the future price of gold without actually dealing in the metal itself. Gold

## Quick Tips

We've all come across those ads for gold-mining stocks that purport to return riches quickly. They sound so alluring, almost too good to be true. I say "stay away!" If you want to double your money, the safest way is to fold it and put it into your pocket.

stocks have some advantages over owning gold directly. Securities are more liquid than the metal, and no assaying or storage costs are involved. However, shares in gold-mining companies are "leveraged instruments." That is, the value of the stock is affected disproportionately by the value of the product being sold. When the value of gold rises, the value of the stock rises even faster, but when the value of gold falls, the value of gold stock falls faster and farther. In addition, most gold stocks pay no dividends, and when the gold originates in a foreign country, it may be subject to international risks.

*Gold certificates:* If you want to buy a small amount of gold (minimum $2500) and do not want to take delivery, certain banks and brokers will allow you to make a purchase and receive a certificate of ownership rather than the gold itself. In essence, you are buying title to gold held at a bank or broker on your behalf. A yearly fee of about 0.5 percent is usually charged. The main advantage of this way of buying gold is that you do not need to have the gold assayed when you decide to sell it. This makes your assets more liquid.

# What Is the Relation Between Gold and Silver?

Is *silver* (the poor person's gold) a better investment as a precious metal? Whereas gold's primary role is monetary, silver's is industrial. Silver has many more commercial uses than gold—Kodak, for example, uses large amounts of silver every year in manufacturing photographic film—and because of the unique physical and chemical properties of silver, no substitute seems likely to be devised. These industrial uses provide a solid foundation for the future value of silver.

The ratio of the price of gold to the price of silver is a useful investment guideline for those interested in buying either of these metals. You can easily determine the current gold/silver ratio by dividing the morning's gold price by that of silver. In past years, the average gold/silver ratio has been 32:1. A high or low gold/silver ratio indicates that one of the metals is currently undervalued in relation to the other, and you will want to consider moving your holdings into the undervalued metal. For example, a gold/silver ratio of 100:1 shows that silver is undervalued and therefore the metal to buy. A ratio of 15:1 means "buy gold." Remember that this ratio is only a basic guideline and certainly does not apply in all economic environments, especially today.

# How Do You Purchase Silver for Investment Purposes?

As with gold, there are several ways to buy silver. One way is to buy junk silver, which consists of a bag of pre-1965 U.S. dimes, quarters, or half dollars with a face value of $1000 and a market value based on the price of silver for the day. Silver bullion is available in 1000-ounce bars, while silver certificates are receipts for the purchase of silver, held at a bank in your name. Like gold certificates, silver certificates have the advantages of being highly liquid and posing no storage or security problems, so your wealth will remain intact.

# How Do Diamonds Compare with Gold in Today's Economy?

A diamond, it has been said, is nothing more than a piece of coal that has made good under pressure. As an investment it has a great deal in common with gold. Both gold and diamonds tend to be costly in terms of brokers' fees and sales markups, but each offers the investor safety as a hedge against inflation. Diamonds are also a good hedge against depression. Have you noticed what happens when you give a diamond to a depressed spouse?

For people with substantial wealth who wish to concentrate a lot of that wealth in a small space, diamonds can be a sound investment. Unlike gold, diamonds don't demand continual monitoring of a highly volatile market; diamond prices don't fluctuate widely.

# How Do You Purchase Diamonds?

If you do decide to buy diamonds as an investment, regard it as a long-term proposal, not a get-rich-quick scheme. Buy gems weighing from 1 to 3 carats and have them evaluated by an appraiser from the Gemological Institute of America (GIA).

# What Are the Major Drawbacks to Investing in Diamonds?

1.  Most diamonds appreciate in value less than 8 percent a year.
2.  Like gold, diamonds are non-income-producing; no interest or dividends are paid on diamonds.
3.  Diamonds are relatively difficult to liquidate.
4.  The jewelry value of a diamond is much higher than its investment value because of heavy retail markups, which range from 40 to 300 percent, with 100 percent being the average. A diamond bought from a jeweler for $8000 is likely to yield only about $4000 if you decide to sell it to another jeweler later.
5.  Diamonds have high storage and insurance costs.
6.  About 85 percent of the world's diamond market is controlled by the DeBeers–Central Selling Organization, headquartered in

London. Therefore, the price of diamonds is dependent on the activities of a single group.

## Get Started

Lots of mumbo-jumbo surrounds diamonds. When you go to buy them, you may be afraid you're not getting the real thing, or the quoted size, or that you're paying too much. And when you go to sell them, dealers may try to play all kinds of money games.

You can avoid all of that. Once you receive your diamond's GIA certificate, it is easy to determine the stone's fair price by consulting a grading table, since the certificate will state the "four C's": color, cut, clarity, and carat.

*Color* refers to how white or yellow a diamond is. The color of a diamond is rated alphabetically from D to Z. The closer a diamond is to the D grade, the whiter its color and the more valuable the stone. *Cut* refers to the shape of the diamond and the skill with which it has been crafted. The brilliance and beauty of a diamond depend largely on how accurately the diamond-cutter did his or her job. Note that round diamonds are generally the most stable. *Clarity* refers to the number and size of the flaws (or "inclusions") contained in the stone. It takes an expert with a magnifying glass to rate the clarity of a stone. Diamonds range from internally flawless (IF) to imperfect (I-3). *Carat* is the unit of weight for the gem, with 1 carat equaling 200 milligrams ($\frac{1}{142}$ ounce). The value of a diamond increases dramatically as its size increases; a 2-carat stone will usually be worth more than twice as much as a 1-carat stone of comparable quality.

# How Would You Summarize Investing in Precious Metals or Gems?

If you want to try your hand at investing in gold, silver, or diamonds, go ahead; if you have educated yourself and follow the market carefully, you may do very well. But most people will probably derive more benefit and happiness from the beauty and sentimental value of gold, silver, and diamond objects than they will from their investment value. And on the topic of happiness, the secret to being happy is to count your blessings while others are adding up their troubles.

*It's a Wrap*

✔ Gold, silver, and diamonds probably have more drawbacks than advantages as investment options for the average, middle-income American.

✔ Gold is not an automatic bulwark in times of economic and social upheaval.

✔ Gold and precious metals carry a high "opportunity cost," if the money you invest in them could be diverted to other assets that produce more immediate income.

✔ There are several ways to invest in gold: bullion, coins, shares and funds, and certificates. Silver, whose primary role is industrial rather than monetary, offers similar investment options.

✔ Diamonds can be a sound buy for well-off investors. Diamond prices are less volatile than those of precious metals.

**The secret to being happy is to count your blessings while others are adding up their troubles.**

# CHAPTER 5

# Money Market Accounts—
# The Parking Lot

*The idea is to make a little money first and
then to make a little money last.*

*Do I Need to Read This Chapter?*

➡ Am I looking for a place to temporarily invest idle cash?

➡ Do I want a relatively safe investment that usually pays slightly higher yields than bank savings accounts and CDs?

➡ Am I interested in an account where I can write checks and earn interest?

➡ Do I understand the major types of money market accounts, including tax-frees?

➡ Have I considered a money market direct account (MMDA)?

➡ Are my money market investments insured? Safe?

As far as I am concerned, the money market is nothing more than a parking lot, a temporary area for buying and selling high-yield, short-term instruments of credit. In the money market, securities such as Treasury bills, certificates of deposit (CDs), and short-term commercial loans are bought and sold. Since these securities carry high interest rates, they make money grow quickly. But they normally require extremely large investments (Treasury bills, $10,000; jumbo CDs and commercial paper, $100,000) that only wealthy individuals or large institutions can afford. That's where money market funds come in. First made available in 1974, money market funds offer the small investor a chance to take advantage of the interest rates prevailing in the money markets by pooling many people's money.

## Quick Tips

You may want to consider using a money market fund in place of a conventional checking account, which earns you no interest. If this feature "interests" you, make note of any restrictions before you choose your fund. Some funds limit the number of checks you are permitted to write (five checks per month, for example). Others stipulate a minimum amount per check ($500, for example)—so that account wouldn't be suitable for daily checking use.

# How Does a Money Market Account Work?

Money market funds operate by combining many small investors' funds to accumulate the kind of money needed to buy costly money market instruments (jumbo CDs, Treasury bills, etc.). Since the instruments purchased by the fund have different maturities, the fund earns interest on a daily basis. Each investor receives his or her share of the interest by means of a regular statement, usually issued monthly. The amount earned on an investment varies continually as the prevalent interest rates in the money market rise and fall.

Money market funds are managed by investment firms and brokerage houses; the management fee is deducted from the fund's earnings. Usually no redemption charges are imposed on the fund. Most firms transact business by mail, so a money market fund headquartered in Illinois, for example, may have shareholders in any of the 50 states. A minimum deposit is required to open a money market account; $1000 is typical. You can add to your investment at any time, and your funds are completely liquid—you can make withdrawals whenever you wish.

# What Types of Money Market Funds Are Offered?

## Get Started

If money markets seem right for you, the first step is to decide which category is most suitable. Money market funds can be broken into three categories, based upon the type of instruments in which the funds invest.

1. *General money market funds:* These invest primarily in non-governmental securities, such as bank certificates of deposit, commercial loans, and banker's acceptances. Of the three types of funds, general money market funds usually pay the highest interest rates.

2. *Government-only money market funds:* These invest only in securities issued by the U.S. government or by a federal agency. Such funds boast a somewhat higher degree of safety than the general money market funds, but they pay a little less.

3. *Tax-free money market funds:* These purchase only short-term, tax-exempt municipal bonds and are especially suitable for investors in high tax brackets. Although this type of money market fund is exempt from federal tax, it could still be subject to state and local income taxes, since most states do not exempt taxes on municipals issued out of state. The exceptions are Alaska, Florida, Indiana, Nebraska, New Mexico, South Dakota, Utah, Vermont, Washington, Wyoming, and the District of Columbia. If you reside in a high-income-tax state, search out those

*Continued*

municipal money market funds that purchase investments only within your state of residence. For example, a fund may obtain only Massachusetts securities so that all the income earned will be "triple tax-free" to Massachusetts investors. However, Illinois, Iowa, Kansas, Oklahoma, and Wisconsin will impose a tax on municipal bonds issued within their state.

Another important point about this type of investment: because of the liquidity of a money market fund, it is an ideal way to invest idle cash that might otherwise find its way into a low-paying passbook savings account. For example, placing the proceeds from the sale of securities into a money market fund until you've decided upon your next investment venture is a good way of earning continuous high interest on your money.

### Don't Forget

Investments are all in the family with many money market funds. The families have names like Fidelity, Vanguard, and T. Rowe Price—to name just a few among hundreds. The relationship is that these money market funds are part of a larger group of other types of funds (known as a *family of funds*). The advantage is that keeping your money "in the family" permits you to move it from one investment to another as financial conditions change. The most prominent funds are listed daily in the financial sections of newspapers. These listings show the average maturity (the shorter the time, the faster the fund reacts to changes in interest rates) and the average yield for the previous 7 days.

# How Do Money Markets Issued by Banks Work?

Banks entered the money market field in 1982 with their version of the money market fund: the *money market deposit account* (MMDA).

**Quick Tips**

You say you're a pretty savvy consumer, yet you haven't heard of MMDAs? No surprise. Banks don't promote them. And that's a shame. But you see, the banks would rather you purchase their CDs, because with CDs they will have your money for a longer period of time.

The MMDA was authorized by Congress in order to stem the $200 billion tide of withdrawals that banks claimed had been lured away by money market funds.

The MMDA is similar in many ways to the money market fund. It too is based on the pooling concept, allowing small investors to earn interest rates otherwise reserved for large institutional investors or wealthy individuals. Like a money market fund, an MMDA requires a minimum initial deposit as well as a minimum balance. However, as of 1986 federal regulations no longer mandated a minimum MMDA balance. Thus banks became free to enforce a minimum balance rule at their discretion, so don't blame the government if your bank requires a high minimum balance.

Finally, as with a money market fund, an MMDA is a good way to invest cash for a short period.

## What Are the Major Differences Between the Money Market Fund and the MMDA?

When you invest in a money market fund, you become a shareholder in the fund. You and the other shareholders receive all the income earned by the fund's investments, less a small management fee (usually about 0.5 percent annually). When you invest in an MMDA, on the other hand, you are not a shareholder but simply a depositor. Investors in MMDAs do not necessarily receive all the interest generated by their investments, but receive whatever interest rate the bank chooses to pay. Furthermore, the bank is free to invest your money any way it sees fit, even in investments that have little or nothing to do with the money market. Therefore, you have no guarantee that the interest rate you receive will truly reflect the money market rate.

Note, too, the difference in the way the money market funds and the MMDAs usually advertise the interest rates they pay. Money market funds normally advertise the current simple interest rate being earned by the fund. This yield, which is not guaranteed, can change daily as conditions in the money markets change. By contrast, banks often promote MMDAs by advertising the effective yield rate, which is usually a fraction of a point higher than the simple interest rate because of compounding. However, the effective yield rate can be misleading, since it assumes that the bank will be giving compound interest on an unchanging interest rate for a full year. Since this is highly unlikely to occur, you should take with a grain of salt the high effective yields claimed by banks.

Therefore, these lower-yielding instruments will lag behind those with shorter maturities and thus could cause a loss in the fund's market value. The average maturity for investments held by general money market funds is about 35 days; for the tax-free funds, about 65 days.

## Get Started

Consider these differences when deciding between money market funds and MMDAs. They can be significant:

1. With an MMDA, you have a person-to-person relationship with a bank officer whom you know, in contrast to the rather anonymous, through-the-mail relationship usually offered by the money market funds. For some investors, dealing with a personal banker is psychologically important.

2.  The money market fund may be preferable if you plan on making frequent withdrawals from your account. You are usually permitted unlimited withdrawals by check from the fund. With an MMDA, there is normally a limit of three checks per month. However, in most banks you can make deposits or withdrawals 24 hours a day by means of the bank's automated teller machines (ATMs). You cannot do this with the money market fund.

3.  With an MMDA, you may lose up to a month's interest if you close out your account anytime within a given month. With a money market fund, this cannot happen because of daily payments of interest.

# Are Both the Money Market Fund and the MMDA Safe Investments?

As with any form of investment, safety is a factor to consider. Your investment in an MMDA offered by a bank or a savings and loan institution is insured by the federal government up to a maximum of $100,000. If safety is of overriding importance to you, choose an MMDA over a money market fund. However, you should realize that the money market funds have an excellent safety track record. This is because they invest only in short-term instruments issued by such secure institutions as government agencies, large corporations, and major banks. Furthermore, the Securities and Exchange Commission (SEC) regulates money market funds very strictly.

Given their relative safety and numerous advantages, money market funds have earned their place as one of today's most popular options. And on the topic of investing, remember that if you hit the ball over the fence, you can take your time going around the bases.

## Quick Tips

Here's a great rule of thumb for the risk-aversive: The shorter the maturity of an investment, the lower the risk. Why is this? If interest rates should rise rapidly, funds holding long-term maturities would find it more difficult to liquidate their low-yielding holdings.

*It's a Wrap*

✔ Money markets are an excellent place to park your money temporarily—and sometimes for the longer haul.

✔ The principal you invest in money markets is safe, although not federally insured (unless you are investing in a money market deposit account, or MMDA, at a bank).

✔ Money markets allow you to withdraw your money at any time with no penalty.

✔ Money markets earn interest rates that reflect current market conditions.

*Remember that if you hit the ball over the fence, you can take your time going around the bases.*

# CHAPTER 6

## Mutual Funds— The Basics

*To be born rich is an accident; to die rich is a miracle.*

**Do I Need to Read This Chapter?**

➡ Am I thinking about getting started in mutual funds?

➡ Is there a way around price fluctuations in the mutual fund arena?

➡ Do mutual funds have advantages over direct stock purchases?

➡ What key factors should I examine when evaluating individual funds and families of funds?

➡ What are the different kinds of stock-based mutual funds?

➡ What are the different kinds of bond-based mutual funds?

Since October 1987, we have experienced stock market plunges and record-breaking rises that today are still causing anxiety among investors. If you still feel uncertain about the market but would like to take some active part, a mutual fund may be ideal.

# How Does the Mutual Fund Work?

A large number of investors put their money together in a pool to be managed by knowledgeable investment professionals. The price of a share in the mutual fund is determined by the value of the fund's holdings. As the value of the stocks owned by the fund increases, the share price increases and the investors make a profit; if the value of the stocks decreases, the shares are worth less and investors suffer a loss. The price of a share in a mutual fund (determined by dividing the net value of the fund's assets by the number of shares outstanding) is usually announced once or twice a day. The mutual fund also earns dividends that may be paid directly to investors or reinvested to buy additional shares in the fund.

Therefore, mutual funds can make money for their investors in three distinct ways:

1.  The shareholders receive dividends earned through the investment that the fund possesses.
2.  If a security in the fund's portfolio is sold at a profit, a capital gains distribution will be made by the fund to its shareholders.
3.  If the value of the fund's portfolio increases, the value of each share also increases.

Mutual funds are normally created and managed by brokerage houses. As you'll learn, there are many kinds of mutual funds, depending on the types of stocks invested in, the degree of risk involved, the financial goals of the fund, and other factors.

## Get Started

You enjoy a definite advantage by investing in a fund that is part of a "family of funds." There are literally hundreds of fund families offered today; entire books, magazines, and newsletters (available at any public library) are devoted to identifying and ranking them.

1. Determine which fund families interest you, then ask for their literature and study their offerings.

2. Pay special attention to the types of stocks each fund invests in, the degree of risk involved, and the financial goals of the fund.

All fund families have the same basic structure: each is a group of mutual funds with differing investment objectives, managed by the same company. Each allows you to move your money from one fund to another (by written notification, telephone, or, in some cases, even by Internet access), thus offering you maximum flexibility with a minimum of paperwork and lost time.

A way to take care of market fluctuations in the mutual fund arena is through dollar cost averaging (DCA). The investor puts into the mutual fund the same amount of money at regular intervals (monthly, for example). This system allows the investor to purchase more shares when prices are low and fewer shares when prices are high.

## Don't Forget

Although dollar cost averaging can work with any investment, it is especially well-suited to mutual funds, because funds have a diversified portfolio and can bounce back quickly from declines. Table 6.1 presents an example. For the investments shown, the average price of a share was $11.25. But the investor using the dollar cost averaging method paid only $8.89 on average. This means that the average cost per share was $2.36 less than the average price.

**TABLE 6.1**   How Dollar Cost Averaging Pays Off

| MONTH | REGULAR INVESTMENT | SHARE PRICE | SHARES ACQUIRED |
|---|---|---|---|
| January | $200 | $10 | 20 |
| February | 200 | 5 | 40 |
| March | 200 | 10 | 20 |
| April | 200 | 20 | 10 |
| TOTAL | $800 | $45 | 90 |

Average share cost: $8.89 ($800/90)

Average share price: $11.25 ($45/4)

One more point on market fluctuations: many funds advertise how high their total return was for a period of time. If you are more interested in knowing the average annual rate of gain rather than the total return, which is the compounded average annual rate, examine Table 6.2.

# What Are the Advantages of Mutual Fund Ownership?

Mutual funds offer eight important benefits to prospective stock market investors:

1. *Diversification and risk control:*   Money invested in a mutual fund is used to buy shares in many different stock issues. This reduces your investment risk, since the failure of one or two companies out of many will not have a devastating effect on your portfolio. It would be impossible for an individual investor to achieve a comparable degree of diversification without

**TABLE 6.2** Average Annual Rates of Return

| TOTAL RETURN | | |
|---|---|---|
| **3 YEARS** | **5 YEARS** | **AVERAGE ANNUAL RATE** |
| 15.76% | 27.63% | 5% |
| 19.10 | 33.82 | 6 |
| 22.50 | 40.26 | 7 |
| 25.97 | 46.93 | 8 |
| 29.50 | 53.86 | 9 |
| 33.10 | 61.05 | 10 |
| 36.76 | 68.51 | 11 |
| 40.49 | 76.23 | 12 |
| 44.29 | 84.24 | 13 |
| 48.15 | 92.54 | 14 |
| 52.09 | 101.14 | 15 |
| 56.09 | 110.03 | 16 |
| 60.16 | 119.24 | 17 |
| 64.30 | 128.78 | 18 |
| 68.52 | 138.64 | 19 |
| 72.80 | 148.83 | 20 |

having a very large sum to invest in a variety of stocks. Also, with a small investment amount, you will find that by "doing it yourself" your transaction costs (commissions) will be very high because you will be transacting in small dollar amounts. Remember that diversification takes both time and a great deal of knowledge. And one more point: in the prospectus, the terms *diversified* or *nondiversified* may be used. A diversified fund must have at least 75 percent of its total portfolio in different securities so that no one investment can make up more than 5 percent of the fund's total assets. In a non-diversified fund, the requirement is reduced from 75 to 50 percent. However, as important as diversification is, the concept that stock funds shield you from stock market plunges is not always true. Even though there is a good amount of diversification (many different stocks in the same fund), if the market should tumble or fluctuate, diluting the risk by spreading your portfolio among many different stocks does nothing when virtually every issue falls.

---

## Quick Tips

It's easy to let your eyes glaze over when you study mutual fund literature. It's also easy—too easy—to concentrate on the fund's past performance, which cannot be guaranteed for the future. Here's an alternative technique that the pros use: pay special attention to the "turnover rate" when evaluating a mutual fund. It speaks volumes about the fund's management and philosophy.

The turnover rate refers to the dollar amount of stock the fund buys or sells in each year, calculated as a percentage of the average value of its stock holdings. A perfect 100 percent means that within a year, the management has turned over the entire value of its portfolio. That shows an extremely aggressive policy. A 25 percent turnover rate indicates a much more conservative, buy and hold concept. However, bear in mind that a high rate does not necessarily mean a bad policy nor a low rate a good one; but in the long run, I would steer toward the lower turnover rate. Thus, turnover can yield information about very active fund managers (who are making profits for the fund or just churning the accounts) or inactive managers (that are steady in their investment policy or just sleeping at the helm of leadership).

---

2. *Professional management:*   Few investors have the time, energy, or expertise to keep track of all the many factors affecting the

stock market, including changes in interest rates and the money supply, new developments in technology, legal and political developments, and foreign competition. Mutual fund companies have the resources to monitor these developments, for they employ staffs of researchers whose sole task is to keep track of business and economic trends that may affect the performance of securities in the fund's portfolio. This expertise works to your benefit when you invest in the fund.

3. *Moderate cost:*   Many mutual funds require only a small initial investment, with management fees averaging 0.5 percent of your investment annually. By buying or selling in large blocks, the mutual fund pays a brokerage commission that is but a fraction of what you, the small investor, might have to pay. Also, certain types of securities should be bought only in large amounts. For example, Treasury bonds produce the best prices on trades of $1 million or higher—far more than most of us can afford—but such trades are no problem for the mutual fund. For more information, see the discussion of load and no-load funds in the section on costs later in this chapter.

4. *Fund-swapping option:*   Many investment firms sponsor more than one type of mutual fund. The firms usually allow their investors to move money from one fund to another by means of letter or phone call. This is a convenient way to take advantage of changing investment conditions.

5. *Automatic deposits:*   You can usually arrange for automatic investments to be made in your mutual fund account by specifying a dollar amount to be withdrawn from your bank account on a regular basis. This provides a painless way of building your investment portfolio month by month.

6. *Automatic reinvestment:*   You can have all dividends, interest, and capital gains earned by your investment automatically reinvested in additional shares in the fund, another painless way of keeping your investment growing.

## Don't Forget

Warning! Some funds may charge a high fee for reinvesting dividends. Make certain that your monthly statement says that the offer is at "net asset value" and not that the reinvestment of the dividend was at the "offering price."

7. *Ease of withdrawal:* You can usually withdraw your funds by means of a letter authorizing the redemption of shares. You'll normally receive your money within 7 days.

## Quick Tips

Please note that I said "*reduction* of record keeping," not elimination of it. Yes, mutual fund ownership requires some paperwork on your part. If you do not identify the specific shares you are selling, the rule of "first in, first out" applies, meaning that the basis of the shares you are turning in will be considered to be the ones that you own for the longest period of time. This will have a major drawback, since the early shares are often the lowest priced. Thus your taxable profit will be higher.

8. *Reduction of record keeping:* The fund handles all stock transactions for you, records any changes in your holdings, and provides periodic statements showing all transactions, dividend distributions, reinvestments, and capital gains. However, always keep a detailed record of how many shares you buy, the date of each purchase and the cost per share. This also includes any dividend reinvestment.

# What Are the Different Types of Mutual Funds?

Depending on your financial circumstances and your investment objectives, there are many types of mutual funds from which to choose. Let's consider the features of the most common types of funds.

## Common-Stock Funds

Many funds invest in common stocks issued by corporations. Stock funds are often classified as either growth funds (holding riskier stocks that may pay low or no dividends but are expected to rise in value rapidly) or income funds (holding low-risk stocks that pay higher dividends but rise in value slowly). Different types include:

- *Aggressive growth:* Small-company growth funds, sector funds, precious metals funds, and others that seek maximum capital appreciation

- *Long-term growth:* Funds whose main objective is long-term growth of capital; income is secondary

- *Global/international:* Funds that invest worldwide, outside the United States only, and single-country funds. It is important to understand the difference between international funds and global funds. International funds invest only in securities of foreign countries while global funds may invest in both foreign countries and in the United States. Remember also that all investments involve risk, but to invest in foreign countries adds additional problems. For example, currency fluctuation is a risk in international and global funds that is not felt by other funds. Global and international funds investments are denominated in foreign currencies and thus the value of its holding depends on the relative strength of the dollar. A weakening dollar will boost the returns of these funds while a strengthening dollar will reduce them. Other risks to be considered are political situations, economic instability, less liquidity, and a decreased availability of investment information. Let's not forget the Hong Kong market fall in 1997 and its rippling effect on all other foreign markets.

## Don't Forget

Most Americans think of the United States as the financial center of the universe, but that's incorrect. The scope of "foreign investments" may surprise you. Seven out of ten of the largest auto companies, eight of ten of the largest insurance companies and airlines, and ten out of ten of the largest banks in the world are all overseas.

## Quick Tips

Just as "turnover rate" can tell you a lot about a stock mutual fund, "duration" is a key factor when evaluating a bond mutual fund. *Duration* measures the sensitivity of a fund to interest-rate abuses. It is stated in years and forecasts the up or down movement of the market value of the fund resulting from a 1 percent shift in interest rates. Naturally, the shorter the "duration," the less volatile the fund's value.

## Bond Funds

Bond funds invest in corporate or government bonds. These funds fall into several categories. High-grade bond funds deal in top-rated bonds with a high degree of safety and modest yields. Speculative bond funds deal in somewhat riskier bonds (with ratings in the high B's) that often pay higher yields. Junk-bond funds carry both the greatest degree of risk and the greatest potential yield. And municipal bond funds invest in tax-free bonds issued by state and local governments.

For example, in a short-term fund, the duration may be two years which would mean that a 1 percent rise in interest rates would cut the market value of the mutual fund by 2 percent (1% × 2 years). A long-term fund with a duration of 10 years would lose 10 percent in value if rates rose by 1 percent.

The concept is to think of duration as a multiplier rather than a time frame. In the long-term example, it would take 10 years for the added income to make up for the lost capital. Ask the company or your broker for the "duration" of its bond fund portfolio. And on the topic of brokers, I call my dog Broker because he does all his trading on the curb.

It's a Wrap

✔ Mutual funds may be ideal for investors who want the action of the stock and bond markets without having to choose and monitor individual stocks and bonds themselves.

✔ With mutual funds, your money has the chance to grow three ways: through dividends, capital gains, and increase in share value.

Investments made regularly, known as dollar cost averaging, help you ride out fluctuations in the markets.

✔ Mutual funds offer an easy way to diversify your money, control risk, and benefit from professional money management at a reasonable cost.

✔ There are as many types of stock mutual funds and bond mutual funds as there are stocks and bonds.

***I call my dog Broker because he does all his trading on the curb.***

# CHAPTER 7

# Mutual Funds— Spreading the Risk

*If you risk nothing, you risk everything.*

→ Do I have a basic knowledge of mutual funds, but want to know more?

→ Is my portfolio properly diversified for my age and investment goals?

→ Do I understand the difference between load and no-load funds?

→ How do mutual fund investments affect my taxes?

→ Have I been double-taxed on mutual funds without realizing it?

→ Am I aware of the best time of year to invest in mutual funds?

→ What information can I glean from the daily mutual fund listings in newspapers?

# How Do You Choose a Mutual Fund?

In order to choose a mutual fund that is best for you, consider these factors:

1. *Past performance:*   It is more likely that a fund with a good performance record will repeat its good record than that a company with a poor performance will turn itself around.

2. *Expenses:*   The less a fund takes out of your payments (management fees, commissions, etc.), the better off you will be since more money is being invested on your behalf.

3. *Risk:*   Risk comes in two forms. The first type of risk is the possibility that rising interest rates will bring down the value of the bond. As you are aware, higher interest rates have a direct reverse effect on fixed-rate securities such as bonds. Thus, short-term bond funds are less risky than intermediate- or long-term bond funds. The second area of risk involves credit risk—the risk that the issuer of the bonds will not pay. Funds that invest in government securities are thus considered very safe.

4. *Management:*   Good management is of course essential for profit. Look at the portfolio turnover of your fund. This will tell you how often a manager sells the instruments in the fund and buys new ones. Remember that the more the selling and buying, the more commissions that have to be paid. Also to be considered with respect to high portfolio turnover is that the manager may be buying instruments, not on their merits, but rather in anticipation of short swings in the market. This is a situation that is risky and may not work in the long run.

## Quick Tips

Warning! Putting the word "government" into the name of a mutual fund is a great sales tool. It implies security and stability. However, what most people do not know is that a fund calling itself "Government Securities Fund" has to invest only 65 percent of its assets in that single security. Thus "Government Securities Fund" can still invest 35 percent of its assets in something that is not government insured. That is the reason some funds are able to pay high yields. A portion of their portfolio may be in junk (high-yielding but risky) obligations.

5. *Your goals:* What is the reason for the creation of your fund? Did you buy it for your child's education? For retirement? The goal you set up will determine the type of mutual fund you will want to purchase. Thus a time horizon is very important for your financial decision making. You may need the money in 10 years for your child's education but in 25 years for your retirement. For a long period, up-front load is not as important as a large annual maintenance charge.

## Get Started

One of the great things about mutual funds is the diversification opportunities they offer. And the key to diversification, in turn, is to assess your investment needs by age and family situation. As your needs change over time, so do the types of funds that are best for you:

1. When you are young, growth funds are usually best. Your financial needs are often modest, and you can afford to take on higher risk in exchange for maximum growth potential.

2. As you and your family grow older, diversification among various types of funds is desirable. Both stock funds and bond funds belong in your portfolio in middle age. For maximum diversity, try a five-prong approach: domestic and international stock and bond funds, and money market funds. In this way you enjoy the potential benefits of three types of financial instruments—stocks, bonds, and cash—in both domestic (United States) and global markets.

3. When you are nearing retirement age, current income becomes paramount. Bond funds are probably your best choice at this point.

4. Investors of any age who find themselves in a high tax bracket should consider one of the tax-free funds that invest in municipal bonds or other tax-free investment. This type of investment can be free of federal, state, and/or local taxes.

# What Are the Costs of Owning a Mutual Fund?

Depending on how they are purchased, mutual funds can be classified as either load or no-load funds. Let's look at the difference.

There are people who use self-service gas pumps and there are those who prefer service; the same goes for mutual funds. If you are not certain as to your current income needs, your risk involvement, and/or the price fluctuations of market investments, or if you simply don't have the time to be "involved," then the load fund is for you.

Shares in a *load fund* are sold through a stockbroker, who charges a sales commission that is a percentage of the purchase price (this is the *front load*). This commission—about three-quarters of which is kept by your individual broker while the balance goes to the sponsor of the fund—is deducted from your account before any investment is made. If you deposit $10,000 in a mutual fund that charges a load of 3 percent, only $9700 will actually be invested in the fund. Depending on the performance of the fund, it could take several months or more for you to recoup the $300 commission. However, if you plan to remain in the fund for a number of years, the initial sales charge will become relatively unimportant over time. An annual management fee of about ½ percent of your investment is usually also charged.

What does your commission fee pay for? Primarily you are paying for the advice and services provided by your broker. As an investment professional, he or she should help you select the best fund or funds for your purposes and should keep you continually informed as to when you should move in or out of a particular instrument. If your broker doesn't provide this kind of expert advice, consider changing brokers; after all, you're paying for it.

*No-load funds* are usually sold through the mail by means of advertisements in newspapers or magazines. No sales broker is involved; therefore, no up-front commission must be paid. However, a service charge is levied each year. Also, you may have to pay an exit or redemption fee (rear-end load) when you withdraw from the fund. No sales advice or investment services are offered with a no-load fund.

No-load funds do not charge commission fees, because their shares are bought directly from the funds and not through the brokers.

However, no-load funds are allowed to have these fees because of a little-known regulation. In 1980, the Securities and Exchange Commission (SEC) added rule 12b-1 to the Investment Company Act, permitting mutual funds to charge shareholders for the cost of getting more assets into the fund. In other words, a fund could charge the investor for advertising, sales literature, and brokers' commissions on new fund sales. Fund managers felt that they were justified in charging these fees since in the long run, fundholders would benefit as operating costs were spread over more assets. Thus expense ratios would go down, and all would benefit. What is considered an equitable expense ratio? A rule of thumb might be that no more than 1 percent annually for stocks and 0.75 percent annually for bonds should be charged.

In the past, funds could hide these 12b-1 costs by scattering them throughout the entire prospectus (a booklet containing information to help evaluate the investment being offered), thereby hiding the fund's true cost. In 1989 the SEC enacted new rules that required funds to disclose all fees and expenses in one table near the front of the prospectus. This table must show all expenses (both direct and indirect) paid by shareholders and must also disclose the cumulative expenses paid on a $100 investment (5 percent return assumed at the end of 1-, 3-, 5-, and 10-year periods).

# How Do You Compute Your Taxes on Mutual Funds?

There are three methods to determine your cost when you have purchased shares over a period of years at different prices.

1. *Average price per share:*   Your cost is the average price of all the shares you bought.

2. *First in–first out (FIFO):*   Here you assume that the shares you sell are the first shares that you bought.

3. *Specific identification:*   Under this method, you identify the specific shares you sold.

---

## Don't Forget

Does all of this seem very confusing? The dollar examples that follow will make things a lot clearer. What you must remember is always to keep a detailed record of the amount of shares purchased, along with the date and price of each share.

---

For example, suppose you bought 1000 shares of the Waller fund during the year and sold 300 shares at $23 per share in December. Under the three different methods, your outcome could be quite different.

| DATE | SHARES BOUGHT | PRICE PER SHARE | COST |
|---|---|---|---|
| January | 200 | $18 | $3600 |
| July | 200 | $20 | $4000 |
| August | 200 | $24 | $4800 |
| September | 200 | $22 | $4400 |
| November | 200 | $23 | $4600 |
| | 1000 | | $21,400 |

1. *Average price:*   $21,400 ÷ 1000 = $21.40

| | |
|---|---|
| Sale Price | $23.00 |
| Cost | $21.40 |
| Profit per Share | $ 1.60 |
| Shares Sold | × 300 |
| **Profit** | **$ 480** |

2. *First in–first out:*

| | SHARES | PRICE PER SHARE | COST |
|---|---|---|---|
| Jan. | 200 shares @ | $18 | $3600 |
| July | 100 shares @ | $20 | $2000 |
| | 300 shares | | $5600 |

| | | |
|---|---|---|
| Selling Price | $6900 ($23 × 300) | |
| Cost | $5600 | |
| **Profit** | **$1300** | |

3. *Specific shares:* Suppose you specified that you wanted to sell the August ($24) and November ($23) shares.

| | |
|---|---|
| August | $24 × 200 = $4800 |
| November | $23 × 100 = $2300 |
| **Total Cost** | **$7100** |

| | | |
|---|---|---|
| Sale | 300 Shares at $23 | $6900 |
| Cost | | −7100 |
| Loss | | ($ 200) |

Regardless which of the three methods you choose, once a method is selected, you must continue to use it for all transactions in that particular fund.

For example, in the last month of the year, you buy 500 shares in a mutual fund selling for $20 a share (NAV). (See page 77.) A few days later, the fund pays a $2 per share distribution which drops the NAV to $18. You did not lose money because you will either receive a check for $1000 ($2 × 500 shares) or have that $1000 payout reinvested in the fund. But even though you haven't made any money either, you will have to pay taxes on this year-end distribution. If you feel you must own the mutual fund, call the company to find out its distribution date and buy the shares the day after.

And a bit more on taxes. There will be three separate areas of gains from mutual funds that could be taxable.

## Quick Tips

While we're on the subject of taxes, I'd like to pass along another important tip. It's almost always better to invest in a mutual fund after the fund makes its distribution, which is usually between September and December. Here's why: Funds buy and sell securities. When profits on trading exceed losses, the difference is passed along to the investor. This is known as a distribution, and you will owe tax on it. Thus, before buying any mutual fund during the last quarter of the year, ask when the next payout will be and get an estimate of its per-share value. As a rule of thumb, if it is more than 5 percent of the NAV, wait until after the payout to buy.

1. Capital gains distributions per year. Include in this figure any shares you bought through a DRIP (Dividend Reinvestment Program). (See page 90.) Remember that the income earned each year on your mutual fund shares is taxable regardless of whether you take it out in cash or reinvest that income in additional shares. Thus, watch out for double taxation from your gains of mutual funds. If you do reinvestment of your dividends in extra shares, those dividends are reported to the IRS and you will be taxed on them. Therefore, make certain that you add the amount of those dividends to the cost of your share holdings. If you do not do this, when you sell your fund shares, your taxable gain will not have taken into consideration already taxed reinvestments, and you will be taxed again.

2. Dividends per year.

3. Capital gains upon sale. When you sell your shares, you will have either a capital gain or loss which is based on the difference between your tax basis (what you paid plus charges) and what you receive from the sale. Prior to May 1997, the capital gains tax rate was 28 percent for any asset held for 12 months or longer. Gains under one year were taxed as ordinary income. The new law increases your holding time to 18 months but reduces the rate to a maximum of 20 percent (10 percent if you are in the lowest tax bracket). And down the road to the year 2006, a new top capital gains rate of 18 percent (8 percent in the lowest bracket) will apply if the assets are held for five years or longer.

# What Information Is Available?

Each newspaper that carries daily information about the value of mutual funds may list data in different ways. Figure 7.1 is a standard reading of mutual funds as listed in the financial section of your newspaper.

Let's look at an example. Yields reported on the same funds may produce different amounts. The yield in an advertisement you read is called the SEC yield because it is based on a strict conservative formula devised by the SEC and can be the only rate used for advertising. The problem with this yield is that the figure suggests income you

| NAME | NAV | BUY | CHANGE |
|------|-----|-----|--------|
| Roseman Fund p | 12.60 | 13.18 | +.12 |
| Highway Fund r | 6.18 | 7.15 | −.15 |
| Harry Fund t | 18.01 | 18.02 | +.21 |
| Madison Fund x | 11.14 | N.L. | −.05 |

Explanations

**NAV** (bid): Net asset value per share (in dollars and cents).

**BUY** (ask): Price paid by investors plus commission.

**CHANGE:** Change in NAV from yesterday.

Symbols

p: Fund imposes a 12b-1 charge.

r: Fund imposes a back-end fee (redemption price).

t: Used when both p and r are applied.

x: The fund's NAV has been reduced by a dividend payout.

N.L.: Signifies no front- or back-end load.

**Figure 7.1**   Sample mutual fund listing.

## Get Started

It's important to understand these rows of numbers, so allow me to provide a little background. The key figure, the NAV (net asset value), states what each fund is worth.

1. The NAV is computed by totaling the market value of all the fund's assets and adding one day's interest and dividends received.

2. The result is then subtracted by one day's expenses and administrative fees.

3. The total is divided by the number of shares outstanding, resulting in the amount for the NAV.

would earn if you were in the fund for a full year and the fund kept paying at its current rate, which may not always be the case. However, some publications may cite the 12-month average yield, which represents all the fund's income payout per share for the past year divided by the NAV. This method expresses what the fund actually paid into fundholders over the past 12 months. Thus, think of yields and NAV as opposite sides of a seesaw. The interest income is in the middle and stays the same as long as the fund's holdings do not change. As the NAV goes up, the yield goes down. As the NAV goes down, the fund's yield from that same amount of income goes up.

And on the topic of information and advice, I have noticed that when a person with money meets a person with experience, the person with the experience gets the money and the person with the money gets the experience.

It's a Wrap

✔ Factors such as past performance, expenses, risk, management, and your own financial goals can help you make your mutual fund choices.

✔ Your age and lifestyle can help you build a portfolio suited to current income and future growth.

Load and no-load mutual funds are available.

✔ Computing taxes owed on earnings from mutual funds can be complicated. Always keep detailed records of your purchases.

✔ It is generally advantageous to buy a mutual fund after its distribution, which is usually made in the last quarter of the year.

*I have noticed that when a person with money*
*meets a person with experience,*
*the person with the experience gets the money*
*and the person with the money gets the experience.*

# CHAPTER 8

# Stock Market—Bulls, Bears, and Pigs

*In the bust of 1987, I made a killing in the market. I shot my broker.*

**Do I Need to Read This Chapter?**

➜ Am I interested in buying stocks, but hesitant to begin?

➜ Exactly what happens when I buy or sell a stock?

➜ What's the difference between common and preferred stocks?

➜ Have I weighed the advantages and disadvantages of stock ownership?

➜ Can I buy stocks directly from a company without using a broker?

J ust prior to October 19, 1987, everyone was witnessing a major surge in the stock market. Money was being made everywhere and the golden bubble of prosperity just grew and grew. Then came the inevitable burst in 1987, again in 1989, and then in the last quarter of 1997. It is said that bulls can make money and bears can make money, but pigs get slaughtered. And that is exactly what happened.

There's no doubt that investing in the stock market can be one of the most exciting ways of making money. Nothing quite compares with the thrill of seeing the little-known stock you picked become a hot property, perhaps doubling in price—and then doubling again and again. Netscape, MicroSoft or many of the hi-tech stocks are good examples. But as with any investment, the potential risks are equal to the rewards. Middle-income investors who want to play the market owe it to themselves to become fully informed before getting involved. This chapter should be only the beginning of a continuing process of education for anyone interested in becoming a successful stock market investor.

## Quick Tips

The following piece of wisdom is aimed especially at newcomers to the stock market. It's a good reminder for seasoned stock investors as well.

Never forget that whenever you buy a stock, there is someone selling it. You may buy the stock because you believe that the investment is good and the price will rise. However, the person selling that same stock believes the opposite, so only one of you will be correct. Think of it in these terms, and you will become a realistic and conservative player.

# How Does the Stock Market Work?

A share of stock represents a unit of ownership in a corporation. When you buy stock, you are becoming a part-owner of the business.

Therefore, you benefit from any increase in the value of the corporation, and you suffer when the corporation performs badly. You're also entitled to share in the profits earned by the corporation.

Stocks are bought and sold in marketplaces known as *stock exchanges*. The exchange itself does not buy or sell stock, nor does it set the price of stock; the exchange is simply a forum in which individuals and institutions may trade in stocks. Stock exchanges play a vital role in a capitalist economy. They provide a way for individuals to purchase shares in thousands of businesses, and they provide businesses with an important source of capital for expansion, growth, research, and development.

There are two types of stock exchanges: organized and unorganized.

There are some 14 organized stock exchanges currently operating in the United States. The New York Stock Exchange (NYSE) is both the best known and the largest (over 1300 members). Only members may trade shares on a stock exchange, and only individuals may become members, although a member may be a partner or an officer in a brokerage firm (known as a *member firm*). To become a member, you must buy a membership, or "seat," from another member or from an estate. The price of a seat varies greatly, depending on the volume of business being transacted, from a low of $35,000 to well over $1 million in the past 20 years.

Most brokerage firms own seats on an exchange, with one of the firm's officers designated as a member. In their role as brokers, members carry out clients' orders to buy or sell certificates on the floor of the exchange. In communication with other exchange members, brokers can carry out buy-and-sell transactions right on the exchange floor. Current sale prices on each stock being traded are constantly updated and made available to all members. Thus the exchange operates as a kind of auction market for the trading of securities.

# How Does an Investor Purchase Stock?

## Get Started

Here, in two steps, is what happens when an investor decides to buy or sell a particular stock.

First, an account executive at the brokerage house receives the buy or sell order, which may take any of several forms:

*Round-lot order:*   An order to buy or sell 100 shares, considered the standard trading unit

*Odd-lot order:*   An order to buy or sell fewer than 100 shares

*Market order:*   An order to buy or sell at the best available price

*Limit order:*   An order to buy or sell at a specified price

*Stop order:*   An order designed to protect profits or limit losses by calling for sale of stock when its price falls to a specified level

*Good till canceled (GTC) order:*   An order that remains open until it is executed or canceled by the investor.

Second, after the order is received, it is sent to the floor of the stock exchange. The brokerage firm's floor broker receives the order and executes it at the appropriate trading post. Confirmation of the transaction is reported back to the account executive at the local office, who notifies the investor. Remarkably, the entire process may take as little as 2 or 3 minutes.

Not all stocks are traded on any of the 14 organized exchanges. Those that are not are traded "over the counter" in the so-called unorganized exchange. Not a physical place, the unorganized exchange consists of thousands of brokers and dealers who trade in about 50,000 different unlisted stocks through telephone or telegraph communication. A computer system, known as the National Association of Securities Dealers Automated Quotations (NASDAQ), is used to provide instant bid and asked prices on stocks.

In the over-the-counter market, transactions are negotiated privately rather than on an auction basis. An investor wishing to purchase a particular unlisted security consults a broker, who contacts other brokers dealing in that stock. The broker offering the stock for sale at the lowest price receives the offer.

Prices of over-the-counter stocks are quoted as both bid and asked prices. The bid price is the final price offered by a buyer, while the asked price is the final price requested by a seller. Trades are normally made when the bid and asked prices approach one another. (See Fig. 8.1.)

# What Kinds of Stocks Are Available?

There are two kinds of stocks: common and preferred.

## Common Stock

Each year, hundreds of new issues of stock, known as initial public offerings (IPOs), are sold to the public. Although human life ends at the hands of the *undertaker,* it begins for common stock at the

| STOCK | BID | ASKED | BID CHANGE |
|-------|-----|-------|------------|
| FRANNIE | 7¼ | 8¼ | +¾ |

**Stock:** The abbreviated name of the issuing company.

**Bid:** This is the price at which dealers are willing to buy the stock—in this case, $7.25 per share.

**Asked:** This is the price at which dealers are willing to sell the stock; it is always higher than the bid price. In this case, it is $8.25 per share.

**Bid Change:** This is the difference between the bid price today and the bid price at the close of the previous day. Since today's bid price is up ¾ from the previous day's close, the bid price yesterday was $6.50 per share.

**Figure 8.1**   Sample OTC stock listing.

hands of the *underwriter,* who sells the stock, at a fixed price, to a group of initial buyers who in turn "farm out" the investment until it reaches the "street"—which is you, the investor.

## Don't Forget

IPOs have their fans *and* detractors. If you're anxious to make big money on an IPO, then the letters stand for "Immediate Profit Opportunity." If you're a skeptic, the acronym has only one meaning: "It's Probably Overpriced."

A share of common stock represents a unit of ownership, or equity, in the issuing corporation. Each share of common stock usually has a par value, which is a more or less arbitrary value established in the corporation's charter and which bears little relation to the stock's actual market value. The market value is influenced by many factors, including the corporation's potential earning power, its financial condition, its earnings record, its record for paying dividends, and general business conditions.

Ownership of a share of common stock carries certain privileges:

1. *A share in earnings:*   Each year, the board of directors of the corporation meets to determine the amount of the corporation's earnings that will be distributed to stockholders. This distribution, known as the *dividend,* will vary depending on the company's current profitability. It may be omitted altogether if the company is earning no current profits or if the board elects to plow back profits into growth.

2. *A share in control:*   Holders of common stock have the right to vote on matters of corporate policy on the basis of one vote per share held. However, the small investor with only a few shares of stock has little or no practical influence on corporate decisions.

3. *A claim on assets:* In the event of the company's liquidation, holders of common stock have the right to share in the firm's assets after all debts and prior claims have been satisfied.

There are four main categories of common stock, each of which is best for a particular investment strategy and purpose.

1. *Blue-chip stocks:* High-grade, or blue-chip, stocks are issued by well-established corporations with many years of proven success, earnings growth, and consistent dividend payments. Blue-chip stocks tend to be relatively high priced and offer a relatively low-income yield. They are a safe investment.

2. *Income stocks:* Income stocks pay a higher-than-average return on investment. They are generally issued by firms in stable businesses which have no need to reinvest a large percentage of profits each year.

3. *Growth stocks:* Issued by firms expected to grow rapidly during the years to come, growth stocks have a current income that is often low, since the company plows back most of its earnings into research and expansion. However, the value of the stock may rise quickly if the company performs up to expectations.

**Quick Tips**

Yes, blue chips are generally safe investments. However, is that your most important concern? Remember, a ship in the harbor is safe, but is that what ships are built for?

4. *Speculative stocks:* Speculative stocks are backed by no proven corporate track record or lengthy dividend history. Stocks issued by little-known companies or newly formed corporations, high-flying "glamour" stocks issued by companies in new business areas, and low-priced "penny stocks" may all be considered speculative stocks. As with any speculative investment, there is a possibility of tremendous profit—but a substantial risk of losing all as well.

## Preferred Stock

Preferred stock, like common stock, represents ownership of a share in a corporation. However, holders of preferred stock have a prior claim on the company's earnings as compared with holders of common stock; hence the name *preferred stock*. Similarly, holders of preferred stock have a prior claim on the company's assets in the event of a liquidation, but they have no voting privileges.

Preferred stock also has certain distinctive features related to dividend payments. A fixed, prespecified annual dividend is usually paid for each share of preferred stock. This fixed dividend may be expressed in dollars (for example, $10 per share) or as a percentage of the stock's par value. It must be paid before dividends are issued to holders of common stock.

However, preferred-stock dividends are not considered a debt of the corporation—unlike, for example, the interest due on corporate bonds—because the firm is not obligated to meet its dividend payments. If the corporation is losing money, the board of directors may decide to withhold the dividend payment for a given year. To protect stockholders against undue losses, most preferred stock is issued with a cumulative feature. If a dividend is not paid on cumulative preferred stock, the amount is carried over to the following period, and both dividends must be paid before holders of common stock can receive any dividend. Also, a few companies may offer adjustable-rate preferred stock (ARPS). These issues have cash dividends that will change every 3 months in accordance with the current market interest rates. This type of stock is designed to be more competitive with bonds and thus to make the dividend rate on preferred stock reflect current market conditions.

# What Are the Advantages and Disadvantages of Stocks?

Like any investment, stocks have distinct advantages and disadvantages. Some of these should have already become apparent. Let's take a systematic look at them. First, the advantages of investing in stocks:

*Growth potential:*    When a company has the potential for growth in value and earnings, so does its stock. If you pick the right stock or group of stocks, you can profit significantly and relatively quickly. History shows that, as a whole, the stock market has had an upward trend in values, with years of gain outnumbering those of decline by better than 3 to 1.

*Liquidity:*    Stocks traded on the major exchanges can be bought and sold quickly and easily at prices readily ascertained.

*Possible tax benefits:*    Growth stocks, which pay low or no dividends so that company profits can be reinvested, provide an effective tax shelter for your profits. As the corporation's value grows, so does the value of your stock, which is a form of tax-deferred income, since no taxes need be paid on these gains until you sell the stock.

Now the disadvantages:

*Risk:*    There can be no guarantee that you will make money investing in stocks. Companies may fail, stock prices may drop, and you may lose your investment. Remember the saying of one concerned investor, "I am not so concerned with the return *on* my investment as I am with the return *of* my investment."

*Brokerage commissions:*    Most investors need the help and advice of a stockbroker when they become involved in the market. However, high brokers' commissions can largely erode your profits. Since one fee is charged when you buy your stocks and another when you sell them, you are, in effect, forced to pay twice. If you're an unusually well-informed investor look into the use of a discount broker, which provides little or no investment counseling but charges greatly reduced commissions when trading your stocks.

*Complexity:*    The stock market is a complicated subject, and the amount of knowledge needed to be consistently successful is tremendous. Investors who lack the patience, time, or skill to inform themselves about the market often buy and sell on impulse, thereby minimizing their profits and maximizing their losses. If you get into the stock market, be prepared to devote

---

## Get Started

More and more investors are considering Dividend Reinvestment Plans (DRIPs), which are direct stock-purchase plans. You might say DRIPs are getting splashier all the time. Like any form of stock ownership, they have pros and cons:

1. DRIPs allow you to purchase shares of a company without any brokerage commission. How? You are buying *directly* from the company, not through a stockbroker.

2. With traditional dividend reinvestment plans, you had to purchase your first shares through a stockbroker before purchasing additional shares directly from the company. Today's DRIPs allow you to buy your first share, and all following shares, directly.

3. Getting into DRIPs is simple, as seen by the ever increasing number of companies that offer them.

4. However, getting out of DRIPs is another story.

You may have to pay a fee to terminate your DRIP as well as tackle the tedious task of attempting to figure your cost basis of shares you have acquired at various different prices. If no records are available for specific identification, the first-in, first out rule applies (see pages 74–75).

---

the time and work necessary to make intelligent decisions instead of haphazard ones.

And on the topic of stocks, what keeps most people out of the stock market is the supermarket.

✔ Playing the stock market requires attention, concentration, and good information. (For more on the latter, please see the next chapter.)

✔ There are four types of common stock: blue-chip, income, growth, and speculative stocks.

✔ Preferred stocks confer certain advantages in regard to earnings and dividend payments.

✔ Stocks offer growth potential, liquidity, and possible tax benefits.

✔ Stocks also involve commission payments and risk.

✔ Dividend Reinvestment Plans (DRIPs) allow you to buy stock directly from issuers, thus bypassing brokers and their commissions.

*What keeps most people out of the stock market is the supermarket.*

# CHAPTER 9

# Stock Market Information— Where to Get It

*It's not the bulls and the bears on Wall Street that make you lose money, it's the bum steers.*

**Do I Need to Read This Chapter?**

➡ Am I eager to jump into the stock market, but feel a little short on general preparation?

➡ Am I totally clear on "P/E," "100s," and all the other shorthand notations for stocks in the financial pages?

➡ Can I identify and analyze the five key indicators in judging a stock's value?

➡ Do I understand the key stock market indexes?

➡ Have I developed the thick skin and commonsense attitude required to play the market?

Now that you know the basic characteristics of the different kinds of stocks, let's take a look at some of the things you should know to get started in stock market investing. People will spend 5 to 10 hours in comparison shopping for a television that costs $300 but will put $5000 into a stock after a 5-minute phone call from a broker. The next time you want to buy a stock, spend time learning about the market and its offerings. Pretend you are shopping for a TV.

## Quick Tips

Newspaper listings are useful, but consider them just a starting point for getting information and analyzing the value of a particular stock. Prudent would-be investors also consult a corporation's annual report, newspaper and magazine articles about the business, stock market newsletters and columnists' comments, and the advice of your broker can all be helpful. An old saying is very appropriate: "Buy on rumor, sell on news." Hearsay aside, facts are your most important asset.

# How Do You Learn About Investing in the Stock Market?

An investor's most important tool is information: information about stock prices, movement in the market, and likely business trends. Without plenty of sound information, investment decisions are pure guesswork. The first place to look for information about any stock is the financial pages of your newspaper, and the best place to start is with the columns listing the current stock prices on one or more of the major organized exchanges. Figure 9.1 provides explanations of the information you'll find in those columns and what it means for you as a prospective investor. It shows a typical listing for a stock traded on one of the major exchanges.

Newspapers can list only a small fraction of the thousands of stocks traded over the counter. Therefore, a phone call to your broker is a must if you are interested in the day's activity in a particular over-the-counter (OTC) stock. Newspaper listings for OTC stocks are simpler than those for stocks traded on a major exchange (see Fig. 8.1).

| HIGH (1) | LOW (1) | STOCK (2) | DIV (3) | P/E (4) | 100S (5) | HIGH (6) | LOW (6) | LAST (7) | CHANGE (8) |
|---|---|---|---|---|---|---|---|---|---|
| 44 | 16 | JLJ | 2.50 | 9 | 33 | 35¼ | 34 | 35 | +½ |

**(1) High and Low:** These are the highest and lowest prices paid for the stock during the previous year (over 52 weeks). This entry shows that the highest price paid for JLJ stock during the previous year was $44 per share; the lowest price, $16 per share.

**(2) Stock:** Stocks are listed alphabetically by an abbreviated form of the corporate name.

**(3) Dividend:** The rate of annual dividend is shown; it is generally an estimate based on the previous quarterly or semiannual payment. This entry shows that JLJ is paying an annual dividend of $2.50 pcr share, or about 7% yield (2.50 ÷ 35). (See page 96.)

**(4) Price/Earnings Ratio:** This is the ratio of the market price of the stock to the annual earnings of the company per share of stock. As you'll learn later, this is an important indicator of corporate success and investor confidence.

**(5) Shares Traded:** This is the number of shares sold for the day, expressed in hundreds. In thc example shown, 3300 shares of JLJ stock were traded. The figure does not include odd-lot sales. Note: if the number in this column is preceded by a "z," it signifies the actual number of shares traded, not hundreds.

**(6) High and Low:** These are the highest and lowest prices paid for JLJ stock during the trading session (that is, the business day). The highest price paid for JLJ stock was $35.25 per share; the lowest price, $34 per share. Stock prices are shown in dollars and fractions of dollars.*

**(7) Closing Price:** The final price of JLJ stock for the day. In this case, it was $35 per share.

**(8) Change:** The difference between the closing price of the stock for this session and the closing price for the previous session. Since JLJ stock closed at $35 per share, up ½ (or 50 cents) from the previous close, yesterday's closing price would have been $34.50.

*Fractions are now reported from ¹⁄₁₆ to ¹⁵⁄₁₆.

**Figure 9.1**   Sample stock listing.

# What Is an Investment Club, and How Can It Help Me?

Investment clubs are popping up all over. There are probably two reasons: the popularity of *The Beardstown Ladies' Common-Sense Investment Guide,* a book about an extremely successful investment club in the heartland of America; and the amazing rise of the stock market.

Investment clubs have a simple premise: a group of friends, family members, or coworkers get together regularly to learn more about stocks and to pool nominal amounts of money into the investments of their choice. Many club members use their new-found knowledge of the stock market to begin their own personal stock portfolios, as well.

## Get Started

1. The beauty of these clubs is that everyone learns together. You need not be an expert to join an investment club, or even to start one. All it takes is the willingness and desire to become a better-educated investor.

2. Most investment clubs—including the Beardstown Ladies—belong to the National Association of Investment Clubs. The NAIC has been promoting the creation of investment clubs and sponsoring Investors' Fairs nationwide since 1951.

3. To learn more about investment clubs, contact the NAIC at 711 West 13 Mile Road, Madison Heights, Michigan 48071, telephone (248) 583-NAIC (6242). Or check them out on the World Wide Web—www.better-investing.org—or by entering GO NAIC on CompuServe.

# What Statistics Should You Know to Evaluate Stocks?

## Get Started

The following statistics are the "Big Five" when it comes to judging the value of a stock's offering:

1. Earnings per share
2. Book value
3. Price/earnings (P/E) ratio
4. Yield
5. Rate of return

These are the building blocks, so let's examine them one by one.

*Earnings per share:* The current earnings-per-share figure is one basic measure of the success of a corporation. It is computed by taking the corporation's net profit after taxes, subtracting any preferred-stock dividends, and dividing the remainder by the number of outstanding shares of common stock. For example, suppose Roseman Corporation earned a net profit of $4,300,000 last year, paid a dividend on preferred stock of $300,000, and has 800,000 outstanding shares of common stock. The earnings per share for the corporation are $5:

|  |  |
|---|---|
| $4,300,000 | Net profit after taxes |
| − 300,000 | Dividend on preferred stock |
| $4,000,000 |  |
| ÷ 800,000 | Outstanding shares of common stock |
| = $5 | Earnings per share |

*Book value:* This is one measure of the value of the assets of the corporation. It is computed by taking the listed value of the assets, subtracting

*Continued*

amounts due to creditors and preferred stockholders, and dividing the remainder by the number of outstanding shares of common stock. To take another simple example, suppose Roseman Corporation owns assets valued at $30 million, has debts totaling $10 million, and has 800,000 shares of common stock outstanding. The book value of Roseman Corporation is $25 per share:

| | | |
|---|---:|---|
| | $30,000,000 | Assets |
| − | 10,000,000 | Debts and value of preferred stock |
| | $20,000,000 | |
| ÷ | 800,000 | Outstanding shares of common stock |
| = | $25 | Book value per share |

*Price/earnings (P/E) ratio:*   This important index allows you to compare the market price of the stock to its demonstrated earning power. A low P/E ratio—say, under 7—shows that the company has high earnings relative to the current market price of its stock and suggests that the market has undervalued the stock. The stock is probably a good buy at its current price. Stocks with low price/earnings ratios can reward you in two ways:

- If they're undervalued, their prices should eventually go up.
- If the market as a whole slumps, they may not sink as much.

For cautious investors, stocks with a low P/E ratio make sense. A host of different studies have shown that, as a group, such stocks perform better, over the years, than a group with medium or high P/E ratios. Conversely, a high P/E ratio (15 or more) shows that the market expects large future gains from the company and has therefore driven up the price of the stock. The P/E ratio is computed by dividing the stock's market price by the company's earnings per share. If stock in a corporation is selling at $35 per share and the company has earnings of $3 per share, the P/E ratio is 35 ÷ 3, or 11.6, which is a bit lower than the average P/E ratio of 13.

*Yield:*   This figure offers another indication as to how reasonable the current price of a stock is. It is a percentage determined by dividing the current annual dividend per share by the current market price of a share. If a corporation is paying an annual dividend of $2.50 per share and the stock is selling at $35 per share, then the yield is 2.50 ÷ 35, or about 7.1 percent.

*Rate of return:*   The rate of return on a given stock is a measure of the total profit you gain from holding that stock for a specified period of time.

Computing the rate of return involves several steps. First, find the total market value of your stock at the end of the period in question. Add to this figure the total amount of dividends earned by the stock during the period. Divide this sum by the total market value of the stock at the start of the period. Subtract 1, and multiply by 100. The resulting figure, expressed as a percentage, is your rate of return for the period. Here's an example. Suppose you bought 100 shares of AJL stock at $24 per share. You've held the stock for 1 year. The stock paid a $2 per share dividend during the course of the year. At the end of the year, it has a market value of $25 per share. The rate of return for this stock is 12.5 percent, calculated in this way:

$2500    Market value of stock at end of period
+  200    Dividend paid during period
―――――
$2700
÷ 2400    Market value of stock at start of period
―――――
1.125

$$1.125 - 1.0 = 0.125 \times 100 = 12.5\% \text{ rate of return}$$

# What Is Dollar Cost Averaging (DCA)?

Although mentioned in the mutual fund section, DCA is so important as a method to limit stock purchase risk that it must be expanded in this section. *Dollar cost averaging* (DCA) can limit your market risk by investing the same sum of money monthly regardless of any stock fluctuations. As prices fall, your fixed amount of money buys more shares. If prices should rise, your amount would purchase less shares but in the long run, DCA results in your buying more shares at low prices than you do at high prices. This method uses time to the best advantage, since over time several market cycles can occur. The best way to understand DCA is to think of it as an installment plan for the investor or as an automatic purchase plan. Arrangements can be made to have this predetermined monthly or quarterly withdrawal come directly from your checking or savings account into the investment of your choice.

**Don't Forget**

Dollar cost averaging sounds ideal, doesn't it? In most ways, it is. However, you should be aware that DCA is not without its problems. If the same amount is invested each month, its inflation-adjusted value will decrease over the years. Also, it does not guarantee that you will protect your investment from losses. If the overall economy and the market is down, you will wind up with a loss for that period of time.

A new investment strategy moves DCA a step further by placing the emphasis on the value of the investment instead of the cost. For example, instead of a fixed investment of $500 monthly, you determine an objective of increasing the value of your investment by $500 monthly. Each month, the value of your investments will then determine how much is needed to bring the value to the level you choose. If the stocks have increased in value since the previous month, you can put in less than the $500 amount. However, if they have decreased, you would put in more than the usual amount in order to replace its lost value. During the crash in October 1987, the amount you would have been required to add would have been extremely high in order to meet your value goal for the next month. Now that's discipline! However, the largest single drop of 554 points on October 27, 1997, comparatively speaking, was short-lived because of succeeding gains. The DCA for the month did not increase that much.

But there is also a downside to this method. You must understand that it is not automatic, as is DCA, which is a fixed amount of money each month. It requires more work on your part. You have to calculate each period the *actual value* of your investments with your *targeted value* so you are able to determine the amount you need to invest.

# What Are Stock Market Indicators?

It has been said that the stock market is a "leading" indicator, meaning that stock prices reflect expectations of future growth and profits. The market is not designed to show current conditions. Thus indexes can yield an idea of what investors are expecting. Most market indexes will move in tandem, but there is a considerable difference in their performances in the long run. The reason is that the indexes are composed of different stocks. Below is a listing of three of the most widely accepted stock market indexes and the types of stocks they include.

1. *Dow Jones Industrial Average (DJIA):* In attempts to gauge or predict large-scale trends in stock market values, the Dow Jones Industrial Average (DJIA) is often cited. The most frequently mentioned of four Dow Jones averages (covering industrial stocks, transportation stocks, utility stocks, and a composite average), the DJIA is a barometer of stock market trends based on prices of 30 large U.S. corporations listed on the NYSE. Every day, the fluctuations in the prices of these stocks are combined by adding up the prices of the 30 stocks and dividing the result by a designated factor 0.3 (used to compensate for complicating situations, such as stock splits and periodic substitutions in the list of stocks used). The 30 stocks that made up the DJIA during 1997 are:

| | |
|---|---|
| Alcoa | (AA) |
| Allied Signal | (ALD) |
| American Express | (AXP) |
| AT&T | (T) |
| Boeing | (BA) |
| Caterpillar | (CAT) |
| Chevron | (CHV) |
| Coca-Cola | (KO) |
| Du Pont | (DD) |
| Eastman Kodak | (EK) |
| Exxon | (XON) |
| General Electric | (GE) |
| General Motors | (GM) |
| Goodyear | (GT) |
| Hewlett-Packard | (HWP) |
| IBM | (IBM) |

| International Paper | (IP) |
| J. P. Morgan | (JPM) |
| Johnson & Johnson | (JNJ) |
| McDonald's | (MCD) |
| Merck | (MRK) |
| Minnesota Mining | (MMM) |
| Philip Morris | (MO) |
| Procter & Gamble | (PG) |
| Sears, Roebuck | (S) |
| Travelers | (TRV) |
| Union Carbide | (UK) |
| United Technologies | (UTX) |
| Wal-Mart | (WMT) |
| Walt Disney | (DIS) |

**Quick Tips**

A glance at this list will tell you why the Dow Jones Industrial Average has been widely criticized as an inaccurate reflection of the U.S. economy and U.S. stock market. The Dow is weighted with older, heavy manufacturing firms and doesn't fully measure the impact of newer, high-tech companies. The mathematical method used in calculating the Dow has also been attacked on various technical grounds. Other indexes, such as the Standard & Poor's Composite Index (see text list), have been created to compete with the Dow. Nonetheless, the Dow Jones Industrial Average remains the most popular and influential measurement of the direction and strength of the U.S. stock market.

2. *Standard & Poor's Composite Index:* This index, better known as the S&P 500, began in 1957 and is presently one of the 12 leading economic indicators. Although the DJIA is much older than the S&P, many investors believe that the S&P better measures the performance of blue-chip stocks because of its broad base of 500 stocks (compared with the DJIA's 30). These 500 stocks, which are traded on the New York and American stock exchanges and on the over-the-counter (OTC) market, are in turn broken up into subindexes (400 industrial, 40 public utilities, 40 financial companies, and 20 transportation companies) so that a broad base is accomplished. Unlike the DJIA, which measures the returns of a small sector of the stock market (large blue-chip stocks), the S&P 500 measures the performance of many relatively smaller stocks as well as the blue chips. Whereas the DJIA simply adds up the current day's prices of its 30

stocks in its index and begins its calculations from that total, the S&P is weighted by market value (number of shares multiplied by price). Thus each stock can influence the result in proportion to its market value. Another point is that the DJIA moves more dramatically than the S&P 500. In a broad market move, the S&P usually moves 1 point for every 7 points lost or gained by the DJIA.

3. *NASDAQ Composite:*   This index, begun in 1971 by the National Association of Securities Dealers, traces 3900 stocks traded on NASDAQ (formally, the National Association of Securities

## Get Started

In summary, the only way to approach the stock market is with good, old-fashioned common sense.

1. *Avoid hot tips:*   If a friend or your brother knows about a hot tip, so do hundreds of other people. Remember, hot tips can get you burnt.

2. *Don't fall in love:*   Don't get married to a stock even if it's your employer's stock that you have accumulated over the years. Weed out those stocks that are not meeting your objectives, even if it's the first stock you ever bought.

3. *Compare your portfolio:*   Check on your total return by adding up the stock's price change and dividends for a specific period and divide the total by the price at the start of that period. Then multiply the result by 100. This will give you a percentage, which is a fair comparison to other types of investments.

4. *Have a bit of patience:*   Except for wild speculation, take your time. Sell, not on the basis of the stock's performance over a short period of time, but rather on the concept of the long run. Remember that the longer the holding period, the more likely you will gain a profit in spite of the inevitable interim ups and downs. On the buy side, the same rule applies. Don't get bullied into purchasing something that "can't wait." Good investments can wait.

Dealers Automated Quotations). Like the S&P 500, the index is market-weighted so that the largest stocks will influence the index more than the smaller ones. Did you know that the 50 largest companies listed on this index have capitalizations of over $1 billion each?

It is true that there is no way to tell where the market will be a year or two from now, but by keeping informed, you stand a better chance in this roller coaster market we are now all experiencing. And on the topic of the market, Wall Street is a place where the day begins with good buys.

*It's a Wrap*

✔ Successful stock investments are based on sound information, not "hot tips" or guesswork.

✔ The five key indicators in judging a stock's value are earnings per share, book value, price/earnings (P/E) ratio, yield, and rate of return.

✔ Dollar cost averaging can limit your market risk, but it is no guarantee against inflation or general loss when the stock market is down.

✔ The three leading market indexes—the Dow Jones Industrial Average, Standard & Poor's Composite Index, and the NASDAQ Composite—attempt to measure the strength and direction of the U.S. stock market.

***Wall Street is a place where the day begins with good buys.***

# CHAPTER 10

# Zero Investment

*Dig a well before you are thirsty.*

**Do I Need to Read This Chapter?**

➔ Do I need to save money towards a particular life event in the future, such as college tuition for my child?

➔ Am I aware of zero coupon bonds?

➔ Can I balance a predictable, long-term investment with a certain degree of risk?

➔ Am I interested in an investment with tax-deferred features?

I s there an instrument that lets you know exactly how much money you will have at a particular future date (whether it be for your child's education, your retirement, etc.) and if administered correctly becomes tax deferred or even tax exempt? Yes, the Zero coupon bond. The Zero coupon bond is a unique financial tool which has become, over the years, an ever increasingly popular instrument for long-term investment.

As you will see in the following pages, zero coupon bonds have some definite advantages over other types of long-term investments. They have become an excellent choice for Individual Retirement Accounts (IRA), 401(k) plans, Keogh and other pension funds, and most certainly for a child's college savings. They are therefore an ideal investment for those of you who are more concerned about "outcome" rather than "income."

### Quick Tips

You're probably wondering what makes zero coupon bonds different from the traditional bonds mentioned in Chap. 3. In short, "zeros" are sold at a price well below the face value. Thus, these bonds are appealing to the small investor because they can be bought far cheaper than ordinary debt obligations. The discount is usually from 50 to 75 percent.

# How Does the Zero Coupon Bond Work?

Bonds are debt obligations issued by a corporation or by a federal, state, or local government agency. When you buy a bond (usually at face value), you are buying a promise from the issuing institution to pay the amount of the face of the bond at maturity.

For example, a zero with a face value of $1000 (at 8 percent) may sell for just $456. You pay $456 today; at the time of maturity—10 years—you can redeem the bond for its full $1000 face value. The extra $544 paid on redemption is the accumulated 10 years' worth of interest on your $456 investment.

- - - - - - - - - - - - - - - - - - - - - - - - - - - - - - - - - - - - - - -

## Don't Forget

As the old saying goes, "good things come to those who wait." If waiting patiently isn't in your nature, zero coupon bonds are not a suitable investment for you. They are strictly for the long term. During the life of the zero, you clip no coupons and receive no interest payments (hence the name "zero coupon bonds"). The entire interest payout comes at once—upon redemption.

- - - - - - - - - - - - - - - - - - - - - - - - - - - - - - - - - - - - - - -

Table 10.1 shows the price for a $1000 zero coupon bond under various interest rates and maturity dates. Naturally, the longer the term of the bond and the higher the interest rate, the greater the discount at which the bond is sold. Note that the amounts are rounded to the nearest dollar.

If you're still in your twenties or thirties, you may purchase a big chunk of retirement money very cheaply by buying a long-term zero right now. For example, at an 8 percent interest rate, you may

**TABLE 10.1** The Cost of a $1000 Zero Coupon Bond

| INTEREST RATE | MATURITY DATE AND COST* | | | | | |
|---|---|---|---|---|---|---|
| | 5 YEARS | 10 YEARS | 15 YEARS | 20 YEARS | 25 YEARS | 30 YEARS |
| 6% | $744 | $544 | $412 | $307 | $228 | $170 |
| 7 | 709 | 502 | 356 | 255 | 179 | 127 |
| 8 | 676 | 456 | 308 | 208 | 141 | 95 |
| 9 | 644 | 415 | 267 | 172 | 111 | 71 |
| 10 | 614 | 377 | 231 | 142 | 87 | 54 |

* Actual price can vary because of availability, fees, and other factors affecting bond prices.

buy a zero redeemable at $1000 in 30 years for under $100. It's hard to imagine a better buy than that.

# What Advantages Do Zeros Offer as an Investment?

## Get Started

Can you tell that I'm a booster when it comes to zero coupon bonds? Objectively speaking, they do offer several distinct advantages:

1. Call protection

2. Liquidity

3. Adaptability

4. Special suitability for tuition savings

Let's look at each of these in depth. And because advantage number 4 is so important these days, we'll examine it on its own.

Zeros have *call protection,* meaning that it is unlikely that they will be called in for early redemption by the issuing company if interest rates should fall. (There'd be no advantage to the corporation in prepaying the interest on zeros unless there were special call provisions in the agreement.) As you are aware, we are presently experiencing major calls in bonds. Thus be certain to find out whether the bond you wish to purchase is callable and if so, ask about its "yield to call." *Yield to call* means that you will be guaranteed a set return if the bond is called in early. Also, if interest rates in the market should fall, with a conventional bond the interest payments you receive would have to be reinvested at the lower existing rate. You avoid this when you purchase zero coupon bonds because the interest is reinvested at the fixed rate (which was higher than the prevailing rate) at which you purchased them.

Zeros also offer *liquidity*. If, for some reason you need to sell your bond before maturity, you can sell it on the so-called secondary market at the current rate. This may produce a gain or loss depending upon interest rates at the time of the sale. For example, if interest rates are higher at the time you dispose of the bonds, you will take a loss. However, a lower interest rate will yield you a profit. And speaking about interest rates, another advantage of zeros is that you avoid the roller coaster ups and downs of interest rates if a bond is kept to maturity. As stated above, the value of a bond will rise if interest rates fall and will drop in value if interest rates rise. With zero bonds, no matter how much their value may fluctuate and fall, at maturity the bond will be redeemed at its face value. This gives you the assurance of knowing exactly what you will receive at a certain time in the future.

Most important, zeros *adapt* themselves very well to a variety of personal financial plans. Because you know exactly how much money you'll be receiving for your investment and exactly when the payout will occur, you can make long-range plans on the basis of your investment in zeros. Thus, they make an excellent choice for your individual retirement account (IRA) or Keogh plan investment, allowing you to accumulate tax-deferred interest at a fixed rate until retirement. This is because the annual earnings of the IRA or Keogh (known as "imputed interest") are not subject to annual tax until they are withdrawn.

# Are Zero Coupon Bonds a Good Investment Vehicle for Education?

Zero coupon bonds are also an excellent way of saving for your child's college tuition. That just-born baby is certainly a joy today but financially a major cost problem years from now. Someone has described a baby as making your days shorter, nights longer, bankrolls smaller, the past forgotten, and the future worth living for. However, it has been estimated that the average cost of 4 years of college could be as high as $200,000 at an Ivy League school by the time that youngster reaches 18 years of age.

You can invest in zeros which will mature at the time your child is ready for school and, at the same time, greatly reduce the tax bite on the interest if the transaction is done properly. Remember, under the Tax Reform Act only the first $1300 of your child's unearned income will be taxed at his or her low rate, with the first $650 being exempt (because of the standard deduction). This means that by reporting the interest each year on the child's return, you will get that exemption 18 times (assuming an 18-year bond), for a total of $11,700. However, if the interest were to be reported in one lump sum only (as with some instruments), you would be able to use the $650 exemption only once. Also, by declaring the tax each year, you do not have to concern yourself about having a taxable lump-sum amount come due just when you are about to pay for your child's college tuition.

One more point on this topic. Make absolutely certain that the zeros mature when the child is past the age of 14, since all income will be subject to the child's lower rate. Before age 14, all income (subject to the $1300 limitation) is taxable at the parent's rate. To avoid any tax to the child, consider the zero coupon municipal bond (tax-free) after annual earnings of $1300 of annual interest income has been reached.

# What Are the Disadvantages of the Zero Coupon Bond?

As a wise person once said, "perfection is not of this earth." Which is another way of saying that zero coupon bonds, good as they are, do have their disadvantages as well.

The degree of risk is one. If the company issuing the bonds is no longer solvent at the time of maturity, you may lose your entire investment. The possibility of default is a serious consideration with bonds of every kind, but the problem is especially significant with zeros. This is because you receive all interest payments at one time, upon maturity, whereas with other types of bonds you receive interest on a regular basis throughout the life of the bond.

A second disadvantage involves the markup that brokers add to the wholesale price of the bonds. The cost to purchase a zero is much higher (in percentage terms) than that of ordinary bonds because of the broker's markup, which is based on face value rather than cost. For example, a $30 commission on an ordinary $1000 (face value) bond is only 3 percent but on the much smaller price of a zero the same $30 commission would be quite high (on a $300 zero it would be 10 percent). It is very difficult for an investor to determine what the markup is on zero coupon bonds because the bonds are sold "net." Brokerage houses buy them at wholesale and resell them to the general public at retail prices. The markup, which is used instead of a sales commission, will increase the price of buying the zero and will reduce the price you get when you sell.

The only way to know whether your broker is charging you a fair price is to shop around. Call other brokerage houses to see what the competition has to offer. Remember that the larger the broker's markup, the more the bond will cost, leaving you with a smaller "yield." Also, prices of zeros change every day, so if you are seeking the best rate, do all your shopping on the *same* day in order to compare fairly.

As a humorous sidelight, those investors who were hurt in the market crash felt that people selling stocks are called brokers because after you take their advice, you are.

A third disadvantage involves taxes. Although you receive no cash payments during the life of the zero coupon bond, you are taxed as if you do, because interest on a zero coupon bond must be reported to the IRS each year. After 18 years, a zero bought for

$200 might grow to $1000 at maturity. To report the $800 interest, you do not take ⅛ of it ($44 each year), but report the interest as it actually accrues. During the first year, a $200 investment earning 8 percent would produce approximately $16. In the second year, your investment would not be $200 but $216 ($200 + $16), and $17.28 would be the interest that year. You do not have to personally compute this every year; you will receive a notice from the issuer or your broker informing you of the amount of interest to report to the IRS. The tax on this "invisible interest," also known as "phantom income," can be considered a major drawback of zero coupon bonds, because you are forced to pay tax on income you haven't received and will not receive for many years. To avoid this problem, look into the *zero coupon municipal bond*.

Another area of taxes involving zeros is the tax basis of these bonds increasing as interest accrues. If you redeem them at maturity, there is no problem, but if you sell before the due date, your basis determines capital gain or loss. Many investors fail to add accrued interest to their original investment, thus forcing them to pay higher taxes. This rule applies to corporate zeros, strips, and tax-free municipal zeros. Your broker can give you the amount of accrued interest annually so that you can add it to your basic cost.

## Get Started

You can minimize the markup disadvantage by comparing brokers. The way to do that is by asking each of them the following questions:

1. How much will I have to invest in order to get the bond (zero) that I want?

2. How much will that investment be worth at maturity?

3. What is the effective yield to maturity?

The broker who can give you the lowest figure for question (1) and the highest figures for (2) and (3) will be getting you your money's worth.

# What Are Zero Coupon Municipal Bonds and Stripped Treasuries?

The zero coupon municipal bond performs the same as a corporate zero coupon bond except that it is issued by a state or local government agency. Maturities range from 7 to 30 years. Because it is a municipal bond, the interest you earn is exempt from all federal taxes and, in many cases, if the bond is issued within your state, from state and local taxes as well. The amount you receive at maturity is considered tax-free income which has accrued annually from the time of the issuance of the bonds.

Those attracted to zero coupon bonds should also consider one more alternative: zeros issued by the U.S. Treasury, the safest of the three types. These are sometimes called by other names, such as *stripped Treasuries,* a name given by brokerage houses which "strip" smaller investment units from large Treasury bonds for sale to investors.

**Quick Tips**

With Treasury zeros, the red flag to watch for is the sensitivity of interest rate fluctuations.

Treasury zeros are 10-year notes and 30-year bonds stripped into units called "pieces." A 30-year bond would consist of 61 pieces (60 semi-annual interest payments and one final principal payment).

You realize that all bonds have an interest-sensitive basis. That means that when interest rates rise, bond values fall and when interest rates fall, bond values rise. Treasury zeros also fall into this category but are more volatile than other types of bond issues. This can occur because of the lack of regular interest payments. For example, if interest rates should rise, the holder of zeros would not be able to reinvest the interest at the new higher rate. However, if interest rates should take a downward turn, earnings on the zero would continue to be reinvested at the older, higher rate.

# Which Type of Zero Is Best for You?

If you're sold on zeros, don't rush out and buy the first one you find. Make your purchasing decision based on the taxable-equivalent yields paid by each type. (*Taxable equivalent* means the amount you have left after all taxes are paid.)

If quality is your first choice, the safety of zero Treasuries should be your choice as there is no risk in a government obligation. If taxes are the prime concern because of your high tax bracket, look at Municipal zeros. Although Corporate usually pay the highest yield, the market choice is small and the risk may be high.

You should consider the purchase of zero coupon bonds over a fixed rate bond when you need to have a predetermined amount of money on a certain date and that you will not need to touch the instrument before maturity. They will also be advantageous to the investor who does not wish to make decisions about reinvesting interest payments twice a year. It is said that you can just let the zero "run on automatic pilot" and thus avoid the semiannual decision on reinvestment that you would have to make with an interest-bearing bond. Tell your broker when you'd like your bonds to mature, and he or she can let you know when zeros that meet your future needs are available. And on the topic of the future, *today is the tomorrow that yesterday you spent money like there was none.*

✔ Zero coupon bonds are extremely well suited to long-term savings, such as tuition needs.

✔ Zeros are appealing to the small investor because they can be bought far cheaper than more traditional types of bonds.

✔ Zeros offer the advantages of call protection, liquidity, and adaptability to a variety of personal financial plans.

✔ The disadvantages of zeros are high initial markups, risk of default by the issuer, and tax complications.

✔ For those seeking deferred or tax-free investments, zero coupon municipal bonds and stripped Treasury bonds should be considered.

**Today is the tomorrow that yesterday you spent money like there was none.**

# PART II

Investment
Instruments:
Government

# CHAPTER 11

# Ginnie Mae—The Misunderstood Instrument

*God gives every bird its food, but doesn't throw it in the nest.*

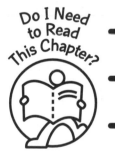

**Do I Need to Read This Chapter?**

➡ Am I looking for an excellent, safe, long-term investment?

➡ Am I aware of Ginnie Maes? of Ginnie Mae mutual funds and trust funds?

➡ Do I understand the relation between Ginnie Maes, current interest rates, and mortgage rates?

I f I had to choose the most misunderstood financial instrument from among the many about which I write, I would pick the government-insured mortgage.

## What Is a Ginnie Mae?

The Government National Mortgage Association (GNMA) was formed by Congress in 1968 as a branch of the Department of Housing and Urban Development. Its objective was to buy government-insured mortgages, similar to those guaranteed by the Federal Housing Administration (FHA) and the Veterans Administration (VA), from the banks which originally made the loans. By doing this, the GNMA provides the lending institutions with the money to offer additional mortgages.

After buying these FHA and VA mortgages, the GNMA groups them into units of a million dollars or more, known as *pools*. These pools are then sold to investment brokerage houses, with an additional guarantee against default added by the GNMA. The brokers, in turn, sell shares in these units of $25,000 or more. These shares are known as *Ginnie Mae pass-through certificates*. The name "Ginnie Mae" is a fanciful pronunciation of GNMA, and the term *pass-through certificate* comes from the fact that, when an investor buys the certificate, the homeowner's mortgage payments are passed through to the investor.

## How Does the Ginnie Mae Work?

To explain how the Ginnie Mae works, let's follow one mortgage as it is created with the borrower and ultimately winds up in the hands of the investor: Robert takes out an FHA mortgage with the Madison National Bank. This bank combines about 50 other similar mortgages totaling approximately $1 million and sells these mort-

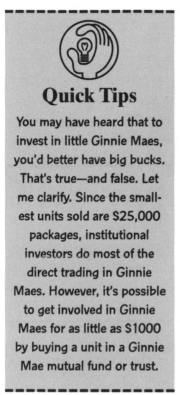

### Quick Tips

You may have heard that to invest in little Ginnie Maes, you'd better have big bucks. That's true—and false. Let me clarify. Since the smallest units sold are $25,000 packages, institutional investors do most of the direct trading in Ginnie Maes. However, it's possible to get involved in Ginnie Maes for as little as $1000 by buying a unit in a Ginnie Mae mutual fund or trust.

gages to the GNMA. This gives the Madison Bank its funds back so that it can lend more money again. The GNMA can either retain this pool of mortgages or sell it to investors. A brokerage house may purchase the pool, carve it up into smaller units, and sell them to its clients, the general public. It then moves out of the picture, leaving the original lender collecting Robert's monthly payment and forwarding it to the investing public who just bought the Ginnie Mae. If he should not be able to meet his mortgage payments, the bank will foreclose and the government will make good that portion of the default.

As you can see, the Ginnie Mae is a way of investing in a large pool of government-guaranteed mortgages simply by purchasing a share in the pool.

## Are Ginnie Maes Safe?

Ginnie Maes are an excellent, safe investment. Because of the involvement of the GNMA, payments of both principal and interest on the mortgage loans are fully guaranteed by the federal government. This guarantee is in addition to the government guarantee which already covers FHA and VA mortgages, so the degree of risk in Ginnie Maes is as small as you're ever likely to get. However, they are not considered obligations of the United States and are therefore subject to federal, state, and any local taxes.

## How Is Income Paid to the Investor?

Income from Ginnie Maes is paid on a monthly basis. If you own a Ginnie Mae, you'll receive (around the fifteenth of each month) a

## Don't Forget

Naturally, it can confuse anyone that Ginnie Maes are considered obligations of the United States when the law of our land reads that "states are not permitted to tax obligations of the United States." What's going on? Don't worry—nothing shady. A two-step safety net is at work. The first obligation to make payment on Ginnie Maes rests with the financial institution that issues the certificates. The U.S. government is only a guarantor in the unlikely event of default.

## Quick Tips

"No principal left." Sounds ominous, doesn't it? Here's where a broker can help. If your broker holds your Ginnie Mae certificates, he or she can move the principal you receive into a cash management account (CMA). Thus you can reinvest in the Ginnie Mae when you have accumulated enough principal to do so.

check representing an installment of the repayment of the mortgages in the pool into which you've bought. A part of each check represents repayment of the principal on the loan; the rest is interest.

An enclosed statement will tell you what portion of the check is interest and what portion is principal—something you'll need to know, since the interest portion is taxable while the principal payments are not. During the early months of the repayment period, you'll mainly receive interest; later payments include a higher percentage of principal. This may be advantageous at times, but it might present a problem. The continual return of your principal can expose you to what is known as *reinvestment risk*. Normally, during times of falling interest rates, your payments accelerate, meaning that you will get money that will be reinvested at lower rates. Also, some people tend to forget that, with each month's payment, they receive, included in the total amount, a portion of their principal. Many times this is ignored and the total amount is spent as if it were all interest. Remember that when those checks stop coming, there is no principal left.

There is a variation of this system by which you can arrange to have the principal remain intact and receive only interest payments. Younger investors may wish to consider this option, since it provides for steady payments of interest on a fixed principal, which itself is paid in full at the time when the certificate matures. Older investors—retirees, for example—will probably prefer the usual interest-plus-principal repayment plan, since they usually have a greater need for monthly income than for a large lump-sum payment at the end.

There is one major drawback to investing in Ginnie Maes—the impossibility of predicting their yield. The monthly checks you'll receive will vary in size, and the period over which the checks keep coming may vary also. The reason is that no one is certain when the mortgages will be paid in full. As you know, some people take a full 30 years to repay their mortgage loans; others sell their houses and repay the mortgages after only a year or two. Since no one can predict how long the homeowners in a particular pool will take to repay their loans, no one can predict exactly how long the payments will last or how large each monthly payment will be. Therefore, one month you might receive a large check that is an unexpected payoff of principal, but then subsequent checks might be smaller, because you will be earning the same rate on a smaller principal.

## Don't Forget

Ginnie Maes do have a bit of a roller-coaster quality about them. If that bothers you, consider these related alternatives. By placing your money in the Federal National Mortgage Association (FNMA) or the Federal Home Loan Mortgage Corporation (FHLMC) (see Chapter 12), you will be involved in at least 1000 mortgages rather than the GNMA's 50. Therefore, the impact of early payback is greatly diminished.

To find the best "deal" from your broker, look for a seasoned pool that has a history of stability. Watch out for any pool based on mortgages with low single-digit interest rates, because with those low rates, homeowners will usually stay with the mortgage until the end (sometimes as long as 30 years). Such a pool will pay out longer than the 12-year average, which will tie up your money and produce even lower returns than you had anticipated.

# When Does the Ginnie Mae Mature?

One rule of thumb brokers often cite is that Ginnie Mae mortgage pools are repaid, on the average, within 12 years. This means that if you buy a Ginnie Mae certificate, you can estimate that you'll continue to receive monthly checks for about 12 years; and those checks will be larger in the beginning than near the end, since the amount of outstanding debt will be greater at that time. Neither prediction is guaranteed. For example, your certificate may continue to pay monthly checks for 15 years or more, or it may be entirely paid out within 5 to 8 years or less.

**Don't Forget**

Warning! Bear in mind that the Ginnie Mae is not a financial instrument to speculate with for a short period of time.

When you purchase one, you are not involved with "Ginnie" for a quick romance; you are in for a long-term relationship. The reason is that the bid/ask spread on this instrument (the difference between what is paid for the instrument and its selling price) is very costly and you could lose a great deal on a short-term basis. It would probably be more beneficial if you bought a Ginnie Mae mutual fund (see the last section of this chapter) even if it costs you about a half point in lower yields. At least you will have the confidence of knowing that you can get out at any time.

# How Do Current Interest Rates Affect the Ginnie Mae?

Changes in the market interest rate on mortgages play an important role here. The interest rate you'll receive on your Ginnie Mae depends, of course, on the mortgage rate at the time the pool was established. If mortgage rates fall below that figure, it's likely that repayment of your Ginnie Mae will be accelerated. This is because the homeowners who took out the mortgages will be eager to repay their high-interest loans and refinance their homes at the new, lower rates. So, you'll get back your money sooner and be forced to reinvest it elsewhere at the new, lower prevailing interest rates. For example, the 1981 high-interest-rate Ginnie Maes (15 to 17 percent) were certainly turned in, as any homeowner with huge debt service would refinance at the earliest opportunity.

By contrast, if mortgage interest rates rise, the life of your Ginnie Mae is likely to be prolonged. Homeowners will be content to keep paying the relatively low rate of interest they locked in at the time they took out their mortgages, and you'll continue to receive checks for longer than the average 12-year repayment period.

## Quick Tips

Here's yet another Ginnie Mae consideration. There is a major secondary market in Ginnie Maes made up of shares in mortgage pools established at some time in the past.

As you can see, Ginnie Maes are not an ideal investment for those who must be able to predict their future monthly income with absolute certainty. If you can afford to be flexible, you can afford to consider Ginnie Maes.

Like previously issued bonds, previously issued Ginnie Maes fluctuate in value owing to market conditions. Depending on the age of the certificate, the number of monthly payments that have already been made, and interest rate considerations, you may be able to buy an older Ginnie Mae certificate at a considerable discount from its face value. A Ginnie Mae quoted at 90 sells for 90 percent of its face value; that is, a $25,000 certificate would cost $22,500.

If you are concerned about taking a loss when selling your Ginnie Mae, consider the following. If the certificate is sold prior to maturity and interest rates rise, your Ginnie Mae would be sold at a loss because it is a fixed-rate instrument. You can avoid any fluctuations by purchasing a Ginnie Mae certificate backed by an adjustable-rate mortgage (ARM) pool. Since the rate of interest is adjusted on the certificate, the Ginnie Mae should trade at close to its original price.

# What Other Factors Should You Know About?

In addition to the quoted price there are two important factors to consider when you look at previously issued Ginnie Maes: the *pool factor* and the *pool speed*.

The *pool factor* is the percentage of the principal that remains unpaid in a particular mortgage pool. The higher the pool factor, the longer it will probably take for the loan repayments to be completed and the longer you will continue to receive checks. The *pool speed* is the relative speed with which repayment of loans in a particular pool is occurring. This will vary depending on economic conditions, the interest rate at the time the pool was established, and the geographic areas in which the mortgages were issued. If the pool speed is high, your Ginnie Mae checks will probably end fairly soon; if the pool speed is low, they will probably last longer.

Therefore, you can readily understand that for the following reasons, Ginnie Mae is an investment worth looking into.

1. Your money is backed by the U.S. government even if the borrowers do not meet their obligations.

2. The loans are liquid and may be resold if necessary.

3. There is a monthly cash flow that allows debt repayment to go from borrower to bank, which will then service you, the investor.

4. You can reinvest your monthly income during periods of higher interest rates.

5. The yields are attractive and higher than Treasury obligations. Also, because mortgages compound every month rather than every 6 months, as with bonds, the yield is higher than what is stated.

# How Can the Small Investor Purchase a Ginnie Mae?

Many people can't afford the $25,000 minimum investment required to buy a Ginnie Mae certificate. If you're one of these people, consider buying a unit in a Ginnie Mae mutual or trust fund. These units usually sell for $1000 and can be bought and sold through brokers. Each fund has its own rules and procedures, as well as its own portfolio of mortgage holdings, which may affect the income you'll receive. When you invest in a Ginnie Mae fund, you may have to pay a sales charge and possibly an annual service or management fee. And on the topic of service, treat a person as he is, and he will remain as he is. Treat him as he could be, and he will become what he should be.

✔ Ginnie Maes are government-insured mortgages that are pooled and sold in shares or "pass-through certificates."

✔ Another form of Ginnie Mae investment is through a Ginnie Mae mutual fund or trust fund, usually sold in $1000 units.

✔ Look into Ginnie Maes if you want an investment that is liquid, usually yields a monthly income, and is backed by the U.S. government.

✔ Be aware that Ginnie Maes are not for investors who must predict their future monthly income with absolute certainty.

*Treat a person as he is, and he will remain as he is. Treat him as he could be, and he will become what he should be.*

# CHAPTER 12

# Ginnie Mae Alternatives

*Some think that Ginnie Mae is just a little girl and that Fannie Mae is her mother.*

Do I Need to Read This Chapter?

→ Am I interested in mortgage-backed investments other than Ginnie Maes?

→ Am I aware of Fannie Maes, Freddie Macs, and collateralized mortgage obligations?

When you investigate Ginnie Maes, you may hear references to two other forms of mortgage-backed securities: Freddie Macs and Fannie Maes. Freddie Macs are issued by the Federal Home Loan Mortgage Corporation (FHLMC) and focus on conventional loans which it purchases in quantity and then resells. A minimum of $25,000 is needed to invest in Freddie Mac *participation certificates* (PCs). The mortgages in the Freddie Mac pools are usually not government-insured loans, like the FHA and VA mortgages in which the GNMA specializes, but are privately issued, nonguaranteed mortgages. As a consequence, the FHLMC does not absolutely guarantee your investment as the GNMA does; instead, you are guaranteed "timely" payments of interest and "ultimate" repayment of principal. It's possible, then, that you might be kept waiting for some of your money when you invest in a Freddie Mac.

As with most forms of investment, the slightly greater risk with a Freddie Mac is counterbalanced by a higher rate of return—usually ¼ to ½ percent or more. Note also that the market for Freddie Macs is much smaller than that for Ginnie Maes, so it might take a while to liquidate your holdings if and when you decide to sell.

## How Do Fannie Maes and Freddie Macs Work?

Fannie Maes are issued by the Federal National Mortgage Association (FNMA). The FNMA serves the secondary mortgage market by buying single and multifamily loans and then reselling them to investors by way of mortgage-backed securities. In most ways, Fannie Maes are similar to Freddie Macs, and, as with Ginnie Maes, timely payments of both interest and principal are guaranteed. Unlike Ginnie Maes, which consist of mortgages insured by the FHA or guaranteed by the VA, Fannie Maes may include either government-backed

## Quick Tips

If the term "privately insured" sends a chill down your spine, here's some reassurance. Do not overly concern yourself about the safety of either the FNMA or FHLMC, as both organizations are government-chartered companies, and their issues are considered to be "moral obligations" of the government. They also yield slightly higher interest rates than the GNMA.

loans or privately insured conventionals. In the latter case, the FNMA (rather than the government) stands behind the debt.

The risk faced by an investor in Ginnie Maes, Fannie Maes, or Freddie Macs is not that the homeowners will not make their monthly payments, but just the opposite, that they might pay off their mortgages too rapidly if mortgage rates should fall. This can occur when homeowners sell, refinance, or exchange a high-interest mortgage for a lower-interest one. The trouble for the investor is that there is a sudden infusion of money because a prepayment by a homeowner will cause all interest payments on the mortgage to stop, and this repaid principal will then have to be reinvested, usually at a lower rate. This early payment problem can now be overcome to a small degree with the introduction of the *collateralized mortgage obligation* (CMO).

## What Backs the CMOs?

CMOs are typically backed by federally sponsored housing agency mortgage pass-through securities of the GNMA (Government National Mortgage Association), the FHLMC (Federal Home Loan Mortgage Corporation) or the FNMA (Federal National Mortgage Association).

CMO issuers include special-purpose subsidiaries of large investment banks, mortgage servicing companies, and U.S. government sponsored agencies. The issuer assembles a large pool of mortgage-backed securities (such as Ginnie Maes (GNMAs), Freddie Macs, and Fannie Maes) in a trust, which is the underlying collateral for the CMO. The mortgages underlying these securities carry U.S. government sponsored agency guarantees.

# What Is the Basic Idea of the CMO?

The interest and principal payments from the underlying mortgage-backed securities are allocated to the CMO investors according to priorities established during the origination process. This payment schedule redistributes the mortgage-backed bonds with sequentially stated maturities call "tranches" (the French word for "slices"). These tranches are offered with short- (fast or first pay), intermediate- (medium pay), and long-term (slow pay) projected average lives. Depending on the structure of the issue, the likelihood of the real average life being very close to the projection may be quite high or subject to considerable variation.

## Don't Forget

CMOs carry another risk you should be aware of. Sometimes institutions begin to carve up the mortgages, dividing principal repayment from interest repayment and then regrouping them back together into bond pools. Thus, the more "slices" in the CMO pie, the more potential problems for the purchaser. The reason is that the "better" slices are offered to the big institutional investors and what is left is then to the public, which is you and me.

# How Do These Payments Work?

Principal repayments will go first to the class with the shortest maturity. When they are retired, the principal will then go to the bonds with the next shortest maturity, and so on, until all classes have been paid off. There could be as many as a dozen different classes of maturity. Instead of one security with a final stated maturity of 20 years, there would be many different classes of maturities (3 years, 5 years, 9 years, etc.). In other words, those holding the "fast pay" will get a portion of the mortgage interest payments and receive all the prepayments on the underlying mortgages until everyone in that group has been fully repaid (2 to 3 years). If investors want higher returns (usually ½ percent) they can choose the "slow pay" option. Under this choice the investor will receive interest for several years (10 to 20 years) but will get no principal until all the shorter-term bonds have been repaid. At that time, payments may continue.

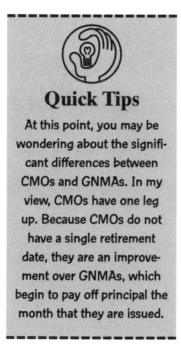

## Quick Tips

At this point, you may be wondering about the significant differences between CMOs and GNMAs. In my view, CMOs have one leg up. Because CMOs do not have a single retirement date, they are an improvement over GNMAs, which begin to pay off principal the month that they are issued.

Bear in mind that CMOs do not carry exact maturity dates as other types of bonds do. A newly issued CMO may have an estimated life of 3 years (1st tranche), 8 years (2d tranche) and 17 years (3d tranche) based upon statistical assumptions. However, the exact speed of prepayment will be determined on what happens in the economy to interest rates. If a CMO paying 10 percent for 8 years falls into an economy that has dropped its interest rate by 3 or 4 percentage points, mortgage holders will refinance their higher mortgages by getting new ones, thus breaking the pool of CMOs and returning money sooner to the investor. Conversely, if interest rates should rise, holders of mortgages will want to keep their mortgages for as long as possible and thus the rate of prepayments of principal would slow down and the investor might end up with a 15-year investment. Because of this uncertainty, you will receive a higher yield than you might receive on comparable securities (at least 100 basis points or 1 percent as compared with U.S. Treasury notes). Bear in mind that the longer and more uncertain the maturity period, the higher the yield.

# How Do You Buy CMOs?

CMOs are issued in book-entry form and are subject to federal and state income tax on their coupon income. CMOs are quoted as a percentage of face value. A $1000 bond (not the $25,000 minimum requirement for a GNMA) quoted at a price of 99 would cost $990. This will include a commission of ½ percent to 3 percent depending on the length of maturity (the longer the period, the higher the commission).

Remember, CMOs can be sold at any time but they are meant to be held until maturity. Also, bear in mind that when comparing the CMO to U.S. Treasury obligations, after the broker's commission, if your CMO does not yield at least 1 percentage point higher than the Treasury notes, there is no reason to purchase the CMO.

## Get Started

For CMO purchasers, here are two important rules of thumb.

1. Don't buy a CMO priced more than a full percentage point below face value. The reason is that if interest rates rise, your projected length of maturity can be much longer than expected (because fewer people will refinance). In other words, you'll be stuck holding a low-yielding investment for a long time.

2. On the other hand, don't purchase a CMO priced more than a full percentage point above par. Why? If interest rates should fall, your premium will disappear, and you won't enjoy healthy returns for the long term because of high prepayments.

# How Safe Are CMOs?

CMOs are backed by the GNMA, FNMA, FHLMC, or by private insurance. Ratings are based not on the credit of the issuer but

## Quick Tips

Warning! At times, private issues may be sold—and you may not know it. If a securities firm is the original issuer and it is not combining or using one of the three agencies (Ginnie, Freddie, or Fannie) that stand behind the issue, don't buy it!

instead on the quality of the underlying collateral. CMOs issued directly by the FNMA and FHLMC are backed by securities which are guaranteed by those agencies. Although they are not rated, they do trade at yields that give them an AAA rating from Standard & Poor's and an Aaa rating from Moody's Investors Service. Those formed by brokerage houses which combine Fannie Maes, Freddie Macs, and Ginnie Maes for resale as CMOs are rated AAA.

## Why Buy CMOs When You Have GNMAs?

The most serious problem of any type of mortgage security is the uncertainty of its maturity. The mortgage security is not the same as a bond that has a fixed maturity date paying the principal back only at that time. Instead, mortgage securities can mature at any time, paying small amounts at different times because of what is known as prepayment risk. For example, 20-year, 9 percent home mortgages issued for $500 million are brought together and sold as bonds by GNMA. Each month, the homeowners make their mortgage payments in which the interest and a small portion of the principal pass through to the bondholders. However, people do change locations, and as they sell their present home and pay off that mortgage, the holder of the mortgage bond will get back his or her principal sooner. Also, if interest rates were to drop substantially to 6 percent (for example) many homeowners holding these 9 percent mortgages might want to refinance their higher-costing mortgage for the new, lower rate. If this happens, the mortgage will be paid off prematurely and the holder of the mortgage bond will get back the principal in lump-sum amounts at a time when interest rates are low and there is little else to invest in.

## Don't Forget

Lower mortgage interest rates put home ownership within the reach of more people. But they also play havoc with mortgage-backed investments. High prepayment rates leave the investor with a choice of investing in the lower yield at the time or seeking riskier issues. That's not much of a choice, but it can happen in a lower-interest-rate market.

The need to reduce this prepayment risk brought the CMO into being. By setting up different time periods (bond classes or tranches) each class would be able to receive its principal in sequential order. In other words, the earliest class (fast or first pay) would get all of the money repaid by the homeowners plus interest until their bond is retired. Then, the next class gets its principal back and after they are retired, the next group and the next, etc. Remember, the group that gets its money first will receive a lower yield than those who wait longer for return of their principal. Monthly checks are sent out to repay each group. If you are in the first tranche you will get both interest and repayment of principal until you are completely paid off. Those holding longer tranches will receive interest only until it is their turn and then the principal begins to move into their group.

If for any reason, you have to sell your CMO before your tranche ends, you have an open market to liquidate, but, as with any fixed-income security, there's an uncertainty which will depend on the number of years and the amount of the principal left in the tranche and, most important, whether interest rates are higher or lower than they were when you bought your CMO. And on the topic of risk, don't be afraid to go out on a limb because that is where the fruit is.

✔ Fannie Maes and Freddie Macs are mortgage-backed securities that offer "timely" payments of interest and "ultimate" repayment of principal, though not necessarily on a fixed schedule.

The drawback of these investments is that homeowners often prepay their mortgages in advance ("prepayment risk"). When this happens, it leaves investors uncertain of the maturity date of their investment.

 Collateralized mortgage obligations (CMOs) reduce prepayment risk.

*Don't be afraid to go out on a limb because that is where the fruit is.*

# CHAPTER 13

# Municipal Bonds—
# The Tax-Free Choice

*You work hard all your life to reach a high tax bracket and then the government goes and lowers it on you.*

**Do I Need to Read This Chapter?**

➜ Do I want, or need, tax-exempt income?

➜ Am I prepared to invest a fair amount of money, usually a minimum of $5000?

➜ Do I understand the problems of investing in municipal bonds while collecting social security benefits?

➜ Would I like a formula that compares tax-exempt municipals to taxable investments?

➜ How can I eliminate the risk in buying municipal bonds?

➜ Do I know how to find the best bond values?

S ince President Clinton brought out his tax plan in 1993 and new tax regulations in 1998, the desire for untaxed income has become stronger than ever. Since tax-exempt bonds yield about 85 percent of comparable taxable instruments, the investor in the 28 to 39.6 percent tax bracket has a chance to lock in excellent returns.

# How Do Municipal Bonds Work?

Today, few local or state governments have on hand the vast sums of money needed to build schools, roads, water and sewer facilities, and other public works. Some towns, cities, and counties are finding it difficult even to meet their daily operating expenses. But these social needs won't just disappear. In order to meet these expenses, communities borrow money from citizens and institutions by issuing debt obligations known as municipal bonds (munis). There are over 40,000 different governmental units and agencies currently issuing municipal bonds. They include states, cities, towns, counties, and such agencies as highway departments and housing authorities.

# What Types of Municipal Bonds Are Available?

Among the more popular varieties of municipal bonds available are the following:

1. *General obligation (GO) bonds:*   These are backed by the full faith and credit of the issuing agency. Interest payments on GO bonds are supported by the taxing authority of the state or city government and are generally considered the safest form of municipal bonds.

2. *Revenue bonds:*   These are usually issued by a government agency or commission that has been charged with operating a self-supporting project, such as a highway or bridge. The money

**Quick Tips**

Revenue bonds pay a slightly higher yield than GO bonds. You can guess why: There's more risk. Here's why. If the project being financed by the bond should earn insufficient income, bondholders may be the ones left holding the bag. The taxpayers of the community are not responsible. Seems unfair? The fact is that if revenue bonds default, the courts are reluctant to auction off the bankrupt assets so that the bonds can be repaid. Municipal assets are viewed as being vital for the public welfare; thus their sale could place the community in jeopardy.

raised through the sale of revenue bonds goes to finance the project, and the income realized from the completed project (tolls, for example) is used to pay the interest and principal on the bonds.

# What Are the Advantages and Disadvantages of Municipal Bonds?

The advantages of municipal bonds are as follows:

1. *Tax exemption:* For the investor, the most important advantage of municipal bonds is the fact that they earn income which is tax-free at the federal level. If you live in the state in which the bonds are issued, the bonds are usually free from state and local taxes as well.

2. *Safety:* Municipal bonds have historically been a very safe form of investment, since states and cities, with their power of taxation, have normally been able to fully meet their debt obligations.

3. *High collateral value:* It's usually possible to borrow up to 90 percent of the market value of your municipal bonds from such lenders as banks and brokerage houses, since municipal bonds

are free of certain restrictions imposed by the Federal Reserve Board on the use of other bonds as collateral.

4. *Diversity:*  Thousands of different municipal bonds are available to suit the requirements of individual investors.

5. *Marketability:*  A large nationwide market for municipal bonds exists, making them easy to sell when necessary.

## Don't Forget

Despite these advantages, I firmly believe that you should never buy municipal bonds for speculation. Purchase them for the tax-free income they produce and only in anticipation of "what you can get from them, not for them."

## Get Started

If municipal bonds sound attractive—and there are many reasons they should—you must now do a preliminary "reality check":

1. *Investment:*  Are you prepared to make a fairly sizable investment? A minimum of $5000 is usually required.

2. *Yield:*  Is your tax bracket high enough to reap the tax-exempt advantage? Remember, tax-exempt municipal bonds usually carry a lower rate of interest than taxable bonds. If you pay a fairly high tax rate, your tax savings will more than make up for the lower return. Those near the bottom of the tax rate tables, however, may be better off with another type of investment.

3. *Social security:*  Are you collecting social security benefits? You may have a problem with munis because, while the interest you receive from these bonds isn't taxable for federal purposes, it may force you to pay federal income tax on up to 85 percent of your social security benefits.

# Are Municipals Your Best Investment?

To determine whether or not you should invest in municipal bonds, you must figure out the taxable rate of return equivalent to that paid by tax-exempt municipals. For example, suppose you have a marginal income tax rate of 28 percent, and you are offered a tax-exempt municipal bond paying 6 percent interest.

To find the equivalent taxable rate of return: (1) take the difference between your marginal tax rate and 100 percent and (2) divide this into the rate paid by the tax-exempt bond. Since your marginal tax rate is 28 percent, the difference between this and 100 percent is 72 percent. Divide 72 percent into 6 percent and you obtain a result of 8.3 percent. Thus, a tax-exempt interest rate of 6 percent is equivalent to a taxable interest rate of 8.3 percent for someone in the 28 percent tax bracket.

## Quick Tips

The following formula will help you determine the equivalent taxable yield (ETY) of any specific municipal bond you may be considering. A filled-in example is included as an illustration.

$$\frac{\text{Yield on MUNI}}{1.00 - \text{tax bracket}} = \text{equivalent taxable yield (ETY)}$$

$$\frac{.06}{1.00 - .28} = \frac{.06}{.72} = .083 \text{ or } 8.3\% \text{ ETY}$$

Table 13.1 shows several typical tax-exempt interest rates along with the equivalent taxable yield for investors in various tax brackets. For example, for an investor in the 28 percent tax bracket, a 6 percent tax-exempt yield is equivalent to an 8.3 percent taxable yield.

This taxable-equivalent yield of 8.3 percent means that you would need a taxable instrument paying almost 9 percent to equal

**TABLE 13.1**    Taxable-Equivalent Yields

| TAX-FREE YIELD, % | FEDERAL TAX RATES | | | | |
|---|---|---|---|---|---|
| | 15% | 28% | 31% | 36% | 39.6% |
| 3.50 | 4.12 | 4.86 | 5.07 | 5.47 | 5.79 |
| 3.75 | 4.41 | 5.21 | 5.43 | 5.86 | 6.21 |
| 4.00 | 4.71 | 5.56 | 5.80 | 6.25 | 6.62 |
| 4.25 | 5.00 | 5.90 | 6.16 | 6.64 | 7.04 |
| 4.50 | 5.29 | 6.25 | 6.52 | 7.03 | 7.45 |
| 4.75 | 5.59 | 6.60 | 6.88 | 7.42 | 7.86 |
| 5.00 | 5.88 | 6.94 | 7.25 | 7.81 | 8.28 |
| 5.25 | 6.18 | 7.29 | 7.61 | 8.20 | 8.69 |
| 5.50 | 6.47 | 7.64 | 7.97 | 8.59 | 9.11 |
| 5.75 | 6.76 | 7.99 | 8.33 | 8.98 | 9.52 |
| (6.00) | 7.06 | (8.33) | 8.70 | 9.38 | 9.93 |
| 6.25 | 7.35 | 8.68 | 9.06 | 9.77 | 10.35 |
| 6.50 | 7.65 | 9.03 | 9.42 | 10.16 | 10.76 |
| 6.75 | 7.94 | 9.37 | 9.78 | 10.55 | 11.18 |
| 7.00 | 8.24 | 9.72 | 10.14 | 10.94 | 11.59 |

your 6 percent tax-exempt bond. By using this table, you will be able to determine the type of taxable return you would have to receive to exceed the tax-exempt return from your muni. Also, bear in mind that state tax is not considered in this example, so your yield is actually higher than 8.3 percent.

# Are Municipals a Risky Investment?

As with any investment, risk is a factor to consider in purchasing municipal bonds. Like corporate bonds, municipal bonds are rated by two major independent rating services: Moody's and Standard & Poor's. The AAA rating is the highest; the C rating is the lowest. In general, the lower the rating, the higher the yield. However, I don't recommend that you purchase bonds with a rating lower than A, since the slightly higher interest rate you may be offered on the lower-rated bond isn't worth the sacrifice in safety. Also, when financial times are uncertain, investors will look for high-quality bonds even though they do produce a lower yield.

Here's how the insurance concept works. When a municipality issues muni bonds, the city's or state's credit is on the line. If bonds are somewhat lower-rated, the municipality must pay higher-than-normal interest on the issued bonds. To save money, it may purchase insurance which guarantees that all payments of principal and interest will be made on time. It thus may appear that the insurance is free to the investor, but that is not true. Since the insurance raises the quality of the municipality's credit, the yield on the bond issued will be lower. And one more point. Because the cost/yield difference between an insured and an uninsured bond is narrow, the insurance has become a "good buy."

## Don't Forget

Believe it or not, you can virtually eliminate the risk in buying municipal bonds. The secret (which isn't so secret) is to buy bonds that carry a third-party guarantee offered by companies such as the Municipal Bond Insurance Association (MBIA), the Financial Guaranty Insurance Company (FGIC), Capital Guaranty (CG), and the American Municipal Bond Assurance Corporation (AMBAC). If the municipality should fail, the insurer will continue to make timely payments of interest and principal as agreed upon at the time of purchase. In addition, the insurance will add to the liquidity of the investment, since potential buyers appreciate the greater safety of the insured bonds.

# Can Municipal Bonds Be Called Back?

Callability is a significant factor affecting the value of municipal bonds. Bonds that offer higher interest rates than what is presently being offered are most likely to be called in, because the issuer will want to redeem these costly older bonds and replace them with new ones paying lower yields. And this is so true today. When a bond is callable, it may be redeemed by the issuing agency prior to the maturity date, usually within 10 years after issue, and usually at a premium (2 percent) $1020 for each $1000 face value of the bond. Of course, this places a lid on potential profits, which may be a significant loss to you if interest rates decline greatly after the bond is issued.

# Are There Strategies in Purchasing Municipal Bonds?

One method of diversifying a bond portfolio is a technique better known as laddering. What is done is that you purchase bonds maturing in different years. Therefore, if rates have risen when a bond matures, you will be able to reinvest the proceeds into an instrument paying the new high yield. Conversely, if interest rates should fall, a portion of your holdings will still earn interest at the higher (earlier) rates.

Also, look into pre-refunded premium bonds. These bonds are issued by states and municipalities in order to reduce the high-double-digit interest costs of bonds issued by them during the early 1980s. What happens is that the issuer will sell, at a lower rate, a second series of bonds maturing on the date when the old bonds can be called in early. The proceeds of the second series are invested in Treasury obligations giving safety to the old issues.

# How Do You Find the Best Bond Value?

Okay. You're ready to buy municipal bonds. Surprise! Unlike stocks, they are not listed on any exchange, making it that much harder to gauge prices. Follow this guidance and you'll be a smart shopper.

## Get Started

1. Get quotes from several brokers before buying bonds. Prices of previously issued bonds vary greatly from dealer to dealer, since each sets his or her own profit margin individually.

2. Be aware that the difference between what the broker pays for the bond (known as the *bid price*) and its selling price (known as the *asking price*) is the "spread." Brokers don't charge commissions on bond trades but make their money on the spread, which is quoted in basis points (hundredths of a percentage point).

3. Remember: The longer the maturity and the smaller the trade, the wider the spread.

4. Ask the broker what he or she would pay to buy back the bond on the following day. The answer will reveal any hidden charges such as fees and markups.

5. Consider buying new issues only. The issuer pays the dealer's markup on those, so you'll get the best price no matter where you buy.

Bottom line: Seek out all information before purchasing.

And on the topic of information, the jawbone of an ass is just as dangerous today as it was in Samson's time.

✔ Tax-free municipal bonds can be a good choice for those in the 28 percent tax bracket and above.

✔ Tax exemption, relative safety, high collateral value, diversity, and marketability make municipal bonds worth considering.

✔ The downside of tax-free munis are high minimum investment requirements, lower yields, and the fact that they can be recalled by the issuer.

✔ Municipal bonds are rated from AAA (least risk) to C (most risk).

✔ Risk can be reduced by purchasing insured bonds, and/or by "laddering" (buying bonds that mature in different years).

*The jawbone of an ass is just as dangerous today as it was in Samson's time.*

# CHAPTER 14

# Municipal Trusts and Funds—Tax-Free Alternatives

*A government is the only vessel known to leak from the top.*

**Do I Need to Read This Chapter?**

➜ Am I in a high enough tax bracket to need tax-free alternatives?

➜ Do I want to know more about municipal bond unit trusts? municipal bond mutual funds?

➜ Am I looking to invest in units as low as $1000?

A t one time, tax-free benefits were available only to the well-to-do because any purchase of municipal bonds under $25,000 was considered an "odd-lot" amount and would cost you extra brokerage commissions (as well as being harder to sell later). Under these conditions, the municipal bond market was strictly a high-priced investor's playground, and the cost of establishing a diversified portfolio of many municipal bonds was extraordinarily high. It was to remedy this situation that the municipal bond unit trust and the municipal bond mutual fund were developed.

# What Are Municipal Funds and Trusts?

In some ways, the municipal bond unit trust and the municipal bond mutual fund are similar. Both offer a way for the small investor to buy a portion of a diversified selection of municipal bonds for as little as $1000. Both offer investments that are free of federal income taxes and, in some cases, state and local taxes (if you live in the state in which the bonds were issued). Also, both pay interest on a monthly basis, unlike the municipal bonds themselves, which pay interest only semiannually.

However, there are many differences between the unit trust and the mutual fund. Let's explore these differences so that you can decide which of the two might be worth considering as an investment for you.

# How Does the Unit Trust Work?

A municipal bond unit trust also known as the Unit Investment Trust (UIT) is established by a sponsor who purchases a substantial share in at least 10, but more often 20 or more, long-term bond issues, usually with maturities ranging from 10 to 30 years. The bonds bought by the trust are left intact and do not change once they have been purchased. Therefore, the yield of the trust remains the same throughout its life span, which has a predetermined length that ends when the bonds in the portfolio mature. When you buy a share in a unit trust, you are buying a portion of this fixed portfolio, and you can predict just how long your investment will last and how much it will pay each year. These units, also called *shares,* trade around $1000 a unit. However, the exact value is based on what each issue in the portfolio is worth.

## Get Started

Unit trusts come in many types, which vary greatly according to length of maturity, degree of risk, tax-exempt status, and yield.

1. Examine your investment needs carefully, to ensure that you choose a trust with the right combination of features for your needs.

2. Decide whether you want to buy your units directly, from a sponsoring firm, or indirectly, through your broker.

3. In my opinion, it pays to work through your broker, who can offer you trusts assembled not only by his or her own firm but by other companies as well.

Once all the units in a particular trust have been sold, no more can be issued. You can dispose of your units without incurring a penalty or sales charge by asking your broker or the sponsoring firm to redeem them. In most cases, unit trust sponsors constitute a secondary market for their own units and will guarantee to buy back your units at their current market value. Of course, this may or may not represent the same amount as you originally paid. If interest rates have risen since the trust was assembled, the rate being paid by the trust may no longer be competitive, and the market value of the units will be less than what you paid for them. On the

## Quick Tips

Remember the "spread," as first discussed in the previous chapter on tax-free municipal bonds. The concept is the same when you are buying and selling units in a bond trust; you must take into consideration the "spread" between the bid price and the asked price. The bid price is what the broker pays for the bond; the asked price is the price the broker charges the investor for the same bond. The gap between the two is the broker's profit. It averages about 2 percent of the value of the bond and is expressed in basis points (hundredths of a percentage point). Each point of the spread reduces your yield by 1/100 of 1 percent and costs you 0.01 percent.

other hand, if interest rates have fallen, you may make a profit when you sell your shares.

Because the portfolio of a unit trust is basically fixed, "managing" the trust is very simple. Therefore, a very small management fee is normally charged. However, when you purchase units in the trust, you must pay a commission which ranges from 2 to 5 percent, depending on the company sponsoring the trust, the length of maturity, and other factors.

What would happen if one of the bonds in the trust should run into financial difficulties? Normally, the trustee may decide to sell that specific issue in the trust; however, unlike fund managers, trust managers are not permitted to add any new issues to a portfolio once it has been created. This tends to make trusts slower to respond when a bond's creditworthiness is in doubt. Also bear in mind the risk of early redemption. Many new issues are callable, meaning that the bonds can be called back after a specified period of time. This may occur if interest rates fall by more than 2 percentage points, so beware of high-yield projections. Every trust prospectus must inform you of which bonds in its portfolio are subject to call and their dates of possible callability.

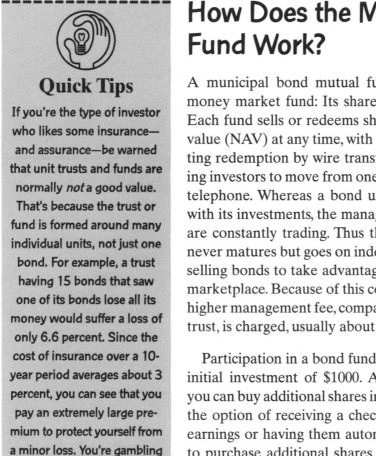

## Quick Tips

If you're the type of investor who likes some insurance—and assurance—be warned that unit trusts and funds are normally *not* a good value. That's because the trust or fund is formed around many individual units, not just one bond. For example, a trust having 15 bonds that saw one of its bonds lose all its money would suffer a loss of only 6.6 percent. Since the cost of insurance over a 10-year period averages about 3 percent, you can see that you pay an extremely large premium to protect yourself from a minor loss. You're gambling on about 100-to-1 odds.

# How Does the Municipal Fund Work?

A municipal bond mutual fund is similar to a money market fund: Its shares are highly liquid. Each fund sells or redeems shares at its net asset value (NAV) at any time, with some funds permitting redemption by wire transfer and even allowing investors to move from one fund to another by telephone. Whereas a bond unit trust stands pat with its investments, the managers of a bond fund are constantly trading. Thus the fund as a whole never matures but goes on indefinitely buying and selling bonds to take advantage of changes in the marketplace. Because of this continuous activity, a higher management fee, compared with that of the trust, is charged, usually about ½ percent annually.

Participation in a bond fund usually requires an initial investment of $1000. Any time thereafter you can buy additional shares in the fund. You have the option of receiving a check for your monthly earnings or having them automatically reinvested to purchase additional shares in the fund. Whenever you wish, you can sell your shares back to the fund. However, since the value of the bonds in the fund's portfolio fluctuates over time, you may or may not get back your original investment when you sell your shares.

# What Are the Basic Differences Between the Trust and the Fund?

The differences between the municipal bond unit trust and the municipal bond mutual fund are summarized in Table 14.1.

**TABLE 14.1** The Municipal Bond Trust
and Fund Compared

| FACTORS | UNIT TRUST | MUTUAL FUND |
|---|---|---|
| Yield | Fixed | Varies with market conditions |
| Life of investment | Ends when bonds mature | Unending; constantly changing portfolio |
| Average maturity of bonds held | 10 to 30 years | 3 years or less |
| Purchase | Fixed number of units offered | Shares always available for purchase |
| Portfolio | Same bonds (15 to 20 issues) held to maturity | 100 or more bonds actively managed |
| Disposal | Units sold through brokers, as with stocks | Shares sold back to fund |

However, you should be aware of how interest-sensitive municipals are. In times of stable interest rates, their after-tax yields are better than most investments (for the high-tax-bracket investor), and should interest rates decline, they can add capital gains as well. It is when rates move upward that the bonds may become a problem, because capital losses can occur upon their sale.

Another problem that funds and trusts are currently experiencing involves two distinct areas: (1) the questionable quality of the bonds bought by funds and trusts looking to boost their yields, and (2) the threat that bond-rating agencies might lower the grades on many munis because of the ever growing financial strains that may cripple state and local governments. Therefore, a word of caution. Look

**Don't Forget**

Not sure which is better for you, a unit trust or mutual fund? Follow this rule of thumb: The unit trust is a better choice if you are certain that you want to hold onto the investment for at least 5 years. If you think you may need to liquidate your holdings sooner than that—or if you anticipate shifting to other investments fairly frequently—the mutual fund is preferable. Either investment, however, is a good way for the small to medium-sized investor to get into municipal bonds with a diversified, professionally selected, tax-free portfolio of holdings.

toward safety when considering muni funds or trusts, staying only with those that invest at least 90 percent of their portfolio in A or better rated bonds. You can get this information from the company's annual report by asking your salesperson or by writing the company.

And on the topic of taxes, Form 1040, the tax return we all file, could just as easily have been numbered 1039 or 1041. The IRS has assured the American public that the number 1040 was a random selection. Still, some taxpayers insist it's not a mere coincidence that in Coventry, England, Lady Godiva, covered only by her long hair, rode naked through the streets protesting the high, oppressive taxes imposed by her husband, the Earl of Coventry, in the year 1040.

✔ Municipal bond unit trusts and mutual funds make it possible for the small investor to buy a portion of a diversified selection of mutual bonds for as little as $1000.

✔ Municipal bond unit trusts vary greatly in terms of their length of maturity, degree of risk, tax-exempt status, and yield.

✔ Municipal bond mutual funds are similar to money market funds.

✔ Insured unit trusts and funds offer poor value, because you must pay a large premium to protect yourself from a minor loss.

✔ Municipal bond unit trusts are generally preferable to municipal bond mutual funds for those planning to hold the investment for at least five years.

✔ Given the volatility of interest rates and markets, it's wise to stick with muni funds and trusts that invest in bonds rated "A" or better.

*Form 1040, the tax return we all file, could just as easily have been numbered 1039 or 1041. The IRS has assured the American public that the number 1040 was a random selection. Still, some taxpayers insist it's not a mere coincidence that in Coventry, England, Lady Godiva, covered only by her long hair, rode naked through the streets protesting the high, oppressive taxes imposed by her husband, the Earl of Coventry, in the year 1040.*

# CHAPTER 15

# Treasuries Are a Treasure

*Everybody wants to eat at the government's table but nobody wants to do the dishes.*

**Do I Need to Read This Chapter?**

→ Am I seeking a safe, secure, short-term investment, perhaps as an alternative to a CD?

→ Am I aware of the different ways to buy Treasury obligations, including at my bank?

→ Would I benefit from direct deposit of interest, discount, and principal payments generated by my Treasury investments?

→ Do I need the telephone number for the Federal Reserve Bank nearest me?

→ Do I know how to read the Treasury price quotations in the daily papers?

→ Are Treasury bills right for me?

→ How about Treasury notes, bonds, and TIPS?

The U.S. Treasury Department has one of the biggest jobs imaginable—providing money for the enormous financial needs of the federal government. No wonder the laws that are created are called "bills." Much of the money the Treasury raises comes from the sale of securities to the general public and institutional investors. These securities are known as *Treasury obligations* and consist of Treasury bills, notes, and bonds.

In a low-interest economy, many people switch to other investments, getting away from their traditional certificates of deposits. If you want a short-term investment, safe and secure, look at the alternative to the CD, the Treasury bill and its longer-term brother and sister, the Treasury note and bond.

# What Is the Best Method of Purchasing Treasury Obligations?

Treasury obligations are tax-exempt at the state and local levels and are backed by "the full faith and credit" of the United States. The credit risk involved in this form of investment is considered practically nil (despite what you may have heard about 12-digit federal deficits). In comparison with similar obligations issued by corporations, Treasury obligations usually pay a yield which is 1 or 2 percentage points lower. However, many people are willing to accept the slightly lower yield in exchange for absolute safety. As the saying goes, you can eat well or sleep well, but you can't do both.

## Get Started

There are several ways to buy Treasury obligations. We'll review each of them in depth:

1. By direct purchase, through banks and brokerage houses
2. Directly from the government, through the Federal Reserve Bank
3. Through the secondary market

## Buying Treasury Issues by Direct Purchase

This method has a certain amount of convenience, because you are buying directly from your brokerage house or bank. (Do note that only *commercial* banks can sell Treasury issues; savings-and-loan institutions cannot.) You will pay a nominal fee, of course, for that convenience. Commercial book entry, available through most financial institutions and brokers, may be most appropriate if you want a third party to manage your account, or if you plan to sell your securities prior to maturity. In the commercial book-entry system, your account records are maintained on the books of the third party you select. Interest and maturity payments are made directly to the third party who disburses the funds to your account.

### Quick Tips

Here is an important warning. Although these securities are absolutely safe, to get the guarantee of the U.S. government, they must be registered in your name.

If you purchase them from a bank or a brokerage house, you are not covered by the government's guarantee because they may not be in your name. However, the bank or brokerage firm will be covered, since the assurance reverts to the registered owner. That may not be a problem as long as financial conditions are sound, but if your bank or brokerage firm should develop financial difficulty, you may have a problem in securing your money. Therefore, have your name on the instrument as registered to you if you purchase Treasuries from banks or firms.

## Buying Treasury Issues Directly from the Government

In my opinion, the best way to purchase Treasury obligations is directly from the government (without a fee) through any of its 12 Federal Reserve banks or their various branches. In 1995, the "Fed" began charging an annual maintenance fee of $25 on each account exceeding $100,000.

You may buy Treasury securities in person or by mail, by submitting a competitive or a noncompetitive bid. These bids are called "tenders." Most competitive bids are made by institutional investors, such as commercial banks and brokers, purchasing large amounts of securities. Competitive bidders must specify the percentage yield they are seeking to two decimal places.

When a competitive bid is made, there is the risk of bidding too high and not getting an allotment of the security, since the Treasury usually will accept the lowest bids.

Virtually all individuals submit noncompetitive tenders, which do not require that a yield be specified. These individuals agree to accept the average yield and equivalent price determined by the accepted competitive tenders. Since the treasury usually accepts all noncompetitive tenders, these bidders do not risk rejection of their bid.

There is no limit on the amount you may purchase in any one name by competitive tender. However, noncompetitive tenders in any one name are limited to $1,000,000 for bills and $5,000,000 for notes and bonds.

Tenders must be submitted before 12 P.M. on the auction day. Auctions are not open to observers. Auction results are announced by the Treasury in the late afternoon of the auction day. This information can be found in the financial section of newspapers the next day. Shortly after they are announced by the Treasury, auction results are also available on the Federal Reserve's 24-hour recorded message. A complete listing of Federal Reserve banks is given in Fig. 15.1.

Treasury securities are issued in book-entry form only. Under the Treasury Direct System, you establish an account master record when you submit your first tender form. You may review your account master record at any Federal Reserve Bank or branch, or request that a statement of account be mailed to you. It consists of name, address, phone number, Treasury Direct account number, tax information, and payment instructions. It also provides detailed information on all your Treasury securities maintained in the Treasury Direct System. Whenever a change is made to the account information, you will receive a copy of the updated record.

**FEDERAL RESERVE BANK INFORMATION**

| | | | |
|---|---|---|---|
| ATLANTA, GA | 404-521-8653 | MIAMI, FL | 305-471-6497 |
| BALTIMORE, MD | 410-576-3553 | MINNEAPOLIS, MN | 612-340-2075 |
| BIRMINGHAM, AL | 205-731-8708 | NASHVILLE, TN | 615-251-7225 |
| BOSTON, MA | 617-973-3810 | EL PASO, TX | 915-521-8272 |
| BUFFALO, NY | 716-849-5000 | NEW ORLEANS, LA | 504-593-3200 |
| CHARLOTTE, NC | 704-358-2100 | NEW YORK, NY | 212-720-6619 |
| CHICAGO, IL | 312-322-5369 | OKLAHOMA CITY, OK | 405-270-8652 |
| CINCINNATI, OH | 513-721-4787 | OMAHA, NE | 402-221-5636 |
| CLEVELAND, OH | 216-579-2000 | PHILADELPHIA, PA | 215-574-6675 |
| DALLAS, TX | 214-922-6770 | PITTSBURGH, PA | 412-261-7802 |
| DENVER, CO | 303-572-2473 | PORTLAND, OR | 503-221-5932 |
| DETROIT, MI | 313-964-6157 | RICHMOND, VA | 804-697-8372 |
| HOUSTON, TX | 713-659-4433 | SALT LAKE CITY, UT | 801-322-7843 |
| JACKSONVILLE, FL | 904-632-1179 | SAN ANTONIO, TX | 210-978-1305 |
| KANSAS CITY, MO | 816-881-2883 | SAN FRANCISCO, CA | 415-974-2330 |
| LITTLE ROCK, AR | 501-324-8272 | SEATTLE, WA | 206-343-3605 |
| LOS ANGELES, CA | 213-624-7398 | ST. LOUIS, MO | 314-444-8703 |
| LOUISVILLE, KY | 502-568-9236 | WASHINGTON, DC | 202-874-4000 |
| MEMPHIS, TN | 901-523-7171 | | |

**Figure 15.1** The Federal Reserve System.

Whenever you purchase a new Treasury security, a statement of account is sent to you listing the description and price associated with each security, and the amount and date of the next interest payment. The statement of account simplifies your record keeping and offers flexibility, since changes can be made quickly.

The Treasury Direct System uses the direct-deposit payment method, whereby interest, discount, and principal payments are electronically deposited into your account at the financial institution you designate. Direct deposit reduces the risk of late payments resulting from lost or stolen checks, ensures that scheduled interest or principal payments will be made to the designated financial institution on the payment date, and allows your funds to earn interest from the payment date if the bank account is interest-bearing. However, your first purchase with the Treasury will not follow the preceding scenario. Instead, you will get your discount by check.

Thus, in most cases it is better to go "Treasury Direct" because:

- It is offered *free of charge* at Federal Reserve offices throughout the country.
- It allows all interest and maturity payments to be deposited on time and automatically into an account of your choice through *direct deposit.* Direct deposit eliminates the possibility of destroyed, lost, or stolen checks.
- It provides a *single master account* for all Treasury securities holdings having the same registration, simplifying your record-keeping. You are mailed a statement of account after any transaction or change that affects your master account, including reinvestments.
- With it, you have the *option of reinvesting* in other Treasury securities being offered at the same time your current holdings mature.

The concept of Treasury Direct has proven to be quite successful with the investing public, but this system does have certain drawbacks. In September 1997, in order to meet investment competition, the U.S. Treasury put out new rules to overcome some of Direct program's problems.

1. The investor is now able to authorize the Treasury to debit his or her account when a security is purchased rather than having to send a check before the auction.
2. The investor can reinvest his or her maturing Treasuries by simply making one call to 800-943-6864, which is open 24 hours a day.
3. The investor will now need only one form to purchase as many different types of Treasuries as desired instead of having to use a separate form for each different issue.
4. The investor can now sell his or her Treasury prior to maturity by going directly through the Chicago Federal Reserve Bank

(fee $34). Under the old ruling, you first had to authorize the Treasury to send your securities to a broker or bank if you wished to sell them before they matured. This procedure could take weeks to complete.

For forms and information, try the Bureau of the Public Debt's Website (http://www.publicdebt.treas.gov) or write to the bureau at 200 Third St., Parkersburg, WV 26106.

When you buy a Treasury obligation, you can have its ownership registered in any of four ways:

1. *Single owner:* For example, Tom Green (social security number 100-10-1000).

2. *Two owners:* For example, Tom Green (100-10-1000) and Betty Green (200-20-2000).

3. *Joint tenancy:* For example, Tom Green (100-10-1000) or Betty Green (200-20-2000).

4. *Guardian or custodian for a minor:* For example, Betty Green, guardian (or custodian) for Tom Green, Jr. (300-30-3000).

Treasury obligations can't be registered solely in the name of a minor.

## Buying Treasury Issues Through the Secondary Market

The third and last method of purchase is to go to the secondary market and buy Treasury issues just as you would any stock or bond. However, this secondary market method does have a hidden transaction cost based on the bid/ask differential (known as the *spread*), to which a retail markup may also be added.

If you purchase in the secondary market, you must keep posted on the market value of the Treasury issue. Newspapers carry the Treasury price quotation each day. Figure 15.2 is an example of part of a one-day's price closing table for U.S. government obligations. The Maturity column shows the maturity date of the issue ("n" depicts Treasury notes). Treasury bond, note, and bill quotes are as of midafternoon. Colons in bid-and-asked quotes represent thirtyseconds. For example 101.02 means 101²⁄₃₂. Treasury bill quotes are in hundredths, quoted on terms of a rate of discount. The "bid" price is the highest price (stated as a percentage of face value) that a buyer is willing to pay. The "asked" price is the lowest price that a seller is willing to accept. The Change column shows the amount of price change from the previous day's closing price to the current day's closing price. The Yield column shows the yield to maturity that the investor would earn if the Treasury were purchased at the current market price and held to the maturity date.

# What Are Treasury Bills and How Do They Work?

Treasury bills, also known as T-bills, are issued with maturities of 3, 6, and 12 months and are sold in minimum amounts of $10,000 and additional multiples of $1000. They are sold at discount (interest becomes yours immediately) and redeemed, upon maturity, at face value.

T-bills are sold at auction on a regular basis. It is at this auction that the interest rate to be paid is set, normally resulting from the competitive bids of large institutional investors. Auctions for 3- and 6-month bills are held every Monday, while auctions for 12- month bills are held once a month on any Thursday the government decides.

If you buy your T-bill from a commercial bank or broker, you'll be charged a small fee (which is tax-deductible). If you buy your T-bill directly from the Federal Reserve, no fee is charged.

Remember, though, that you will lose the opportunity to earn interest during the period from the auction to the settlement date. If you buy your Treasury bill from a commercial bank, although there is a fee of about $50, you continue to earn interest on your money right up to the settlement date because the bank will not transfer your funds until that date.

| TREASURY BILLS | | | | | |
|---|---|---|---|---|---|
| MATURITY | DAYS TO MAT. | BID | ASKED | CHG. | ASK YLD. |
| Mar 27 '97 | 2 | 5.04 | 5.00 | +0.14 | 5.07 |
| Apr 03 '97 | 9 | 5.12 | 5.08 | −0.05 | 5.16 |
| Apr 10 '97 | 16 | 5.13 | 5.09 | −0.04 | 5.17 |
| Apr 17 '97 | 23 | 5.32 | 5.28 | −0.02 | 5.37 |
| Apr 24 '97 | 30 | 5.22 | 5.18 | −0.05 | 5.27 |
| May 01 '97 | 37 | 5.20 | 5.16 | −0.07 | 5.26 |
| May 08 '97 | 44 | 5.22 | 5.18 | −0.04 | 5.29 |
| May 15 '97 | 51 | 5.25 | 5.21 | −0.03 | 5.32 |
| May 22 '97 | 58 | 5.22 | 5.18 | −0.06 | 5.30 |
| May 29 '97 | 65 | 5.23 | 5.21 | −0.04 | 5.33 |
| Jun 05 '97 | 72 | 5.22 | 5.20 | −0.03 | 5.33 |
| Jun 12 '97 | 79 | 5.24 | 5.23 | −0.01 | 5.36 |
| Jun 19 '97 | 86 | 5.25 | 5.24 | −0.01 | 5.38 |
| Jun 26 '97 | 93 | 5.27 | 5.25 | −0.03 | 5.40 |
| **Jun 26 '97** | **93** | **5.25** | **5.24** | **−0.03** | **5.39** |
| Jul 03 '97 | 100 | 5.25 | 5.23 | −0.03 | 5.38 |
| Jul 10 '97 | 107 | 5.26 | 5.24 | −0.02 | 5.40 |
| Jul 17 '97 | 114 | 5.25 | 5.23 | −0.03 | 5.39 |
| Jul 24 '97 | 121 | 5.29 | 5.27 | −0.02 | 5.44 |
| Jul 31 '97 | 128 | 5.15 | 5.13 | −0.04 | 5.30 |
| Aug 07 '97 | 135 | 5.28 | 5.26 | −0.02 | 5.44 |
| Aug 14 '97 | 142 | 5.28 | 5.26 | .... | 5.45 |
| Aug 21 '97 | 149 | 5.32 | 5.30 | −0.01 | 5.49 |
| Aug 28 '97 | 156 | 5.31 | 5.29 | −0.01 | 5.49 |
| Sep 04 '97 | 163 | 5.33 | 5.32 | .... | 5.53 |
| Sep 11 '97 | 170 | 5.34 | 5.32 | .... | 5.53 |
| Sep 18 '97 | 177 | 5.36 | 5.34 | .... | 5.56 |
| **Sep 25 '97** | **184** | **5.34** | **5.32** | **−0.01** | **5.54** |
| Oct 16 '97 | 205 | 5.37 | 5.36 | −0.01 | 5.59 |
| Nov 13 '97 | 233 | 5.44 | 5.42 | .... | 5.66 |
| Dec 11 '97 | 261 | 5.46 | 5.44 | .... | 5.69 |
| Jan 08 '98 | 289 | 5.49 | 5.47 | +0.01 | 5.74 |
| Feb 05 '98 | 317 | 5.52 | 5.50 | .... | 5.79 |
| Mar 05 '98 | 345 | 5.53 | 5.52 | .... | 5.83 |
| Apr 02 '98 | 373 | 5.59 | 5.58 | .... | 5.92 |

| GOVT. BONDS & NOTES | | | | | |
|---|---|---|---|---|---|
| MATURITY RATE | MO/YR | BID | ASKED | CHG. | ASK YLD. |
| 6⅝ | Mar 97n | 100:00 | 100:01 | .... | 4.58 |
| 6⅞ | Mar 97n | 100:00 | 100:01 | .... | 4.82 |
| 8½ | Apr 97n | 100:04 | 100:06 | .... | 5.05 |
| 6½ | Apr 97n | 100:02 | 100:04 | .... | 5.10 |
| 6⅞ | Apr 97n | 100:03 | 100:05 | .... | 5.15 |
| 6½ | May 97n | 100:03 | 100:05 | .... | 5.26 |
| 8½ | May 97n | 100:12 | 100:14 | .... | 5.21 |
| 6⅛ | May 97n | 100:01 | 100:03 | .... | 5.50 |
| 6¾ | May 97n | 100:05 | 100:07 | +1 | 5.43 |
| 5⅝ | Jun 97n | 100:00 | 100:02 | .... | 5.32 |
| 6⅜ | Jun 97n | 100:06 | 100:08 | .... | 5.35 |
| 8½ | Jul 97n | 100:27 | 100:29 | .... | 5.43 |
| 5½ | Jul 97n | 99:30 | 100:00 | +1 | 5.46 |
| 5⅞ | Jul 97n | 100:02 | 100:04 | +1 | 5.47 |
| 6½ | Aug 97n | 100:09 | 100:11 | .... | 5.57 |
| 8⅝ | Aug 97n | 101:03 | 101:05 | −1 | 5.58 |
| 5⅝ | Aug 97n | 99:29 | 99:31 | +1 | 5.68 |
| 6 | Aug 97n | 100:01 | 100:03 | .... | 5.75 |
| 5½ | Sep 97n | 99:27 | 99:29 | .... | 5.68 |
| 5¾ | Sep 97n | 99:31 | 100:01 | .... | 5.69 |
| 8¾ | Oct 97n | 101:19 | 101:21 | .... | 5.68 |
| 5⅝ | Oct 97n | 99:28 | 99:30 | .... | 5.72 |
| 5¾ | Oct 97n | 99:30 | 100:00 | .... | 5.74 |
| 7⅞ | Nov 97n | 100:29 | 100:31 | .... | 5.80 |
| 8⅞ | Nov 97n | 101:26 | 101:28 | −1 | 5.83 |
| 5⅞ | Nov 97n | 99:21 | 99:23 | .... | 5.79 |
| 6 | Nov 97n | 100:02 | 100:04 | .... | 5.80 |
| 5¼ | Dec 97n | 99:17 | 99:19 | .... | 5.79 |
| 6 | Dec 97n | 100:03 | 100:05 | .... | 5.77 |
| 7⅞ | Jan 98n | 101:16 | 101:18 | .... | 5.85 |
| 5 | Jan 98n | 99:06 | 99:08 | .... | 5.90 |
| 5⅝ | Jan 98n | 99:22 | 99:24 | .... | 5.92 |
| 7¼ | Feb 98n | 101:02 | 101:04 | .... | 5.93 |
| 8⅛ | Feb 98n | 101:26 | 101:28 | .... | 5.93 |
| 5⅛ | Feb 98n | 99:07 | 99:09 | .... | 5.92 |
| 5⅛ | Mar 98n | 99:05 | 99:07 | .... | 5.93 |
| 6⅛ | Mar 98n | 100:04 | 100:06 | .... | 5.93 |
| 7⅞ | Apr 98n | 101:27 | 101:29 | .... | 5.98 |

**Figure 15.2**  Price closing table for U.S. government obligations.

## Get Started

Buying a T-bill directly from the Federal Reserve is like one of those recipes that looks complicated, but really isn't. Most of the "ingredients" are minor, like salt and pepper. By following these steps, you'll save yourself the aforementioned fee.

1. Bring your payment for a T-bill in the denomination you prefer to a branch of the Federal Reserve bank, making certain that it is received prior to 12 P.M. Eastern Standard Time on the day of the auction.

2. The payment must be by cash, a certified personal check, a bank check, or a matured U.S. Treasury note or bond, and it must be for the full face value of the T-bill.

3. When the auction takes place, the interest rate for the bills sold that day is set, and the amount of the discount to which you are entitled is determined accordingly. You are then sent a check (within 4 banking days of purchase) for the amount of the discount.

4. If no Federal Reserve bank is nearby, you can send for an application by writing either to the Bureau of the public Debt, Division of Customer Services, or to your local Federal Reserve bank. Request the booklet "Basic Information on Treasury Securities—Treasury Direct."

5. If you do not have an application, you can send a letter with a certified check and the following information: your name, address, social security number, and daytime phone number; a statement saying that your bill is noncompetitive; the amount (face value) you wish to purchase; the maturity of the bill (3, 6, or 12 months); and your account number at your bank (for direct deposit).

# Do You Receive a Certificate When You Purchase a T-Bill?

The sale of Treasury bills is recorded in book-entry form, meaning that you will not be sent a certificate. The securities are held through the Federal Reserve records in a Treasury Direct account that will be opened when you purchase the securities. Thereafter, all future Treasury transactions will be entered in that account when an order is placed on the tender form. When the maturity date of the T-bill arrives, you can redeem the bill for its full face value. And since you received the interest (in the form of the discount) in advance, the yield is actually higher than the nominal interest rate.

# How Is Interest Paid and What Are the Tax Consequences?

Suppose you buy a $10,000, 1-year T-bill with an interest rate set by auction at 6 percent. After paying your $10,000, you'll receive by mail (see the discussion of Treasury Direct) a check for the 6 percent discount, or $600. Thus the effective price of the T-bill is just $9400. Since you've now received $600 income on that $9400 investment, your true yield is 6.4 percent. To summarize:

$10,000 × .06 = $600          Discount sent to you
$10,000 − $600 = $9400        Net cost
$600 ÷ $9400 = 6.4%           True yield on an annual basis

Also, you can take the $600, invest it somewhere else for the rest of the year, and further increase your income.

For federal income tax purposes, the $600 is considered ordinary income to be reported at the time the T-bill matures, not at the time you receive it. For example, if you bought a 1-year T-bill in Jan. 1998, you'd receive your full discount ($600) immediately. However, this amount would not be considered income until Jan. 1999 when the T-bill matures. Therefore, the $600 would not have to be declared for tax purposes, nor taxes paid on it, until as late as April 2000. (Estimated tax is not considered in the example.)

## Don't Forget

For most of us, state and even local taxes have a tax impact. However, T-bills have no state or local tax. Therefore, beyond the calculation for the true yield of a Treasury Bill, you must factor them as well to get the actual yield. In the preceding example, if your state and local tax totaled 7 percent, your true yield would even be higher. To calculate, subtract the tax from 100 percent (100 − 7 = 93). Then divide the remainder into the T-bill's calculated yield (6.4 ÷ 93 = 6.9). Thus the above 6 percent T-bill has an actual yield of nearly 7 percent.

# What Happens at the Time of Maturity?

When it's time to redeem your T-bill, if you bought it through a bank or a broker, you'll follow the procedure arranged at the time of purchase. If you bought it directly from a Federal Reserve bank, the Treasury Department will make a direct deposit for you into your bank. This procedure smooths the way for you by having the interest payments and proceeds (when the security matures) automatically deposited into your account at any bank of your choosing.

If for any reason you have to cash in your T-bill before it matures and you bought it at a Federal Reserve bank, you must first transfer it to a bank or broker for sale on the open market. You will need to obtain a securities transfer request (STR) and submit it to the bank from which you bought the T-bill (see page 167 for the exception). The amount of proceeds will vary from day to day because the maturity value of the bill is affected by (1) interest rates prevailing on the sale date, (2) the number of days remaining before the T-bill matures, and (3) the bank or brokerage fee.

# What Are Treasury Notes and Bonds?

Treasury notes, like T-bills, pay interest rates determined by auction. However, they are not sold at a discount. Instead, they pay interest every 6 months at a rate fixed at the time of purchase. In this respect, they resemble corporate bonds. Because you will be receiving interest every 6 months, if you should have a change of address (Form PD345) or a problem with any interest checks, contact Bureau of Public Debt, Dept. A, Washington, DC 20239-1000.

Treasury notes also have a longer life span than T-bills (up to 10 years from the date of issue). Notes that mature in 2 or 3 years are offered by the Treasury in minimum denominations of $5000, with $1000 increments thereafter. Those notes maturing in 5 or 10 years are sold in minimum denominations of $1000.

Like corporate bonds, Treasury notes can be bought and sold on the secondary market by both brokers and banks. The U.S. Treasury doesn't buy back Treasury notes: however, you can exchange notes of one denomination for those of another. The market price for a Treasury note will fluctuate, depending on changes in interest rates. You can find current prices in the financial pages of your newspaper (see Fig. 15.2). However, the actual price you'll pay a broker—or the amount you'll receive when selling your note—will differ from the price shown, because of the broker's fee and the slightly higher costs involved in buying or selling odd-lot amounts (which include purchases of less than $1 million worth of Treasury notes).

Treasury bonds are much like Treasury notes, with a few differences. They have the longest maturity periods—30 years—and are auctioned semiannually in August and February. The minimum investment is $1000.

## What Are TIPS?

TIPS don't refer to gratuities. In 1997, the government introduced a new type of Treasury obligation known as *Treasury Inflation Pro-*

## Quick Tips

Yes, it is possible to lose on a Treasury obligation. The reason is that Treasury bonds tend to fluctuate in price on the secondary market more than Treasury notes do. Study the following example as an illustration.

Suppose that the $1000, 30-year Treasury bond you bought last year appears on your statement valued at only $970. What happened to the remaining $30? Nothing really, as you will get back your $1000 at maturity, so no risk is involved. But there is a risk on the secondary market (where Treasury obligations are traded) if you decide to sell the bond before it matures in 30 years. The proceeds from the sale are based on the market value of the bond, which depends on the direction of interest rates. When these rates rise, bond prices will tend to decrease. For example, if you bought a 30-year, 7 percent Treasury bond for $1000 today and in 3 years interest rates should rise to 8 percent, the market value of your T-bond would be less than the $1000 face value. The reason is that buyers would rather purchase a T-bond with an 8 percent return for the same $1000 than buy your 7 percent bond.

*tection Securities,* or *TIPS,* which were designed to protect the investor against future inflation. As you are aware, Treasuries are absolutely safe in the face of their value but during inflationary periods, their value loses ground. Thus, the government came up with TIPS whose principal is adjusted daily to keep up with increases in the CPI (Consumer Price Index). Payments are made to the investor twice a year being based on that adjusted value. For example, if inflation becomes 4 percent for the year, the principal value of a $10,000 TIP would rise to $10,400. However, there are always disadvantages. TIPS offer a much lower coupon rate and have a terrible tax computation. These inflation adjustments to the principal are considered taxable income even though you do not receive it annually. You do not get your inflation in cash as it is added to the bond's underlying value and paid only when you cash them in. You are paying tax on money you have not yet received. Thus they work best for tax-deferred accounts [IRAs, 401(k)s] that can be set up through brokers and employers.

# Where Can I Learn More About Treasury Issues?

For more information about any Treasury obligations, write to the Bureau of the Public Debt, Dept. A, Washington, DC 20239-1000 and request the "Treasury Direct Package." Also, the Department of Treasury Website (www.ustreas.gov) offers bond-pricing tools for downloading. One example of what's available: the Current Redemption Value tool has you enter the denomination of your bond, its issue date, type of series, and redemption date. It then generates the current redemption value and the amount of interest the bond has accrued.

There is a wealth of information about these instruments. And on the topic of wealth, it is good to have money and the things that money can buy, but it is also good to check up once in a while and make certain you haven't lost the things that money can't buy.

✔ The federal government raises money by selling securities known as Treasury obligations, available as T-bills, notes, and bonds, and TIPS (Treasury Inflation Protection Securities).

✔ Treasury issues are exempt from state and local taxes and offer virtually no risk.

✔ Treasury issues can be purchased through commercial banks and brokerage houses, directly from the government, or through the secondary market.

✔ "Treasury Direct" offers safe, convenient, direct deposit of interest, discount, and principal payments generated by Treasury investments.

*It is good to have money and the things that money can buy, but it is also good to check up once in a while and make certain you haven't lost the things that money can't buy.*

# CHAPTER 16

# U.S. Savings Bonds—
# Safety First

*Patriotism is not so much protecting the land of our ancestors as preserving the land for our children.*

**Do I Need to Read This Chapter?**

→ Am I interested in an affordable, long-term investment with relatively low yields but unmatched safety?

→ Do I know about the newer, easier way to buy U.S. bonds?

→ Do I understand the difference between EE and HH bonds?

→ Am I aware of changes in how savings bond interest is calculated and credited?

→ If I'm buying bonds as a gift for children, do I understand how their tax liability works?

→ Am I aware of the pros and cons of savings bonds used for college tuition?

When I was in public school, World War II was under way and the sale of war bonds was very popular. Every adult bought them. Children could purchase, in small amounts, freedom stamps (10 cents or 25 cents) that were then pasted into a "victory book." When this booklet was filled ($18.75), it was turned into the bank and exchanged for a savings bond with a face value at maturity of $25. Well, things have certainly changed. Years ago savings bonds were purchased to help our country finance and win World War II, but today they're purchased for completely different reasons.

U.S. Savings Bonds have been sold by the Treasury for more than 50 years. In that half century, these bonds have kept their appeal because they are affordable and safe. They also offer certain tax advantages and have changed with the times as the interest rate environment has changed. Savings bonds are intended for investors who want to save for the long-term yet are flexible enough for those who must have funds available, if needed. Two series of savings bonds are now issued, EE bonds and HH bonds.

Extended Maturities

| SERIES | DATE OF ISSUE | TERM TO FINAL MATURITY |
|--------|---------------|------------------------|
| E | May 1941–November 1965 | 40 years |
|   | December 1965 and later | 30 years |
| EE | All Issues | 30 years |
| HH | All Issues | 20 years |

# How Do EE Bonds Work?

The EE bond is a nonnegotiable security against the credit of the U.S. Treasury—nonnegotiable because once it is purchased, it can-

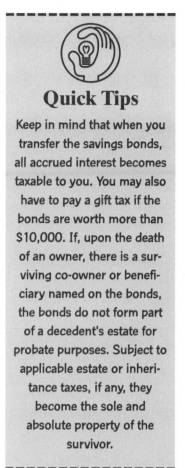

## Quick Tips

Keep in mind that when you transfer the savings bonds, all accrued interest becomes taxable to you. You may also have to pay a gift tax if the bonds are worth more than $10,000. If, upon the death of an owner, there is a surviving co-owner or beneficiary named on the bonds, the bonds do not form part of a decedent's estate for probate purposes. Subject to applicable estate or inheritance taxes, if any, they become the sole and absolute property of the survivor.

not be resold to anyone else but may be sold back only to the government at a fixed price. However, you are permitted to transfer the bonds to someone else by using Form PD3360 to register them in the person's name. This form is available at any Federal Reserve district bank.

Series EE bonds are sold at half their face value and are available in denominations of $100, $200, $500, $1000, $5000, and $10,000. Thus savings bonds are available for as little as $50, making them a practical choice for the investor with only a minimal amount of money to set aside.

The annual limit on the amount of Series EE bonds an individual may buy is $15,000 issue price ($30,000 face amount). This limit applies to the amount of bonds that may be purchased in the name of any one person in any one calendar year; it has no effect on cumulative holdings. Purchasing bonds in co-ownership form effectively doubles the limit, if neither co-owner has purchased other bonds.

## Get Started

U.S. savings bonds are very easy to buy. You can purchase them in two ways, each of which we'll look at more closely:

1. Over the counter
2. Through payroll deduction

In 1992 a new method for issuing savings bonds purchased over the counter was implemented by the Treasury. Referred to as the *regional delivery system* (RDS), it consolidates responsibility for the inscription and issuance of savings bonds with the Federal Reserve banks. Banks, savings and loans, and other financial institutions continue to receive bond purchase applications and payments from their customers. However, instead of each financial institution issuing bonds directly, with RDS the purchase information is forwarded to a Federal Reserve bank, which issues and mails the bonds to customers, usually within 2 or 3 weeks. If you like buying savings bonds as last-minute gifts, the bank will give you a gift certificate.

You can also buy savings bonds on a regular basis through your employer's payroll-deduction plan. This is a very valuable service for those who find it hard to save unless forced to do so. With payroll deduction, the money to buy your bonds is taken out of your salary check before you get it, thus reducing the pain involved in saving and eliminating the temptation to spend the money rather than put it aside.

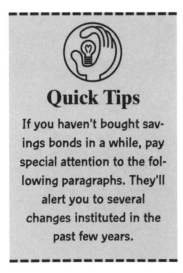

### Quick Tips

If you haven't bought savings bonds in a while, pay special attention to the following paragraphs. They'll alert you to several changes instituted in the past few years.

# How Do You Purchase Savings Bonds?

The registration on a savings bond (owner's name) is conclusive of ownership. Bonds may be registered in the names of individuals in one of three ways: single ownership, co-ownership, or beneficiary form.

# How Do Bonds Earn Interest?

Each May 1 and November 1, the Treasury will announce the rate that will apply to Series EE bonds. In May 1997, it raised the interest rate formula to 90% (up from 85%) of the average of five-year

Registration Options

| CATEGORY | EXAMPLE | RIGHTS |
|---|---|---|
| Single Ownership | 123-45-6789 Rob Kincaid | Only the registered owner may cash. On the death of the owner, bond becomes part of the owner's estate. |
| Co-ownership | 123-45-6789 Rob Kincaid or Fran Kincaid | Either may cash the bond without the knowledge or approval of the other. On the death of one co-owner, the other becomes the sole owner of the bond. |
| Beneficiary | 123-45-6789 Rob Kincaid P.O.D. Fran Kincaid | Only the owner may cash the bond during his or her lifetime. The beneficiary, if he or she survives the owner, automatically becomes the sole owner of the bond when the original owner dies. In order to redeem the bond the beneficiary must present a certified copy of the registered owner's death certificate. |

Treasuries. This rate is effective from the time of purchase, whereas before May 1997 you previously had to wait five years to earn the market-based rate.

Another major change. There used to be a guarantee that EE bonds would pay at least 4 percent no matter what happened to the market. Now there is no floor so they can fall below the 4 percent rate. However, the maximum length of time for maturity is 17 years, regardless of the rate in effect.

One more new factor to consider is the method of calculation of older bonds. Bonds, issued prior to November 1986, earned a guaranteed minimum of 7.5 percent. Although they will pay interest for 30 years, the guaranteed minimum is good only for the original maturity period—in this case, approximately 10 years. After that time period, the original minimum expires and the new "no minimum" takes effect. For example, if a bond was bought in 1983, the new calculation for 1998 would be 10 years at 7.5 percent minimum and 5 years at the current rate for 1998. To find out the current interest rates for these bonds, call 1-800-4US BONDS.

### Are Bonds Right for Me?

It is undeniable that U.S. savings bonds do not match the rates of other, more competitive financial instruments. However—and especially if interest rates rise—they do provide an acceptable yield along with their unmatched safety—safety not only for their guarantee of principal and interest, but also for their repayment should they be stolen, lost, or destroyed.

If any of these three situations occurs, by the way, simply file form PD 1048. These bonds can be replaced by notifying the Bureau of Public Debt, 200 Third Street, Parkersburg, WV 26101-1328.

# How Do You Redeem Savings Bonds?

No matter on what day of the month you buy your EE bonds, you will be credited with interest for the full month. This means that even if you buy the bonds on the last day of the month, you will get credit for interest beginning on the first day of the month. That rule of buying applies no matter when you purchase the bonds.

---

## Don't Forget

Because EE bonds earn interest every six months, follow this important rule when redeeming them: "In whatever month you purchase a savings bond (the month and year are stamped on the bond), consider that month as the first month of a 6-month cycle and sell the bond in the 7th month."

---

For example, if you bought the bond in June, you should redeem it (regardless of the year) in December so that you would be certain of receiving the 6 months of interest. If you had cashed it in one month sooner, you would lose the entire one-half year's interest. A table of redemption values can be received free by requesting Form PD3600 from U.S. Savings Bond Office, 800 K St. NW, Suite 800, Washington, DC 20001.

# How Do Taxes Affect Savings Bonds?

The interest payout on U.S. savings bonds is tax-exempt at the state and local levels but is subject to inheritance and estate taxes levied by states and localities. It is tax-deferred at the federal level. That is, the interest you receive is paid in one lump sum at the time of redemption and is fully taxable in that year. You can avoid this tax liability by buying bonds in your child's name, either alone or with a parent as beneficiary (not co-owner). Interest income can then be reported on behalf of the child annually as it is earned or reporting can be deferred until the bonds are redeemed. In either case the child will be liable for any federal income tax on the interest. After the first year of purchases the parents may file a federal income tax return in the child's name (the child will need to have a social security number) reporting the year's accrued interest on all bonds registered to the child. The intention to report savings bond interest annually should be noted on the form. (For most purposes, a Form 1040EZ should suffice.)

No tax will be due until the child has unearned income (interest and dividends) of $650 or more in a single year, and no further returns need to be filed until that annual level has been reached. For children under age 14, income over $1300 will be taxed at the parent's rate. If the child is 14 or over, income will be taxed at the child's rate. Limits are adjusted annually for inflation.

With this system, the tax liability on the bond interest is gradually absorbed so that when the bonds are redeemed, only the most recent year's accrual will have to be reported for tax purposes. Why is this? Because the youngster is entitled to the standard deduction as a separate tax return (Form 1040) has been filed in his or her name. If the bond interest is the major source of income, he or she will pay little or no tax on this income. Also, the parents will not lose their child's personal exemption, as they are still permitted to take the child as a deduction on their own return.

**Get Started**

It makes a lot of sense to ensure that the tax liability on bond interest is gradually absorbed. However, if you intend to use this method to save on taxes, be sure to take two precautions:

1. Save copies of your child's income tax forms until you've redeemed the bonds.

2. Don't put your name or anyone else's on the bond as co-owner. The instrument must be in the child's name only, so that the child is presumed to be the owner no matter who paid for the bond.

This tax-saving technique is most appropriate for use with bonds that are intended for savings to benefit the child—a college tuition fund, for example. Remember that the earlier you start saving, the more you will have when your child is ready for college.

# What Role Do Bonds Play in Plans for College?

On January 1, 1990, a new education savings bond program began. Known as the Technical and Miscellaneous Revenue Act of 1988 (TAMRA '88), it permitted qualified taxpayers to exclude from their gross income all or a part of the interest earned on savings

## Quick Tips

This program sounds great, but is it? Not really—because the conditions that must be met are quite numerous and will in essence disallow this tax loophole for most people. Read on and see if you qualify.

bonds bought after that date. This tax-free income (federal, state, and local) is permitted if the proceeds of the bonds are used only for the child's college fees, which do not include room, board, or books.

In order to get this tax-free income, the following conditions must prevail:

1. The child cannot own the bond. The bond must be owned by a parent, who must be over 24 years of age.

2. If the parents' "modified" adjusted gross income is more than $60,000, or $40,000 if you are single (this income level is considered at the time of redemption and not at the purchase date), the bonds will begin to lose their tax-free nature. A portion of the interest can be still considered tax-exempt over these levels, but parents with high incomes will get no tax exemption and these income limits will rise each year with the inflation rate. However, you will not know what they will be until you finally redeem the bonds. The problem is obvious. You could invest money in these savings bonds for years and then find out when your child enters college that you fail to qualify because your income has outpaced inflation. In other words, if you finally "make it financially," you will be penalized.

3. Your yearly expenses for college tuition must be more than what you receive in the same year from the bonds you redeem. For example, if you receive $8000 for the bonds, $4000 of which is interest, and you spend $6000 in college costs, you will be allowed only $3000 as an exemption (75 percent of the $4000 interest). The 75 percent figure derives from the fact that only $6000 of the $8000 (that is, three-fourths, or 75 percent) has been used for acceptable college expenses. Therefore, it is important that you balance interest each year with your annual tuition costs.

4. You do not have to declare how you intend to use the money from the savings bonds when you purchase them, but you must be ready to show evidence that the money was used for educational purposes when you cash in the bonds.

5. The standard limitation of $30,000 face value or $15,000 purchase price (or $60,000 and $30,000 for husband and wife holding bonds as co-owners) in bonds per year applies to the education bond program as well as to all EE issues. However, there is no limit to the amount of bonds that can be accumulated for educational expenses over time.

For more information about savings bonds for college education write to the Office of Public Affairs, U.S. Savings Bond Division, Department CT, Washington, DC 20226.

# How Do HH Bonds Work?

Up to this point, we've been discussing EE bonds only. The HH bonds are different in several ways. Unlike EE bonds, HH bonds pay interest on a semiannual basis. Therefore, the interest income is taxable as it is earned throughout the life of the bond. HH bonds mature in 20 years, pay 6 percent (if bought before March 1, 1993; 4% after that date), and are available in denominations of $500, $1000, $5000, and $10,000.

You can't buy HH bonds for cash. They can be acquired only in exchange for (1) EE bonds, or (2) the older E bonds. You have 1 year from the final maturity date of your Series E bonds to transfer them to Series HH. By making this transfer, you can continue to defer taxes. Therefore, if your income is likely to drop over the next 20 years (the life of HH bonds), you will benefit from this deferral. These exchanges can be made by any of the 12 Federal Reserve banks and their 24 branches, or by using Form PD3253, which can be secured at any bank.

## Don't Forget

You must time your switch. Any month after June is a good time. For example, if you were to swap EE bonds for HH bonds during July 1998, the first payment of HH interest to you won't be made until January 1999. This means that you will not have to declare the income—can you believe this—until 2000 when you file your 1999 return?

Why would anyone turn in their EE bonds to get HH bonds? It's a way of stretching out and so limiting the income tax liability that goes along with the lump-sum interest payout charactcristic of EE bonds. The interest payable on your mature EE bonds isn't taxable at the time you exchange them for HH bonds. Instead, the amount of interest accumulated on the EE bonds is stamped on the face of the HH bonds. That amount is not taxable as current income until you cash in your HH bonds, which may not happen for quite a while—not until after retirement, for example, at which time your income and tax bracket could be lower. If you're planning on retiring fairly soon, it's a good idea to exchange your EE bonds for HH bonds rather than simply cashing them in. And on the topic of retirement, remember it is always better to retire too soon than too late.

✔ U.S. savings bonds are affordable, long-term investments that emphasize safety over yield.

✔ Series EE bonds are sold at half their face value and mature in 30 years.

✔ Interest on EE bonds is credited every six months.

✔ Savings bond interest is federally tax-deferred and tax-exempt at the state and local levels.

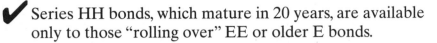 Savings bonds can play a role in long-term college tuition savings, but be aware of the drawbacks.

✔ Series HH bonds, which mature in 20 years, are available only to those "rolling over" EE or older E bonds.

***Remember it is always better to retire too soon than too late.***

# PART III

Other Financial Considerations

# CHAPTER 17

# Life Insurance— The Risk Protector

*For 3 days after death, hair and fingernails continue to grow but phone calls do taper off.*

**Do I Need to Read This Chapter?**

➡ Have I thought about the need to protect my dependents when I die?

➡ Am I under the false illusion that my kids under age 21 need life insurance?

➡ Do I understand the different types of life insurance?

➡ Am I aware of the pros and cons (mostly cons!) of insurance as an investment?

➡ Can I decipher the ratings (like AA or Ba3) given to insurance companies?

➡ Have I determined, free of sales pitches, the best life insurance for my situation?

# What Is the Purpose of Life Insurance?

The basic purpose of life insurance is to offer financial protection to your loved ones in the event of your death. The benefit it provides is one which you hope you won't need—at least not soon—but which most people would be foolish to do without. Remember that:

1. Life insurance is usually the major source of liquidity to beneficiaries.
2. Life insurance proceeds, in most states, are exempt from the claims of the deceased's creditors.
3. Life insurance proceeds are usually not subject to probate, thus eliminating both probate expenses and probate delays.

Because beneficiaries avoid probate and receive the face value of the policy tax-free, be certain to name contingent beneficiaries. If not, and your primary beneficiary predeceases you, the insurance proceeds of your policy upon your death will become part of your will and will end up in probate court. Also, naming young children as beneficiaries may not always be a smart move. An insurance company will not pay proceeds upon death to a minor. The money will be held until a court approved guardian is established. A needless delay!

## Get Started

"Just enough and no more." That's the right amount of life insurance to buy. Follow these guidelines and you'll be in the ballpark:

1. Insure yourself for five times your annual income, after taxes, if your family is completely dependent on what you earn.
2. Raise that figure to seven times your annual take-home pay if you have very young children.
3. Naturally, if you and your spouse both work, you can combine your efforts to the stated needs.

## Should I Buy Life Insurance for My Children?

Speaking bluntly, I do not believe in life insurance for children. If your son or daughter is a famous movie or rock star, bringing into the family huge sums of money, then I can accept the notion of insurance. But if your child is just a normal kid, you don't need it. The absolute purpose of life insurance is to provide (in the case of death) for your dependents. Children do not have dependents.

Also, the argument by insurance salespeople that a child insured today will be insured forever holds no basis. The scenario goes something like this: "What happens to your son or daughter if they should be stricken by some dread disease and become uninsurable?" The answer is simple. You should purchase, under your policy, a rider insuring the child to age 25. If a salesperson touts you on the concept of using such a policy as a method of saving for the child's college education, you would be far better off with most other financial instruments that do not charge for the added expenses of mortality (life insurance costs) and commissions. Stay away.

## What About the Investment Benefits of Life Insurance?

Many life insurance policies contain investment features which can be used to provide additional income for you and your family. You probably won't want to buy life insurance primarily for its investment value—other forms of investments are generally more lucrative—but the investment benefits can be a significant secondary reason for buying insurance, as well as a factor in choosing among the available policies. So it pays to understand the different types of life insurance and their varying values as investments.

Let's consider the most popular forms of life insurance today; with special attention to their investment potential: (1) term insurance, (2) straight life insurance, and (3) universal life insurance. Table 17.1 provides a summary.

**TABLE 17.1**   Summary of Life Insurance Programs

| FEATURES | TYPE OF INSURANCE PROGRAM | | |
| | TERM | WHOLE LIFE | UNIVERSAL LIFE |
| --- | --- | --- | --- |
| Premium | Lowest cost; increases in cost at the end of each term | Fixed premium; reinvestment of interest reduces payments insured for life | Flexible premiums; insured for specified period |
| Cash value | None | Some cash value | Varies with amount invested |
| Objectives | Protection for a limited time period to cover specific and temporary risks | Protection for life with cash value for insured | Life insurance protection plus high rate of return on savings component |

# How Does Term Insurance Work?

*Term* life insurance offers the greatest amount of financial protection at the lowest cost in premiums. This is because when you buy term insurance, you buy the possible death benefit only; there is no savings or investment of a specified sum if you die during the life of the policy (the "term" from which this type of insurance gets its name). Term policies are usually issued for a specific period of years, after which the insurance coverage can be renewed but only at a higher premium rate.

Two variations on the term insurance policy are the *decreasing term* policy, in which the premiums remain the same but the amount of the death benefits decreases as you get older, and the level term policy, in which the amount of the death benefit remains the same but the size of the premium increases over time.

Term insurance is popular in instances where the need for life insurance protection is temporary or where other, more costly forms of insurance are unaffordable. For example, term insurance may be an ideal choice for a young family with children, where insurance protection is vital but the family income may still be modest. As the family grows older and the parents' careers take wing, the family income will probably increase, and other types of policies may become more attractive.

## Don't Forget

Rates for term insurance may seem "off" in relation to other types of life insurance. But remember this: Although the premiums of term will eventually become more expensive than cash-value policies mentioned in the next few pages, term has the advantage of being far less costly at the time in people's lives when large amounts of coverage are most needed.

# How Does Straight Life Insurance Work?

Also known as *whole life insurance,* a straight life policy offers a specified death benefit (the face value of the policy) in exchange for an unchanging premium payment. The size of the premium depends mainly on your age at the time you purchase the policy; the younger you are, the lower your annual premium will be. At the time of your death, the face value of the policy will be paid to your beneficiary.

Unlike term insurance, straight life insurance includes an investment feature. Part of your premium payment is placed in a savings fund and invested by the insurance company. As the years pass, the amount of money in this fund will grow, both from your contributions and from the company's investment earnings. This growing sum is known as the policy's *cash surrender value.* It is quite small at first but, after a number of years, can become a substantial amount of money. The cash surrender value of your policy can benefit you in two ways. First, if you terminate the policy, you can receive the cash surrender value as a lump sum (unlike term insurance, in which you walk away with nothing). Second, while the policy is in force, you can borrow against the cash surrender value at a favorable interest rate, even if you may not qualify for other types of loans. This provision can be useful, for example, when college tuition bills come due.

**Quick Tips**

Here's an easy and accurate way to assess the relative costs of similar policies. Ask your insurance broker, or the insurer itself, for "cost indexes" that encompass the factors detailed earlier. Then compare the index number given for each policy. The lower the cost index number, the less the policy will cost you. It's as simple as that.

The investment value of straight life insurance gives it an advantage over term insurance. However, it is considerably more costly. The amount of savings you'll accumulate through your insurance policy is probably smaller than the amount you could save through other investment plans. And, of course, in order for your beneficiary to receive the death benefit, you must continue to pay premiums until you die. This can be a financial strain, especially for older people whose earnings have fallen after retirement. So consider the pros and cons carefully before opting for a straight life policy.

Another factor to consider is the term *cost*. This is the difference between what you pay in premiums and what you will get back. If you buy term insurance, you will pay a premium and get nothing back; thus your cost for insuring your life is the premium. If there is a cash surrender value, as in the other types of life insurance, your cost is smaller than the premium. Cost can also be reduced by dividends in the "participating" policies, but not all policies carry this feature. Thus, in order to evaluate the costs of different policies, you need to compare the premiums, cash surrender values, and dividends, if any.

# How Does Universal Life Insurance Work?

Because of much criticism about insurance companies' low returns on whole life policies, the concept of *universal life insurance* was born. Unlike deferred annuities, the universal life policy is bought mainly for its insurance feature. It was first introduced in 1979 as a type of life insurance which combines insurance protection (in the form of term insurance coverage) with a savings plan that builds tax-deferred income at highly competitive rates. This income becomes taxable only when the policy lapses or is surrendered. The holder of a universal life policy chooses the amount of life insurance protection he or she wants, and part of the premium goes to cover that protection. The insurance company invests the rest of the premium payment in various high-yielding instruments. Watch out for these yields, though. Although high, they are usually "gross" rates, meaning that administrative and other costs have not been considered in the computation. The insurance company's investment managers usually decide on the investment policy, so your growth or yield is determined by their decisions. If the managers make a series of bad investment decisions, the cash value of your policy will decline. This doesn't happen with straight life insurance, in which cash values are projected using a fixed interest rate, so that you know in advance just what your policy's cash surrender value will be at any time.

Another important feature to consider is that this type of policy is very flexible. At any time, the amount of insurance coverage can be increased or decreased, the size of the premiums can be adjusted, and the accumulated cash value can be withdrawn by means of an automatic policy loan.

An interesting option that is offered with some universal life policies, known as a vanishing premium, allows you to discontinue your payments after a certain period of time. Assume you are 40 years old. You will pay a larger premium for a fixed number of years (I'll use 25 years as an example). After the twenty-fifth year the earnings on the premiums will have accumulated, and the premiums will be paid from the earnings. So, by the time you are ready for retirement, you no longer have to worry about paying life insurance premiums. Remember that the death benefit does not decline when you stop paying premiums.

**Don't Forget**

As times change, so do life insurance projections and yields. When approaching any type of insurance/investment relationship, you must be realistic. For example, many policies bought in the 1980s had interest rates projected at 12 percent (and higher)—at that time the current rate. These projections are no longer valid, and policyholders may find that their idea of using cash surrender value to supplement their retirement income is at risk. Also, people who bought "vanishing premium" policies may discover that, because of lower yields, they have to continue making premium payments long after the period of "no premiums" has expired.

One last point. If the earnings on the universal life policy are more than what the company had projected, you may find that the death benefit actually increases. The reason is that by tax law, the cash value of the policy cannot be allowed to come too close to the policy's death benefit. If this should occur, the death benefit must be increased or the policy would lose its tax-favored status.

Therefore, when you shop for universal life insurance, it's very important to compare the investment policies of different insurance companies. Some are more successful than others. Also find out about the fees charged by the companies you're considering. Some charge heavy sales commissions, which may run as high as 50 percent of your first year's premium; others charge large surrender fees (known as *back-end loads*) in the event you decide to cancel your policy. Ask before you buy.

# Why Is It Important to Know About Insurance Company Ratings?

The issue of the financial strength of an insurance company to meet its obligations is a most important item for the investor to understand. The role of a rating agency is to evaluate an insurance company's financial position and its ability to pay policyholder claims. Insurance customers and prospective customers can benefit greatly from seeing these valuative ratings so that they can compare one company with another. Thus the reader can better determine which companies possess the stability and financial resources needed in today's economy and then select the best company according to its product, its service, and its performance. The three leading independent analysts are A. M. Best, Standard & Poor's, and Moody's. Although they have common characteristics in their evaluations, adopt the same accounting methods, and issue letter grades (including the use of modifiers), their rating methodologies differ. Each has its own basic approach to evaluating the data and performance of insurance companies. Table 17.2 provides a summary.

Information can be obtained by calling these firms directly:

Standard & Poor's (212) 208-1527
Moody's (212) 553-0377
A. M. Best (900) 555-2378

## Don't Forget

Your state's Department of Insurance can also supply valuable information about insurers. You can find the department's number under the state government listings in your telephone directory.

# What Other Types of Insurance Policies or Options Are Available?

Although an enormous array of choices exist, the "Second to Die" policy and the accelerated death benefit (ADB) option should be mentioned.

**TABLE 17.2** Insurance Company Ratings

| DESCRIPTION | A. M. BEST | S&P | MOODY'S |
|---|---|---|---|
| **Superior** <br> Smallest degree of risk | A+ | AAA | Aaa |
| **Excellent** <br> Capacity to meet <br> obligations differs <br> only slightly from <br> highest-rated category | A+(c) <br> A, A(c) <br> A– | AA+ <br> AA <br> AA– | Aa1 <br> Aa2 <br> Aa3 |
| **Good** <br> Strong financial <br> security, but somewhat <br> more susceptible to <br> adverse changes in <br> the economy | A– (c) <br> B+ <br> B+(c) | A+ <br> A <br> A– | A1 <br> A2 <br> A3 |
| **Adequate** <br> Financially secure, but <br> may develop risk in the <br> future | B <br> B(c) <br> B– | BBB+ <br> BBB <br> BBB– | Baa1 <br> Baa2 <br> Baa3 |
| **Below average** <br> Judged to have <br> speculative elements | B– (c) <br> C+ <br> C+(c) | BB+ <br> BB <br> BB– | Ba1 <br> Ba2 <br> Ba3 |
| **Financially weak** <br> High vulnerability to <br> adverse economic <br> conditions | C <br> C(c) <br> C– | B+ <br> B <br> B– | B1 <br> B2 <br> B3 |
| **Nonviable** <br> Ability to meet <br> obligations is highly <br> questionable | | CCC <br> CC, D | Caa <br> Ca, C |

(c) = Best's contingency rating, indicating it sees a temporary decline in profitability or liquidity.

Under the 1981 Economic Recovery Tax Act, an unlimited federal marital deduction was allowed at the first death. That meant that all federal estate tax payments would not be levied until the death of the surviving spouse. This was not always the case. Prior to 1981, estate taxes were levied on 50 percent of the assets left to the surviving spouse—an immediate tax. A new type of insurance arose from this procedure. Known as the "second to die" policy, it is used primarily for paying estate taxes, adding to a lowering inheritance, reducing insurance premiums, and caring for children with special problems.

**Quick Tips**

Before signing up for any "second to die" policy, I strongly recommend that you speak with your attorney. One short consultation can head off a long string of complications down the road.

The concept works in this way. Instead of one policy on one spouse's life or one policy on each spouse, there is one policy insuring both lives payable at the death of the second insured. It is much cheaper than having two policies and more efficient. However, there are certain disadvantages to such a policy. Income may be needed immediately after the death of the first insured, especially if there are large debts to be paid. Also, in the light of so many second marriages, individuals may want to leave their estate directly to their children and not to the surviving spouse.

# What Should You Remember About Choosing a Policy?

On the basis of the brief descriptions in this chapter, if you consider your objectives, you will now be able to choose the best type of policy for you. Term insurance is your choice if your needs require large amounts of insurance and you cannot afford cash value policies. Consider straight life or universal life only if you can afford the higher premiums. Remember that you should not forsake important coverage for investment yield. Also, the tax-deferred features of the investment-type policies are of most benefit to people in high tax brackets. If you are not in a high tax bracket, you may be better off in a taxable investment paying a higher rate even though the interest is subject to tax.

By the way, if a policy is lost, you can send a self-addressed stamped envelope to The American Council of Life Insurance, 1001 Pennsylvania Avenue, NW, Washington, DC 20004 and request a "policy search form." And on the topic of life insurance, as the insurance agent said, "Don't let me push you into making a hasty decision. Sleep on it tonight. If you should wake up tomorrow, let me know what you've decided."

 The chief purpose of life insurance is to provide for your dependents in the case of your death.

 Generally speaking, minors do not need life insurance.

 Term life insurance provides a death benefit only. Its cost usually rises as you age.

 Straight or whole life insurance provides a specified death benefit in exchange for a premium payment that never changes. It also accrues a lump sum called "cash surrender value."

 Universal life insurance combines term coverage with a savings plan that builds tax-deferred income.

 Insurance companies are objectively rated to evaluate their financial position and ability to pay claims.

*As the insurance agent said, "Don't let me push you into making a hasty decision. Sleep on it tonight. If you should wake up tomorrow, let me know what you've decided."*

# CHAPTER 18

# Real Estate as Security and Investment

*A lot of homeowners have discovered that trees grow on money.*

**Do I Need to Read This Chapter?**

➡ Am I curious about real estate as an investment?

➡ Do I understand its unique risks?

➡ Am I thinking of selling my home?

➡ Am I aware of real estate investment trusts?

The real estate market has cooled down since its fantastic rise in the preceding decade. However, regardless of economic conditions, there are certain basic concepts that should be understood.

# What Are the Benefits of Real Estate?

When you buy real estate for use as rental property, you can benefit by the purchase in at least three ways: It provides current income; it provides tax benefits through business expense deductions and depreciation; and, if you like, it can provide a place to live when you retire.

Let's consider first the tax benefits which result from offering property you own for rental purposes. First, any expenses you incur in operating the rental property are deductible from your income as business expenses. These might include repair and maintenance of the house or other property, interest payments on a mortgage, or an occasional trip to inspect the property if it is outside your own residential area.

Second, depreciation can be deducted from your income as well. This is the annual decline in value of any property which results from its increasing age and is determined according to a fixed schedule depending on the nature of the property. This is a noncash deduction, since you are not actually expending any money; yet you reap tax benefits just as if you were.

Interestingly, real estate values usually increase each year rather than decrease, despite what happens in "soft" markets such as in the early 1990s. Therefore, you could say that you benefit twice: the actual resale value of your real property will generally grow, while you get a tax deduction because of the theoretical decrease in the value of your property over time.

Real estate, then, offers decided advantages to the canny investor. But like any other investment, it carries risks as well. The greatest is the risk of buying a property whose rental or resale value is minimal.

## Quick Tips

Experts will tell you that nothing can replace first-hand knowledge of a property. Examining it "up close and personal" is the only way to judge actual value. Never buy property you haven't personally visited and inspected. Photos or videotapes shown by an agent are no substitute; you'll never see the drawbacks of the property in that way.

It has been said that the three most important rules of real estate investment are location, location, and location, and that advice is pretty sound.

There are plenty of places in the world where no one is living and where no one will ever want to live. If you buy one of them, your chance of renting or selling the property is small, and mortgage payments, taxes, and other expenses will still have to be met. So above all, make sure you know the property before you buy.

# What Rules Govern Investing in Real Estate?

Real estate is such a major undertaking that you must tread very carefully before investing. Remember, above all, that property just doesn't offer the liquidity of most other investments. Therefore, consider these points carefully before taking the real estate plunge.

# What Are the Tax Benefits of Selling a Home?

Another important aspect of real estate investments is the selling of your home and its tax ramifications. When you sell your home and a profit is realized, you will get two favorable tax treatments:

1. You will be able to postpone the tax on the profit indefinitely if you purchase another primary residence within 2 years.

2. Before May 1997, a one-time tax exclusion of $125,000 was available to anyone over the age of 55 while other homeowners could be taxed on any profit from the sale of their home as a capital gains. Under the Taxpayers Relief Act of 1997 that

## Get Started

1. Never buy property solely for its depreciation value. If a piece of real estate isn't a good investment in its own right, its tax benefits will not make it worthwhile.

2. Don't buy commercial property if you're a beginner in real estate investing. Single homes and small apartment houses are safer investments and more reliable sources of income.

3. Buy property within your own community, where you know property values and can anticipate trends. Your chance of success in the real estate field decreases as the distance from your home base increases.

4. Use as little cash as possible when buying real estate for investment purposes. Make a small down payment and take out the largest fixed-rate mortgage you can afford.

5. Don't invest in real estate unless you can reasonably foresee an annual profit from your investment (after deducting expenses and taxes) of at least 15 percent. The property itself should have a reasonable prospect for appreciation of about 10 percent annually.

6. Remember that renting can mean headaches for you as a landlord. The property must be maintained according to health and safety standards set by local governments, and complaints from tenants can be annoying. You might consider having a professional manager operate your property, but his or her fee, ranging from 6 to 10 percent of the rent, will cut heavily into your profit.

exclusion, regardless of age, has been raised to $500,000 for gains on the sale of the home for married couples and $250,000 for single filers as long as the property was held, as a primary residence, for two of the past five years. However, homeowners can no longer plow their gains in excess of the exclusion into a new house.

# Is There an Alternative to a Direct Real Estate Purchase?

If you're interested in real estate investment but somewhat hesitant to get involved directly, consider a real estate investment trust (REIT). It is the simplest and most direct way to invest in real estate. Like a mutual fund, a REIT pools money from many investors who buy shares in the trust's portfolio. However, rather than investing in stocks or bonds, a REIT invests in real estate.

Purchasing a REIT could be looked at as investing your money in real estate by the share instead of by the brick. When you receive shares in a trust, you are buying a stock that trades on a stock exchange just as any other stock does. Income from rent or interest on the mortgages is paid as dividends to the shareholders. These securities are required by law to pass through 95 percent of the income they generate to shareholders in the form of dividends. When the property is sold, capital gains will be given to the stockholders as a special dividend; or the sale may increase the earnings per share, thus raising the value of the stock.

## What Are the Pros and Cons of REITs?

REITs have a number of advantages for investors. They allow small investors to participate in real estate investments that would otherwise be unavailable. Shares in a REIT are liquid and can normally be sold at or near their full value. They are a liquid method of owning what is traditionally an illiquid asset and are easier to buy and sell than physical property.

As long as a REIT meets certain requirements, it pays no corporate tax. Thus, while other investments, such as mutual funds, pay after-tax dividends, the REIT can distribute pretax dollars. One additional point. Under the old law, pension funds were not permitted to invest in REITs. However, in 1993 this ban was lifted.

## Get Started

REITs fall into two basic categories. Chances are that one will appeal to you much more strongly than the other, based on your investment needs:

1. *Equity:* These REITs get their income from rental and lease payments and at times from the sale of property (capital gains). It has excellent growth potential. This type of REIT should be chosen if you feel that there will be higher inflation. Remember that the higher the inflation, the greater the chance that your property values will increase and rents will rise.

2. *Mortgage:* If you feel that inflation will remain low, then the mortgage REITs' yields will look very attractive against a background of stable or even falling interest rates. All REITs, like bonds, rise in value when interest rates fall as investors run to higher-yielding securities. But because they are highly leveraged, these mortgage REITs will react much more intensely to interest rate movements than the equity REITs.

Naturally, REITs have their disadvantages. Management and operating fees reduce the net earnings of the trust and the amount of investor distributions as well. The tax benefits normally associated with real estate ownership—including deductions for depreciation, interest, and maintenance costs—are absorbed by the trust rather than passed on to individual investors. REITs normally do not have to pay taxes. However, you, the investor, do, since most dividends received from these trusts are taxable at regular rates. There is an exception. Dividends paid out to shareholders' equity (which represents a return of capital) are not taxable. Also, remember that any loss occurring from your REIT can be used to offset capital gains you made during the year and that any loss over gain can be deducted from your income for up to $3000 annually.

REIT investments may be very conservative or highly speculative, depending upon the policy set by the management of the trust.

## Quick Tips

Here's another nugget for anyone who is considering this form of investment: REITs do not always get the best real estate choices, since many of the smaller REITs have trouble competing for properties with real estate syndicates, insurance companies, and large pension funds.

You'll want to make sure that the objectives of the trust match your own investment plans before you get involved.

## To REIT or Not to REIT?

By now you probably realize that REITs are little more complicated than, say, savings accounts. Think about these six points as you decide whether REITs are right for you:

1. How do you know which REIT to buy? A little research based upon demographic and economic trends could certainly help. For example, a REIT involved in regional apartments would involve knowing about vacancy rates and rents, new apartment construction, and affordability of homeownership. As an example, because of the very high cost of residential homes, only a third of San Francisco's population can afford a house. Therefore, a REIT for apartments in this location might make an ideal investment.

2. Make certain you examine the proxy statement to see what management's stake has in its own investment. The people who are in charge of the REIT must have a substantial position in it. If you find that management had a large share and then sold it recently, the red flag is up. If the REIT is new, the prospectus will show the management's track record in other ventures.

3. Be careful about selecting trusts that use large amounts of short-term debt to finance long-term mortgages. If short-term rates go up, your holdings could face serious trouble.

4. The total management fees and other charges should not exceed 1 percent of gross assets a year. Try to choose a REIT that is "self-administered," meaning that the managers are employed by the trust.

5. Avoid newly formed REITs. As far as I am concerned, the trust should have a track record of at least 3 years. Also, look for a dividend growth of at least 10 percent annually.

6. The major difference between a REIT and a stock of a company is that earnings per share is not the major concern for the REIT investor. Rather REITs use funds from operations (FFO), which is net income excluding gains (losses) from property sale and adding back depreciation. If you want to see how well your REIT is doing, look at its FFO growth.

Over the past 3 decades, real estate values in the United States have soared, with few other investments showing such a comparable growth. If the U.S. economy continues to prosper, real estate will continue to benefit. As long as you know what you're buying, the chances are that you can do very well by investing in real estate. And on the topic of real estate, by the time you finish paying for a house in the country, it's no longer the country.

*It's a Wrap*

✔ Real estate has distinct advantages for the canny investor.

✔ Real estate investment offers some great tax benefits, but never buy a property for the latter alone.

✔ You should net a 15 percent annual profit, after expenses, to make a real estate investment worthwhile.

✔ The gain on the sale of your home could give you up to $500,000 ($250,000/single) tax free if certain conditions are met.

✔ If you're interested in a mutual fund–type investment in properties, consider real estate investment trusts, or REITs.

***By the time you finish paying for a house in the country, it's no longer the country.***

# CHAPTER 19

# Condominiums and Co-ops—A Living Investment

*Rents are so high, leases are breaking tenants.*

Do I Need to Read This Chapter?

➡ Would you love your own space, yet can't afford to buy a house?

➡ Would you prefer to live in a townhouse or apartment, with much of the maintenance and repairs done by others (albeit for a fee)?

➡ Do you understand how condominium ownership works?

➡ Do you know if cooperatives, or co-ops, are available in your area? If so, are you acquainted with their pros and cons?

Chapter 18 discussed real estate and home ownership. But what if you can't afford to buy your own home? You may want to consider buying a condominium or cooperative apartment as an alternative.

# What Is a Condominium?

A *condominium,* or *condo,* is an arrangement in which you own your own dwelling unit, usually an apartment but sometimes an individual house, row house, duplex, or other unit. Therefore, you have the same control over your property as does the owner of a conventional house. However, you also own a share of the common properties used by all the owners in a particular building or complex, including the land, the lobby, the heating and electrical system, and the parking lots, as well as any community facilities such as a golf course, recreation hall, or swimming pool. In these areas you do not have full control. Control (including maintenance) of the land and amenities (pool, tennis court, etc.) lies in the hands of the owners' association, and your input into the decisions of the association is limited to the size of your shareholdings. You must pay a monthly maintenance fee to the developer of the condominium; this fee covers your share of the operating costs. In addition, you must pay your own property taxes and any mortgage you need to buy the apartment, just as most homeowners do.

## Quick Tips

Like a house, a condo is a tax-wise investment. The portion of your mortgage payments devoted to interest payment is deductible from your income prior to federal taxation—a substantial benefit for condominium owners. Your property tax payments, too, are deductible from your income for federal tax purposes.

Since you are the owner of your own condominium unit, the finances of condominium ownership resemble those of buying a house. You must arrange for your own financing, generally by taking out a mortgage from the bank or other financial institution. Mortgage money for condominiums is usually readily available, sometimes at interest rates slightly lower than those charged for home mortgages.

Also, since you own your condominium unit, you have the right to sell the apartment without the permission of the board, providing that the board has been allowed to exercise its right of first refusal. You also have the right, in most cases, to rent out your apartment, but the management also has the right to charge fees for this privilege. These fees can become excessive and can create a deterrent for rentals.

# What Are the Advantages and Disadvantages of Condominium Ownership?

As you can see, condominium ownership can offer some important benefits. Here are some of the other advantages of owning a condo unit:

- It usually costs less to buy a condominium than to buy a private home, and, as already mentioned, condo financing is often easier to arrange.

- Condominium projects are professionally maintained, thereby alleviating much of the anxiety of owning your own home. This can be especially important for the elderly, who may want to escape chores such as painting, shoveling snow, and trimming hedges.

- Safety and security are usually tighter in a multiple dwelling such as a condo apartment complex than in an isolated private home—another important consideration for older people in particular.

- Finally, the sharing of costs among a large group of owners permits luxuries that individual homeowners usually can't afford—swimming pools, tennis courts, golf courses, and the like.

This is not to say that condo ownership is without drawbacks or pitfalls. Here are some cautionary notes to consider before making a condo purchase:

- When investigating a particular condominium project, check the quality and condition of the property carefully. Make sure the plumbing, electrical, and heating systems are in good working order. The developer should be willing to certify the condition of the structure. If the condominium is in a newly built development, don't rely on assurances that special facilities, such as a pool or golf course will "soon be available." If these amenities aren't in place and operating when you buy, you may never see them.

- When you own a condo, all decisions concerning the common properties of the condominium project are made by a management committee and ratified by a vote of the individual owners. The weight of your vote depends on the size of your unit: the bigger your apartment, the more votes you'll have. Nonetheless, the wishes of the majority of owners will normally prevail. Can this become a problem? Yes, if decisions are made which affect living conditions at the condo in ways you don't approve—the prohibition of pets, for example.

- The maintenance fee you pay is not permanently fixed. It may increase because of ordinary price inflation. It may also have to be boosted if the maintenance budget initially set by the developer was unrealistically low. This is something to consider carefully before buying.

- Monthly carrying charges (building maintenance of lobbies, driveways, systems, services, etc.) can be lower than they are for co-op apartments of similar size, because there is no building mortgage to amortize. But not owning common property may not always be an advantage. If a condo building needs money for major repairs, there is no common property to borrow from. If there is no cash reserve available, each condo owner is assessed for the cost of the repair.

# What Is Needed in Order to Own a Condo?

Every investment involves much paperwork, and you must be extremely careful to understand the many documents needed in condo ownership.

- The declaration or master deed will describe the physical details of your condo ownership. The deed contains the conditions and restrictions of ownership.

- The condo association's bylaws are also an important document for you to examine. These bylaws contain all the rules and regulations of the condo.

- The condo management agreement (if the project is managed by a professional management company) will disclose who operates the condo, the duties of the managers, and the rates charged by the management company.

- The title insurance commitment, or an abstract certified to date, will disclose whether the seller has clear title to the condo (free of any mortgages or liens). This document is essential when you are contemplating the purchase of a condo.

- The purchase agreement (offer) is the most important document in your condo transactions, because once it is signed by you and accepted by the seller, it will govern every aspect of the purchase, including condition of the property, repairs to be made, construction of amenities, and simple things such as color of paint, fixtures to be included, and appliances. Verbal descriptions are not binding, so any representations must be in writing. Therefore, you should employ experienced counsel well in advance of signing any papers.

## Get Started

As you can see, condo ownership can be ideal for many people. But be sure to understand the terms of the arrangement before getting involved:

1. See that the maintenance fees are spelled out.

2. Read the rules and restrictions carefully.

3. Have the condition of the property checked out thoroughly.

4. Above all, be sure you're dealing with an established, reputable developer. Talk to friends, call the local Better Business Bureau, and ask at your bank. If anything you hear makes you doubt the reliability of the seller, back off.

# What Is a Cooperative?

As the name implies, the *cooperative,* or *co-op,* was considered to be a cooperative living arrangement with people who had a common interest (union membership as an example) and who ran the building as a corporation. A cooperative differs from a condominium in several ways. When you buy a co-op, you buy a share or a number of shares in the corporation that owns and manages the land and the buildings. These shares entitle you to occupy a particular apartment for a specified term. However, you do not own the apartment, as you would when buying a condo.

As a co-op owner, you must pay a monthly maintenance fee, which includes not only your share of the cost of maintaining the building and grounds (like the condo maintenance fee) but also your share of the mortgage costs and taxes on the entire property, which are paid by the corporation as a whole. Note that you can deduct from your income, for tax purposes, the portion of your monthly maintenance fee which goes to pay for interest on the corporate mortgage and property taxes. In addition, of course, you may have to make payments on the mortgage loan you took out to purchase your shares in the co-op. If you get a co-op loan, unlike a condo loan, you will not have to pay a mortgage recording tax, because buying a co-op is not considered a real estate investment but is deemed ownership of shares in a corporation.

# What Other Differences Should the Investor Know Of?

There are other differences between a condo and a co-op. When decisions affecting the management of the development must be made, condo owners have voting power weighted according to the size of the units they own. A co-op owner has a single vote, per share, and the number of shares he or she has is usually deter-

## Don't Forget

One of the major problems of co-op ownership is that the co-op board holds the right of approval on your financial application. Yet this would-be obstacle is not usually as important as boards make it. Read on and see why.

Any shareholder purchasing an apartment with financing from a bank signs a "recognition agreement" in which the lender agrees that its loan is subordinate to the co-op's right to collect maintenance charges from the shareholder. In practice this means that if a shareholder defaults, the lender will begin paying the monthly maintenance to the co-op almost immediately to protect its collateral.

If no lender is involved, the process is more difficult, since the burden of collecting falls on the co-op, but the co-op still has a first lien on the apartment.

## Quick Tips

Thinking of buying a co-op to rent out as an investment? It may not be possible. The reason is that many co-op boards can deny its shareholders permission to sublet. Although this may not sound fair, many owners do feel that they want to live in a building where "outsiders" cannot come and go as they please.

mined by the size and value of the apartment owned. A condo owner may sell the unit to anyone (although the management usually has the first right of refusal). By contrast, the corporation which manages the co-op has complete control over the buying and selling of apartments. You may be required to sell your apartment only to the corporation; you will certainly have to obtain permission before you can sell it to anyone else.

Co-op boards have the right to reject applicants without giving them a reason for nonacceptance. The only method of protest is to prove that the decision was based on race, creed, color, sexual orientation, marital status, or disability. Also, some co-ops will charge their shareholders a fee (known as a flip charge, usually 2 to 4 percent of the selling price) when they sell their apartment.

Finally, the co-op board will probably also have to approve any major alterations a shareholder wishes to make in an apartment. However, as with a condo, any appreciation in the value of a co-op apartment during the period of ownership will be of benefit when the time comes to sell.

## Will Co-op Ownership Bring Restrictions or Possible Liabilities?

The strict control over the property held by a co-op's management can be both an advantage and a disadvantage to the individual owner. On the one hand, it restricts your freedom to do as you like with the apartment. On the other hand, as a voting shareholder in the corporation, you may like the idea that the corporation can limit and control the uses to which the property is put and, to some extent, the people who move in. In fact, this feature of the co-op has been used by many wealthy people as a way of preventing those whom they consider "undesirable" from becoming their neighbors. If you're a typical middle-class person, this feature will probably not have much appeal to you.

There is one more important difference between condo and co-op ownership. When you buy shares in a co-op, you are investing in a corporation, and, in effect, becoming business partners with the other co-op owners. This means that you can be held responsible for the solvency of the enterprise. And if a co-op owner defaults on his or her maintenance payments, you and the other co-op owners will have to help make up the difference. Therefore, the reliability of those buying shares in the co-op should be an important consideration in deciding whether or not to get involved. That is the reason that lenders such as banks usually charge more for a co-op loan than for a condo loan. This extra potential liability adds to the charges. In contrast, condo ownership means responsibility only for your own unit, and a default on a condo loan cannot be passed on to other condo owners.

On balance, the condominium is probably a more favorable choice for most people than the co-op.

## The Building Where I Rent Is "Going Co-op"— What Should I Do Next?

Co-op conversions have slowed greatly from their frantic pace in the past decade. However, if you're an apartment renter, you may find one day that the owner of your building has decided to "go co-op"—that is, to attempt to convert the building from rentals to co-ops, with the former owner as the manager of the newly formed corporation. If this happens, you will, of course, be faced with the decision of whether or not to purchase shares in the co-op. If you decide that you do wish to purchase, on the basis of your financial situation and how well you like your apartment, fine. If for some reasons you prefer not to join the co-op, you should be aware of the rights you have as a renter in a building going co-op. It is impossible to list these rights here, as they will vary from one state and city to another, because of local laws, but you can find out about them by contacting any local realtor or attorney who specializes in real estate.

As you can see, either a condominium or a co-op can be a worthwhile investment. Both provide tax advantages that renting cannot offer, and with both arrangements you own a property (either the actual dwelling unit or a share in the co-op) which has a good chance of growing in value while you use it. Therefore, if you're currently renting the home in which you live and buying a house is either impractical or just not your cup of tea, look into the local condo and co-op markets. Both are options well worth considering. And on the topic of real estate, for what I paid for my townhouse today, 100 years ago I could have bought the town.

✔ Both condominiums and cooperatives ("co-ops") can be worthwhile investments.

✔ As alternatives to single-family home ownership, both provide tax advantages that renting cannot offer.

Condo owners hold title to their actual units (apartments, townhouses, or whatever), whereas co-op owners hold shares in the building corporation.

✔ Co-ops tend to have more stringent restrictions on financing, subletting, and other factors than condos do.

*For what I paid for my townhouse today, 100 years ago I could have bought the town.*

# CHAPTER 20

# Mortgages—The Finances of Home Ownership

*Love your neighbor—but don't pull down the fences.*

Do I Need to Read This Chapter?

→ Are you moving up to home ownership and want an overview of your financing options?

→ Are you a current owner interested in refinancing?

→ Do you understand the many different types of mortgages?

→ Do you wonder if you will qualify financially for a mortgage?

→ Are you clear on the tax benefits and implications of holding a mortgage, especially where "points" are concerned?

→ Are you considering a home equity loan, which entails borrowing money against your house?

For most people, buying a home, condo, or co-op entails taking out a mortgage to help meet the cost of purchase. You are normally required to pay a percentage of the purchase price in cash; this is called the *down payment*. The remainder of the purchase price is covered by the mortgage, with your title to the house used as security for the unpaid balance on your mortgage. This means that if you are unable to repay your mortgage, the lender has the right to foreclose—that is, to take possession of the property. Most mortgage loans are made by banks and savings and loan associations, though other institutions and individuals may sometimes offer mortgages.

# What Types of Mortgages Are Offered?

Many mortgages provide for repayment over a 10- to 30-year period in equal monthly payment amounts based on a fixed rate of interest. Each payment includes both repayment of principal and payment of interest, with early payments representing interest and later payments representing mainly principal. This is known as the fixed-rate mortgage payment.

However, the volatile economic climate of the late 1970s—in particular, soaring interest rates—led to the increased use of another type of mortgage, the *adjustable-rate mortgage* (ARM). This type of mortgage is usually a long-term loan, providing for repayment in 20 to 30 years. It differs from the traditional fixed-rate mortgage in that the interest rate on the loan changes at stated intervals. Thus, as interest rates rise, the amount you must pay the bank each month rises too; as interest rates fall, so do your monthly payments.

# How Does the ARM Work?

The amount you must pay each month on an adjustable-rate mortgage loan depends on three factors:

## Get Started

Mortgages have become financial "products" with all sorts of variations. However, most of the differences are mere window dressing. If you acquaint yourself with following four terms, you'll understand the basics of every type of mortgage:

1. *Origination fee:*   This is a one-time charge that the lender will add as a cost of the mortgage.

2. *Simple interest rate:*   This is the quoted rate of the loan. If a mortgage is negotiated for 15 years at 8 percent with a 3 point origination fee, the simple interest is still 8 percent.

3. *Effective interest rate:*   This is different from the simple rate in that it is the actual cost of borrowing after considering origination fees. In the preceding example the effective rate would be 8.2 percent.

4. *PITI:*   This stands for the total monthly payment of *p*rincipal, *i*nterest, *t*axes, and *i*nsurance that is so important to know when a family budgets for the purchase of a home.

1. *Interval:*   The period of time between adjustments of the interest rate. Typical intervals are 6 months and 1 year.

2. *Index:*   A guideline used in determining the current interest rate on the mortgage. The index will be clearly defined at the time the mortgage is made. Any of a number of widely accepted financial guidelines may be used as an index; one typical index is the current interest rate on 6-month U.S. Treasury bills. As the index goes up or down, so does the interest rate on your mortgage, and along with it your monthly payment.

3. *Cap:*   A predetermined figure limiting the movement of the interest rate on your mortgage in any single interval. If an adjustable-rate mortgage includes a cap, and not all do, the interest rate may not change by an amount greater than the cap, even though the variation in the index would normally call for a greater change.

As you can see, an adjustable-rate mortgage has one major disadvantage for the borrower: it's impossible to know beforehand how large your monthly payments will be in the future. Thus much of the security of the traditional fixed-rate mortgage is forfeited.

---

**Don't Forget**

Adjustable-rate mortgages have earned their place in the mortgage market. They have great appeal because they usually offer lower initial interest rates than comparable fixed-rate mortgages. The tradeoff, however, is that you won't know how long this advantage will last. In my opinion, it's better for most home buyers to choose fixed-rate mortgages, especially for those planning to "stay put" for a while. In volatile economic times, fixed rates offer peace of mind—you always know exactly how much you will owe.

---

# What Are the Basic Requirements for a Mortgage?

Lenders usually require that your housing costs do not exceed 28 percent of your family gross income. When you add to the 28 percent your fixed payments for auto, credit cards, loans, and the like, your total fixed debt should not be more than 36 percent of gross monthly income. Also, do not attempt to secure a mortgage whose cost will be more than 2½ times your annual income. A $70,000 annual family income is just enough to purchase a home with a mortgage of $175,000.

# How Does Refinancing a Mortgage Work in Today's Market?

When possible, it may be advantageous for you to switch mortgage methods by refinancing if interest rates go down. But it is not always

**Quick Tips**

Home-financing experts suggest this rule of thumb: do not refinance your existing mortgage unless you can benefit by at least 2 percentage points off the old mortgage rate.

true that a lower interest rate alone means that refinancing is the way to go. For example, it could take many years to recoup the cost of the up-front fees, which could include lawyer's fees, title search and insurance, recording taxes, and, possibly, bank origination fees. In comparing figures, you must also consider the tax consequences before any refinancing decision can take place. Remember, by reducing your mortgage payment (which includes tax-deductible interest), you reduce the only tax deduction for interest which is left for the middle-income investor. This then raises your taxable income. So think carefully and weigh all the factors necessary to make an intelligent choice.

Table 20.1 gives the monthly mortgage payments under a fixed-rate mortgage. For example, a $75,000 mortgage at 8 percent for 15 years would be calculated as follows:

1. Look across the 8 percent line to the column titled 15 years.
2. The amount is $9.56.
3. Multiply the $9.56 by 75 (represents $75,000).
4. The result is $717 monthly payment.

A $100,000 mortgage would be computed as $9.56 × 100 = $956.

A further consideration, however, is pretax versus after-tax money. Assume that you have a 30-year, 10 percent, $100,000 mortgage that you will refinance at 7.5 percent. According to Table 20.1, your present monthly mortgage payment would be $878 (10 percent) while your new refinanced monthly payment would be only $700 (7.5 percent). You would consider that it would be a monthly savings of $178 ($878 − 700), but that is based upon pretax money. In order for you to get your aftertax savings, you must multiply your tax bracket rate (e.g., 28 percent) by the pretax savings ($178) and then subtract:

| | |
|---|---|
| $178 | Pretax savings |
| −50 | ($178 × .28, rounded off) |
| $128 | Aftertax savings |

**TABLE 20.1**  Monthly Mortgage Payments for Each $1000 Owed

| INTEREST RATE (%) | YEARS | | | | |
|---|---|---|---|---|---|
| | 10 | 15 | 20 | 25 | 30 |
| 6.00 | $11.11 | $8.44 | $7.17 | $6.45 | $6.00 |
| 6.25 | 11.23 | 8.58 | 7.31 | 6.60 | 6.16 |
| 6.50 | 11.36 | 8.72 | 7.46 | 6.76 | 6.33 |
| 6.75 | 11.49 | 8.85 | 7.61 | 6.91 | 6.49 |
| 7.00 | 11.62 | 8.99 | 7.76 | 7.07 | 6.63 |
| 7.25 | 11.75 | 9.13 | 7.91 | 7.23 | 6.83 |
| 7.50 | 11.88 | 9.28 | 8.06 | 7.39 | 7.00 |
| 7.75 | 12.01 | 9.42 | 8.21 | 7.56 | 7.17 |
| 8.00 | 12.14 | 9.56 | 8.37 | 7.72 | 7.34 |
| 8.25 | 12.27 | 9.71 | 8.53 | 7.89 | 7.52 |
| 8.50 | 12.40 | 9.85 | 8.68 | 8.06 | 7.69 |
| 8.75 | 12.54 | 10.00 | 8.84 | 8.23 | 7.87 |
| 9.00 | 12.67 | 10.15 | 9.00 | 8.40 | 8.05 |
| 9.50 | 12.94 | 10.45 | 9.33 | 8.74 | 8.41 |
| 10.00 | 13.22 | 10.75 | 9.66 | 9.09 | 8.78 |
| 10.50 | 13.50 | 11.06 | 9.99 | 9.45 | 9.14 |
| 11.00 | 13.78 | 11.37 | 10.33 | 9.81 | 9.51 |
| 11.50 | 14.06 | 11.69 | 10.67 | 10.17 | 9.90 |
| 12.00 | 14.35 | 12.01 | 11.02 | 10.54 | 10.28 |

# What Are the Tax Considerations in Mortgage Financing?

No matter which type of mortgage you obtain, you'll receive significant tax benefits during the repayment period. These benefits arise from the fact that interest payments on the original purchase of a home, up to $1 million, are deductible from your taxable income for federal income tax purposes. For most homeowners, that's a substantial amount.

If you're currently shopping for a home (and a mortgage), you should be aware of two other factors which will affect the cost of home buying: closing costs and points.

*Closing costs* are one-time expenses that include the cost of a title search, title insurance, surveying fees, attorneys' fees, mortgage recording tax, and many other smaller fees that can total as much as 5 percent of the value of the home you're buying. Before purchase, you should receive from the lending institution a good-faith estimate of what your closing costs will be.

*Points* are one-time lump-sum charges levied by the bank at the time you buy your home. A point is 1 percent of the total amount of the loan; the bank may charge from 2 to 4 points. For example, if you take out a $60,000 mortgage from a bank which charges 4 points for the loan, you will have to pay the bank a $2400 fee at the time of purchase. To receive the most for your money, you should estimate how long you intend to own the home. Then decide on the best combination of interest rate and points. Because points are an up-front fee, whether you sell your house and pay off the loan after only 15 years or 30 years, remember that the longer you hold the loan, the smaller the impact the points will have on the effective rate of mortgage.

For example, if you have a 15-year mortgage at 8 percent and are charged 3 points, your effective rate is 8.2 percent. Simply divide the

## Don't Forget

Keep in mind that points are overhead—a one-time, up-front fee. You pay the same points whether you hold your mortgage for the full term or sell your home and pay it off a year later. Thus, the longer you hold your mortgage, the smaller the impact on your effective mortgage rate. Use this three-step formula to compare loans:

1. Estimate how long you intend to keep the loan.
2. Divide that period into the number of points contracted.
3. Add your result to the interest rate agreed upon.

3 points by 15 years and add the result to the interest charged to find your effective yield:

$$3 \div 15 = .002 \text{ or } 0.2\%$$
$$8\% + 0.2\% = 8.2\%$$

Here is another way to compare mortgage loans. Assume you are offered this choice: a 30-year, $100,000 mortgage with 3 points (costing you $3000 up front) at 7.5 percent ($700 monthly) versus a no-point 8 percent ($734 monthly) mortgage. Which would be more advantageous to you? The difference in your monthly payments would be $34 ($734 − $700). If you took the 7.5 percent loan, the $34 monthly savings would go toward your getting back your $3000 (3 points), and you would break even in less than 8 years. This means that every month after the eighth year, you would be ahead by $34 a month. Over the 30-year mortgage, you could save close to $9000.

## Any Other Pointers on Points?

Points paid in connection with a loan taken to purchase real estate are tax deductible as interest in the year the loan is closed. Points paid in connection with a refinance must be amortized over the life

## Quick Tips

Here's the bottom line on points. A buyer who plans to keep property for a short time should shop for a loan with a higher interest rate but lower points while a buyer who intends to keep property long term should look for a lower interest rate and be willing to pay more points up front.

of the loan. For example, if a borrower pays 3 points to refinance a $100,000 loan to be paid over 30 years, a total of $3000 will be paid in points. The deductible interest for the points will be $100 per year.

Generally, the more points a borrower pays, the lower the interest rate on the loan. Generally, every one-half point change in points is accompanied by a one-eighth point change in the interest rate in the opposite direction. So an 8.75 percent mortgage with 2 points would become an 8.5 percent mortgage with 3 points.

# What Is a Home Equity Loan?

Up to this point, we've been concentrating on the most common type of mortgage loan—the "first mortgage"—normally taken out to make home purchase possible. However, many homeowners who already have mortgages are taking advantage of the equity they have built up in their homes by borrowing against that equity. These loans are called *home equity loans* and are a convenient source of needed cash. Many banks will lend up to 80 percent of the equity of your home—that is, the value of your home less the unpaid balance of your mortgage—without requiring lengthy loan applications or long waits for approval. However, do not fall into the trap of thinking that the net value of your home (after mortgage liability is considered) always becomes the amount you will be able to borrow on a home equity loan.

Consider this scenario: You have a $200,000 home with a $75,000 mortgage remaining. The bank states that its limit for a home equity loan is 80 percent of the appraised value. Therefore, you assume that the loan amount will be:

| | |
|---|---|
| $200,000 | Value of home |
| − 75,000 | Mortgage remaining |
| $125,000 | Equity in home |
| × 80% | Bank's appraisal limit rate |
| $100,000 | Line of credit for home equity loan |

*Wrong!* Because of little home appreciation in the early and mid 1990s, many lenders have become very conservative in their method of computation. In the above example, even if you have $125,000 of equity in your home, you may not be able to receive 80 percent of it. Rather, the lender could compute your line of credit in the following manner:

| | |
|---|---|
| $200,000 | Value of home |
| × 80% | Bank's appraisal limit rate |
| $160,000 | Bank's appraisal limit |
| − 75,000 | Mortgage remaining |
| $85,000 | Line of credit for home equity loan |

Also remember that after you take out a home equity loan, you will have to make two monthly loan repayments (one for the original mortgage and one for the second mortgage) to retain your ownership of a single piece of property.

## What Are the Basic Types of Home Equity Loans?

Home equity loans come in two basic flavors. A *revolving line of credit account* is much like a standard credit card account—with the advantages of potential tax deductions. Customers can borrow as much as they like, up to a predetermined credit limit. For the first five years they can make interest payments only, giving them the power to manage their cash flow. After the interest-only period, they pay off the balance in monthly installments at a variable rate of interest. Variable rates make the most sense for investors who know they are going to sell the property they are paying off in five to ten years.

With a *fixed-rate home equity loan,* the borrower pays off the loan with regular monthly payments at a constant rate of interest. Fixed rates are usually best for long-term borrowers looking to lock in a favorable interest rate. Although the points are deductible for refinancing on home equity loans, as stated before, they cannot be deducted all at once but must be gradually written off over the years that you remain in the house. On the original purchase of a home, however, you can deduct the cost of the points at one time.

# What Tax Ramifications Are There with Home Equity Refinancing?

Immediately after the 1986 Tax Reform Act, U.S. taxpayers found that they had lost most of their interest deductions on personal debt. But by taking out a home equity loan, they were still able to deduct the interest charges regardless of the purpose the funds were used for. The laws have changed slightly, but within the limits of sensible debt management, it is still advantageous to secure a home equity loan when you need money. For other than home equity debt, a cap of $100,000 (on top of the loan you took out to purchase the home) is deductible. You cannot use the money, however, for the purchase of tax-exempt bonds.

## Don't Forget

A home equity loan can turn some impossible dreams into reality. For example, such a loan is ideal for financing a child's education: it is often less expensive than a normal personal loan, the interest you are charged is usually tax-deductible, and the payback period can be spread over 20 years. Or you may use the funds for that dream "retreat" that you were never able to afford. In today's economy, financing for vacation homes is not always readily available, and when it is, it is usually encumbered with stringent restrictions. Now, through home equity loans, these impossible dreams can become a reality.

And on the topic of mortgages, it is amazing that yesterday's nest egg can't buy today's birdhouse.

✔ Mortgages come in two basic types: fixed-rate and adjustable-rate.

✔ If adjustable-rate mortgages appeal to you, be sure to evaluate how often the rate will be adjusted, what index governs the change, and whether the rate is "capped" at a stated maximum.

✔ Generally you will qualify financially for a mortgage if your housing costs don't exceed 28 percent of the family's monthly gross income. Another benchmark is that your total fixed debt (including car payments and the like) shouldn't exceed 36 percent of your gross monthly income.

✔ It may pay to refinance your mortgage if the new rate is at least 2 percentage points below the old one.

✔ Closing costs and "points" (one-time bank charges) affect the true rate of any mortgage or refinancing.

✔ Once you've paid off a fair percentage of your mortgage, home equity loans can be an excellent source of credit.

***It's amazing that yesterday's nest egg can't buy today's birdhouse.***

# CHAPTER 21

# Mortgages— In Reverse

*A conventional mortgage will turn your income into equity, while a reverse mortgage will turn your equity into income.*

**Do I Need to Read This Chapter?**

→ Am I house-rich but cash-poor?

→ Do I need income during retirement?

→ Am I aware of the advantages and drawbacks of reverse mortgages?

→ Do I realize that such mortgages offer a variety of payment plans?

I n the previous chapter, we discussed the conventional mortgage. Let's reverse the topic and take a regular mortgage and stand it on its head. In other words, rather than borrowing a lump sum of money and paying it back monthly, let's get the entire loan in monthly payments sent to us and then pay it back, only if we sell the house or, better still, have our heirs pay for it at our demise.

## How Can Reverse Mortgages Make Retirement Easier?

The beauty of reverse mortgages will be appreciated by the millions of retirees who have found it difficult, in today's economy, to make ends meet. It is true that most retirees own their own home, with a great deal of equity in it, but they do not have sufficient income to live their remaining years in the lifestyle that they have dreamed about. Most of these people are house-rich and cash-poor. Certainly they can sell their home for additional cash, but then where would they live? They can borrow through home equity loans (only if they qualify and have sufficient current income which most do not), but they must still pay back a portion of the debt each month.

What to do? The answer is the reverse mortgage (RM)! Bear in mind that the topic of reverse mortgages can be a lengthy and complicated one. I will attempt in the next few pages to give you a clear, concise overview of what this program is all about, but more research on your part is needed.

# What Is a Reverse Mortgage (RM)?

The reverse mortgage is a home loan that is treated in the opposite fashion of a standard mortgage because the money goes from the lender (a bank, for example) to you, the homeowner. In other words, instead of you borrowing a large amount of money and making small monthly repayments back to the lender, you borrow small amounts over a period of year, even for the rest of your life.

You do not give up any ownership when you take out an RM. All privileges of ownership stay with you as well as all responsibilities

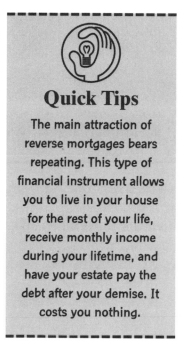

**Quick Tips**

The main attraction of reverse mortgages bears repeating. This type of financial instrument allows you to live in your house for the rest of your life, receive monthly income during your lifetime, and have your estate pay the debt after your demise. It costs you nothing.

(taxes, insurance, maintenance, etc.). If you sell your home, the money that is owed becomes due and will come from the proceeds of the sale of the home. If you die before any sale is made, your estate will pay the amount that is owed.

## Who Is Eligible for a Reverse Mortgage?

To be eligible for an RM (lenders have different requirements) you must own your home (usually with little or no debt) and you must be of a minimum age. You do not want to be too young (in your early sixties) to take this out, since your monthly income will be much less than if you were 10 years older. The reason that higher monthly income increases for older people is that the number of years that they have left to live will be less, the value of their home will have increased, and the possibility of one of the spouses becoming widowed is greater.

**Get Started**

As for payout methods, many possibilities are available to you: there are many different methods of payments to you.

1. Single lump-sum payment
2. Lifetime monthly advances (most popular)
3. Monthly advances for a specific period of time
4. A line of credit
5. Any combination of these payment methods

Monthly payments, credit line withdrawals, and lump-sum payments to homeowners are not to be considered as income for tax purposes. The income also does not affect Social Security and Medicare benefits.

# What Is the Structure of the Reverse Mortgage?

All reverse mortgages are known as "rising debt" loans because the amount you owe grows larger over a period of time. After you receive your first monthly advance, that is the amount that you will owe. But the next month you will receive more money and that is added to what you already owe from the month before. The pattern goes on for each and every month that you live. You own the home during your lifetime, and the title rests with you. However, if your heirs fail to repay the loan when the due date arrives (usually upon your death), the lender has the right to foreclose the property. Most RMs allow you to prepay the loan at any time.

Medicare and social security eligibility are not based on either your assets or your income. Therefore, whatever advances you receive from the RM will not affect any benefits you receive from public programs. If you receive SSI, RM monthly advances will not affect your benefits as long as you spend the money within the month you receive it.

Bear in mind, and this is most important, that all income you receive from the RM (whether monthly or in a lump sum) is non-taxable. That means that you get to keep every penny you receive.

## What Are the Drawbacks?

Of course, certain disadvantages are attached to the RM. The costs attributed to reverse mortgages (closing fees, point, etc.) are usually higher than the costs of other loans, and the interest rates charged by the lender are on a compounding basis. Because these fees can be high, you should plan to take out the RM only if you intend to live in the house for a long period of time. Under the Fannie Mae RM, for example, a 75-year old living in a $150,000 home could incur as much as $8,000 in origination, closing, and insurance costs. Also, this type of mortgage will give your heirs less equity in the home you leave them.

And another point to ponder: if RMs are as good as they appear to be for older homeowners, why have so few seniors made use of them? The reason lies in the fact that the terms of such agreements are harder to understand than those of other types of loans, sometimes going beyond the comprehension of most retirees. Another question to raise is that if reverse mortgages do represent a very lucrative market for lenders, why have most of the financial institutions ignored them? The answer is that an insured RM is neither a simple loan agreement backed by real estate nor a simple life insurance or annuity policy funded with cash. In other words, both banks and insurance companies must stretch their expertise way beyond their normal boundaries in order to design and market this product, which is both risky and expensive.

# How Is the Amount of Payment to You Determined?

The amount of money you receive from your lender will depend upon three factors:

1. *Age:* How old you are at the closing of the mortgage will determine in part the amount of your income. Naturally the older you are, the more money you will receive, since you have fewer years left to receive this income. If you are married, some lenders will use the age of the younger spouse; others will average the two life ages together in order to determine their payment to you.

2. *Equity:* The value of your home will determine the monthly income you will receive. Some lenders may have minimums or maximums on the value of your home.

3. *Costs:* The costs of closing fees, insurance, and interest will determine the net amount of your monthly receipt. There is now a method for homeowners to determine the potential cost of a loan. It is known as Total Annual Loan Cost (TALC), which is a disclosure form that all lenders must provide to anyone interested in securing a reverse mortgage. This program will inform

the borrower of the approximate total annual cost of the loan expressed as an interest rate. It gives the homeowner the real cost of the loan by showing the total annual percentage rate (a) after two years, (b) at life expectancy of the home owner, and (c) at some point beyond life expectancy. Because the effective cost of an RM decreases the longer it is held, the form reflects different costs for different time periods. TALC rates make it possible for homeowners to compare the actual cost of reverse mortgage programs with very different types of itemized costs.

## Don't Forget

Let me clarify the major difference between a standard (also known as forward) mortgage and a reverse mortgage. In a standard mortgage, your monthly payments to the lender become equity for you in the future, whereas in a reverse mortgage you turn your present equity into monthly income (as a debt). In other words, a standard mortgage builds up your equity with each payment you make, while a reverse mortgage spends down your equity with each payment you receive. Remember you can never fall behind or even have late payments since there are never any payments due on your part.

# What Types of Reverse Mortgages Exist?

Basically, there are three major categories of RMs:

1. *Home Equity Conversion Mortgage (HECM):* This FHA reverse mortgage appears to be the most popular. Congress passed in 1987, and amended in 1989, housing legislation authorizing 25,000 federally insured reverse mortgages under the Federal Housing Administration (FHA) and the Department of Housing and Urban Development (HUD). Under the HUD agreement, the range of value (at maximum) is between $70,000 and $152,000 depending upon location (urban vs. rural) and is available in 47 states (exceptions are Alaska, South Dakota, and Texas). In order

## Get Started

You'll want to select the method of income payment that suits your lifestyle and situation. Generally, lenders offer three plans:

1. The *tenure plan* provides monthly repayments to you for as long as you live in your home. These payments will continue until you die, sell, or move away.

2. The *term plan* provides a monthly advance for a specific number of months that you select (higher income each month than the tenure plan). When the time period runs out and the lender's repayments to you cease, you are not required to make payments back to the lender as long as you live in the house.

3. The *line of credit* lets you decide when you would like additional cash. If you combine the tenure or term plan with the line-of-credit plan, you will have not just income each month but also the option of meeting any unexpected expenses (having to leave your home for health reasons, for example) that may occur in the future. Remember that your concern is in the future, because that is where you will be spending the rest of your life.

to be eligible for the RM, the borrower must own a single-family dwelling. Condominiums must be FHA approved to be eligible, whereas co-ops and mobile homes do not qualify. Homeowners living in duplexes, triplexes, and four-unit buildings are now eligible for the Home Equity Conversion Mortgage (HECM) insured by the Federal Housing Administration (FHA).

2. *Fannie Mae:* This new reverse mortgage, offered by the largest supplier of mortgage capital, is known as the "Home Keeper." Its major advantage over the FHA mortgage is that it will consider homes with up to $207,000 value rather than the maximum of FHA's $152,000. This has become the most significant development in the history of reverse mortgages because it may now attract more lenders including banks, S&Ls, and credit unions.

3. *Private Reverse Mortgages:*   This type of loan is based on the concept that lenders will create their own private pool of insurance with FHA help. This plan generally has the same procedures and benefits as the FHA reverse mortgage, but the amount of its advances is usually greater. Under this insured plan, you can request only a percentage of your home equity to go toward the RM, thus reserving part of the value of your home for yourself or your heirs. For example, on a $100,000 equity, you may decide to mortgage only 70 percent ($70,000) and keep the balance ($30,000) for the future. Thus the lender, at payoff time would recover, at most, only the $70,000 that was loaned. Your 30 percent share would always be in your estate.

## How About Uninsured Reverse Mortgages?

The uninsured reverse mortgage (also known as the fixed-term RM) is structured differently. The loan is paid out to you for a fixed period of time (usually 5 to 10 years) in monthly payments. The length of the loan will have a major impact on the amount of money you receive monthly. A 5-year term, for example, can pay you as much as three times the monthly amount as a 10-year term. This imbalance occurs because you are allocating the same value of your home over a longer period of time, and the longer the term of the loan, the more the effect that compounding interest has on its cost. When the time period ends, no additional income is sent to you. The loan must be repaid at that point.

### Quick Tips

It's worth remembering that lender-insured loans can become very expensive if homes appreciate at a high rate. Yet the overall cost of this type of loan is low if you exceed your life expectancy and the home appreciates at a low rate.

This type of loan is designed only for a person who needs monthly income for a specific period of time and who intends to sell the home at that point. Do not consider this type of RM if your plans are indefinite or if you intend to live in your home forever.

# What Other Information Should You Know About the Reverse Mortgage?

1. Watch out for the "default" clause that appears in some contracts. This acceleration means that certain conditions could force you to sell your home before you die. These may include an extended stay at a nursing-care facility, failure to pay property tax, failure to maintain and insure the property, personal bankruptcy, fraud, and condemnation proceedings.

2. Look to see if there is an "Appreciation Sharing" clause that permits the lending institution to share in any appreciation or increase in value of the home upon its ultimate sale.

3. Remember that an RM is a loan only against your home equity; thus you can never owe more than the value of your home at any time. This limited liability is known as the "nonrecourse" limit, stopping the lender from seeking more money from your other assets or from your heirs. In other words, if you should live many years more than was initially anticipated (thus receiving more income than your house is worth) the lender cannot go after your estate to make up the difference.

4. Look at the RM in the same manner as a single-premium annuity policy. Under the annuity concept, you receive a monthly income for the rest of your life by taking money out of your capital and paying one lump-sum payment in advance. The reverse mortgage works in similar fashion but instead of giving the lender a large amount of money, you merely put up your house as the collateral for the funds. The big difference is that you still have your capital.

5. The lending institution that holds your reverse mortgage will get the money it paid to you (principal, interest, and costs) when the home is sold. Let me emphasize how crucial it is to examine these costs carefully. Although the interest rate that is charged to you is the one that is most visible, expenses can vary considerably and may

include origination and insurance fees, interest on loan advances, and of course closing costs. The best method to treat all the various charges involved in the process is to insist that all loan costs be combined into one single rate. This is known as the total annual percentage rate (TAPR) which will become due at the loan's maturity.

6. The lender must send you monthly advances until you sell, give away your home, or die. At that time, under any of these conditions, the money owed is paid back to the lender. However, the vast majority of homeowners will never themselves actually pay back the money that has been advanced to them. Rather, the amount owed will be paid after the death by their estate, normally from the sale of the house. What you are actually doing, then, is using and enjoying the money "while you are living." After your demise, your heirs will meet your obligations and retain whatever is left for themselves. Remember that you are not taking any money out of your childrens' pockets, as they are not paying anything that you owe from their own personal assets. What you are doing instead is leaving them a little less. In other words, you are spending part of your childrens' inheritance. And on the topic of children, *when you teach your child, you teach your child's child.*

**It's a Wrap**

✔ Reverse mortgages may be an ideal solution for those who own their homes "free and clear" but have little or no income.

✔ You do not give up any of the benefits or responsibilities of home ownership by holding a reverse mortgage.

✔ Reverse mortgages allow you to draw down the equity in your home through a lump-sum payment, monthly advances, or a line of credit.

✔ Payments enjoyed through reverse mortgages are not considered as income for purposes of tax, Social Security, or Medicare.

Reverse mortgage lenders may be hard to find. If you do locate one, you may pay high closing costs to secure your loan.

✔ You can prepay a reverse mortgage at any time.

✔ If you still owe money on your reverse mortgage when you die, your heirs must pay the balance (normally from the sale of the house).

*When you teach your child, you teach your child's child.*

# PART IV

Financial Planning for the Future

# CHAPTER 22

# Planning Your Retirement—An Overview

*Retirement takes all the fun out of Sundays.*

**Do I Need to Read This Chapter?**

→ Am I thinking about the financial and emotional implications of retirement?

→ Do I know at what age I want to retire?

→ Do I understand how pension payouts work?

→ Am I clear on IRA rollover rules?

In the following chapters, various retirement plans are discussed. Whether you are employed by a corporation or a government agency, are self-employed, or are working part time, some of the options explained in the following pages will affect your future financial plans.

## Quick Tips

Are you puzzled at this point? Are you thinking that there are thousands of books and magazines on retirement? Of course there are. But few of them cover the key point: the feeling of being retired. Today's unanswered question seems to be not so much what happens physically to people when they retire as what happens to them emotionally. The American public, the government, and the medical profession put more effort into helping folks reach old age than in helping them enjoy it. Can you imagine filling 10 hours a day (3650 hours a year) in leisure? That huge amount of time hangs over every retired person like unspent capital.

# How Does Early Retirement Play a Role in the Various Plans?

There is a story of a beautiful bird who was powerful and free. It had magnificent, colorful plumage, of which it was very proud. One day the bird decided to pluck its feathers, one by one, in order to make a nest in which it could rest in comfort and security. Now it cannot fly.

Don't consider retiring until you are both financially and emotionally ready. Why? Because people have not been properly prepared for retirement in America. We spend a third of our lifetime preparing for a career but almost no time in preparing for the period afterward.

## How Long Will My Money Last?

Lots of decisions, not all of them voluntary, help to determine when you will retire. If you have any say in the matter, I advise being very careful about what age you will leave the workforce. The decision to retire will be based on your financial status, and careful planning is mandatory. For example, people who are nearing retirement or have begun retirement with a fixed asset base may be concerned whether their money will last

**TABLE 22.1**  Earnings and Withdrawals

| IF PRINCIPAL IS EARNING AT THIS RATE | AND YOU ARE WITHDRAWING AT THIS RATE | | | | | | | | | | |
| | 16% | 15% | 14% | 13% | 12% | 11% | 10% | 9% | 8% | 7% | 6% |
|---|---|---|---|---|---|---|---|---|---|---|---|
| 12% | 12 | 14 | 17 | 23 | Here's how many years your | | | | | | |
| 11 | 11 | 13 | 15 | 18 | 24 | principal will last | | | | | |
| 10 | 10 | 12 | 13 | 15 | 19 | 25 | | | | | |
| 9 | 10 | 11 | 12 | 14 | 16 | 20 | 27 | | | | |
| 8 | 9 | 10 | 11 | 12 | 14 | 17 | 21 | 28 | | | |
| 7 | 9 | 9 | 10 | 11 | 13 | 15 | 18 | 22 | 31 | | |
| 6 | 8 | 9 | 10 | 11 | 12 | 13 | 16 | 19 | 24 | 33 | |
| 5 | 8 | 8 | 9 | 10 | 11 | 12 | 14 | 17 | 20 | 26 | 37 |

as long as it will be needed. If you are forced to dip into your principal in order to make ends meet, Table 22.1 may be of great help to you. It shows how long your money will last if you must draw from it at a rate faster than it is growing. As an illustration, suppose your assets are earning an 8 percent annual return and you must withdraw 15 percent of your principal each year in order to live comfortably in retirement. As shown in the table, your money should last approximately 10 years.

# How Do Lump-Sum Distributions Work?

Every day, for various reasons, people receive large lump-sum distributions representing the accumulated value of their pension plans. This may occur when you retire, or it may occur sooner if you become disabled, if you leave your present employer, or if the company decides to terminate your pension plan. In any case, when you receive such a lump-sum distribution, you face a problem: How do you minimize the taxes on this often sizable payment?

**Get Started**

Basically, you have two ways to handle lump-sum distributions:

1. 5-year forward averaging for tax purposes

2. Rollover into an individual retirement account (IRA)

Let's look at both in depth.

# What Is the 5-Year Forward-Averaging Plan?

You may be acquainted with ordinary income averaging, which is a way of reducing your income taxes for a year in which your income is markedly higher than in previous years. Five-year forward averaging is slightly different in that it allows your lump-sum distribution to be taxed at a different, lower rate than your other income. Here's how it works.

When you use 5-year forward averaging, your lump-sum distribution is taxed as if you were receiving it in five equal annual payments. For each of the 5 years, you pay taxes on just one-fifth of the total distribution. Furthermore, the tax on each installment is computed as though the lump-sum distribution were your only source of income for the year, which is then added to your other income tax payments for the year. The tax is likely to be far less than it would be if it were computed as part of your entire year's income. Under the Tax Reform Act (TRA), if you were age 50 by January 1986, you can use 10 years instead of 5 years in computing forward averaging, if you use specific tax rate tables.

In order for you to use either method, your distribution must come from a qualified plan in which you have been enrolled for at least 5 years, the sum must represent your entire interest in the plan, and you must be at least age 59½.

If you decide to forward-average (under either a 5- or 10-year plan), the tax law requires you to use the method on all other lump sums you receive in the same year from any other tax-deferred plan. In other words, you cannot forward-average one lump sum and roll over others into an IRA.

---

### Don't Forget

Warning! Be aware that this 5-year plan will be repealed beginning in the year 2000. Thus if you were thinking of using this plan on future distributions, you must consider taking it before 1999 runs out.

---

# What Is an IRA Rollover?

Another way to reduce the taxes on your lump-sum distribution is to roll it over—that is, reinvest it—in an IRA. This must be done within 60 days of receiving the distribution, or you will lose the tax-shelter status otherwise conferred by the IRA. You don't have to pay any current income taxes on the distribution amount if you deposit it in an IRA, nor will you owe taxes on the income which accumulates in the account. The IRA funds become taxable only upon withdrawal, which may begin after you reach age 59½ and must begin by age 70½. See Chap. 23 for specific rulings on IRA rollovers.

# Which Method—5-Year Averaging or IRA Rollover—Is Better?

The answer to this question depends on your personal financial situation. If you plan to retire and liquidate your IRA in a short time—say, 4 years or less—then the 5-year forward-averaging method is likely to save you more money. This is because, once you begin withdrawing your IRA funds, the money is usually taxed at a higher rate than that called for under 5-year averaging.

Another consideration is the level of income you expect to enjoy after retirement. If you expect your income to decline sharply upon retirement, then an IRA rollover plan is probably your best choice. Chances are that, under those circumstances, the taxes you'll pay when withdrawing your IRA funds will be relatively low. On the other hand, if income from other sources will keep you in a fairly high tax bracket when you retire, then the 5-year forward averaging plan is best. Pay the low 5-year averaging rate and invest the distribution amount in an appropriate tax-saving instrument such as municipal bonds. As with most financial decisions, several factors must be taken into account, and only you can decide which is most important to you.

And on the topic of doing for yourself, remember that the only person you can redo is yourself, because it is easier to put on cloth slippers than to carpet the entire world.

It's a Wrap

✔ Retirement is a major life change, financially and emotionally.

✔ In cashing out a pension, look to minimize taxes.

✔ Act soon if you are in a position to take advantage of 5-year forward averaging, because this option will be repealed in the year 2000.

***The only person you can redo is yourself, because it is easier to put on cloth slippers than to carpet the entire world.***

# CHAPTER 23

# The IRA

*You can plan for tomorrow today but you can't plan for today tomorrow.*

**Do I Need to Read This Chapter?**

➜ Am I eligible for an IRA?

➜ Am I aware of the recent changes in IRA rules?

➜ Do I know that I can withdraw from my IRA before age 59½ without penalty, under certain conditions?

➜ Am I clear on the rules for mandatory IRA withdrawals after age 70½?

➜ Have I investigated various investment options for my IRA?

➜ Do I understand the difference between transfers and rollovers?

The *individual retirement account* (*IRA*) is a method of investing originally designed to help individuals not covered by company pension plans save for their retirement. On January 1, 1982, the law governing IRAs was changed to make them available to anyone with earned income (wages, fees), whether or not the individual was covered by a company pension plan. The law was changed again in January 1987, again in 1993, and still again in 1997 to limit the amount deductible from your income tax.

# How Does the IRA Work?

First, some basic ground rules. Your IRA is a savings account containing funds that can be invested in any of a number of different financial instruments. (I'll offer some guidelines on your options in a moment.) By law, you may contribute to your IRA up to 100 percent of the first $2000 that you earn each year. If a husband and wife are both working, they can establish an IRA and contribute up to $2000 per year to each account, for a family total of $4000.

Previously, a nonworking spouse and a working spouse could invest together into an IRA a combined total of $2250. In 1997, a change was made that permits stay-at-home spouses and their employed mate a total contribution up to $4000, which puts them on par with families in which both spouses work.

## How Will My IRA Grow?

Many advertisers are touting the fact that a $2000 annual deposit into an IRA (at 10 percent) by a 25-year-old would be worth nearly $1 million ($973,704) when the person reached age 65. Table 23.1 shows the value for different years and rate yields for a constant $2000 annual contribution. The figures are impressive.

But here is where the rules have changed. If you or your spouse is considered an active participant in a qualified pension plan (even if you do not as yet have vested rights), you will have limits imposed on your IRA contribution. You can still contribute up to

## Quick Tips

By establishing the spousal IRA, the government finally recognized the value of the work that women do in their households. More important, the spousal IRA recognizes that women who don't work outside the house still need to think about saving for retirement. The reason was stated before but must be addressed again. Women fail to save enough for their own retirement because they tend, during their lifetime, to move in and out of the workforce causing their savings to be sporadic. Also, they live longer than men, thus requiring their savings to be stretched further. And, of course, women still earn less than men, which compounds the reasons just mentioned.

**TABLE 23.1**   Value of Principal for $2000 Yearly IRA Contribution

| | INTEREST RATE | | | |
| YEAR | 6% | 8% | 10% | 12% |
|---|---|---|---|---|
| 1 | $2120 | $2160 | $2200 | $2240 |
| 5 | 11,951 | 12,672 | 13,431 | 14,230 |
| 10 | 27,943 | 31,291 | 35,062 | 39,309 |
| 15 | 49,345 | 58,649 | 69,900 | 83,507 |
| 20 | 77,985 | 98,846 | 126,005 | 161,397 |
| 25 | 116,313 | 157,909 | 216,364 | 298,668 |
| 30 | 167,603 | 244,692 | 361,887 | 540,585 |
| 35 | 236,242 | 372,204 | 596,254 | 966,927 |
| 40 | 328,095 | 599,562 | 973,704 | 1,718,285 |

---

### Don't Forget

January may not be your favorite month weather-wise, but if you're investing in an IRA you should learn to love it. It is very important that you make your IRA contribution in the beginning of the year. Over the long run, the tax deferral you get from the compounding of your earnings on that money can actually be more valuable than your IRA contribution. If you earn 6 percent on your $2000 annual contribution, the $120 interest on the money you earn each year is compounded from the beginning of the year. If you wait until the end of the year, you will lose a whole year's compounded interest.

---

$2000 as long as your adjusted gross income (AGI) is not more than $50,000 (individual) or $80,000 (joint) (1998).

# What Are the Tax Consequences of the IRA?

The money you contribute to your IRA is deducted from your income for tax purposes, providing immediate tax benefits, and is called a *deductible contribution*.

In 1998, a new form of IRA was initiated—the Roth IRA. Although the contributions you make (up to $2000) are not tax deductible, the investment earnings are eliminated while the traditional IRA simply defers them. The longer you have till you retire, the more the earnings will be and the more you will save by avoiding taxes on those gains. Only joint filers with adjusted gross income of $150,000 or less and single filers with less than $95,000 of income can set up the Roth IRA. Since this new IRA has just been authorized, I suggest you check with your accountant on the ramifications of the new law and how it can affect you.

# What Are the Rules for IRA Distributions?

Since the IRA was created specifically to make it easier for working people to save for their retirement, there are built-in restrictions on your access to IRA funds.

## Get Started

1. You can begin withdrawing your IRA money without penalty after reaching age 59½.

2. If you must withdraw money from your IRA before that time, you must pay an extra 10 percent penalty tax on the amount you withdraw, unless you are disabled.

3. You *must* start withdrawing from your IRA at age 70½.

However, as with everything in life—especially where the government is concerned—there are exceptions. Read on!

You can now make penalty-free IRA withdrawals if the money is used to pay medical expenses that exceed 7.5 percent of adjusted gross income or to purchase health insurance if you've been receiving unemployment compensation for more than 12 weeks. This provision took effect on January 1, 1997. There is also no early withdrawal penalty for any IRA distribution before age 59½ if the money is used to help a first-time home buyer (immediate family) purchase a home with a $10,000 lifetime limit. The penalty is also waived if you use the money to pay higher education expenses of the taxpayer or child, spouse, or grandchild of the taxpayer.

Another exception is that an individual may also withdraw funds from an IRA without penalty (before age 59½) as long as the individual makes equal withdrawals each year in predetermined amounts. This method of withdrawal (called *annuitizing*) is designed to deplete the amount of money in the IRA over the life expectancy of the person. To those individuals who wish to retire in their fifties, this withdrawal option is of great benefit because it allows them to supplement their income until their social security benefits begin at age 62. Also, parents can now tap their IRAs before age 59½ to help pay the high costs of education for their children.

What is important is that the IRA funds are able to be withdrawn under the annuity plan for any purpose without any justification needed. Even if the person was not able or eligible for the $2000 contribution, proceeds from pension plans, for example, can be rolled over into the IRA and the withdrawal plan option can be utilized for these funds. Also, and most important, once the yearly withdrawals begin, they must continue at the same rate for at least 5 years. A change after that period of time is permitted as long as the person is over 59½. Therefore, a 55-year-old would be able to (1) stop making annual withdrawals, (2) change the amount of withdrawal, or (3) withdraw the entire balance at age 60. Just remember that by tapping the IRA funds, you are reducing the basic financial structure for your retirement years and also your ability to have your money grow through tax-deferred savings.

## How Bad Are the IRA Penalties?

The penalty for early withdrawal deters many young people from opening IRAs. When you're 25 years old, 59½ may seem an eternity away, and more than 30 years may seem like an impossibly long time to tie up your money. However, the effects of the penalty aren't nearly as severe as you might think. Because of the tax benefits derived both at the time of the contribution and during the accumulation of tax-free interest, IRA accounts become profitable fairly quickly even when the penalty for early withdrawal is taken into account. With 5 or 6 years of compounding, your income will compensate for the withdrawal penalty. After that time, even if you incur the 10 percent penalty, you will have increased your money faster than otherwise possible because of the tax benefits.

Therefore, don't let the early withdrawal penalty discourage you unduly. An IRA is still a highly beneficial investment.

## I'm Turning 70½. What Now?

When you reach age 70½, you must begin to take money out of your IRA. The first year, however, the government gives you a grace period until April 1 of the following year. After that first year, your withdrawal must be made by December 31. Remember, that if you take advantage of the delay in the first year, you will have to take 2 years' worth of withdrawals, which could push you into a higher tax bracket and make your social security benefits more exposed to tax.

### Quick Tips

Here's a point to ponder. Under a little-known and confusing ruling, if you are still working past age 70½, you are not required to begin taking the mandatory distributions from your qualified retirement plans. You don't have to do anything until you retire. However, this rule does not apply to IRAs. The mandatory law of April 1 withdrawal of the year following your 70½th birthday still pertains to IRAs.

The minimum amount of withdrawal each year is based on your life expectancy or, if a beneficiary is named, on the joint life expectancy of both. To compute the withdrawal, you divide the amount in the IRA by the appropriate life expectancy figure. At age 70, a life expectancy of 15 years would mean $\frac{1}{15}$ of your total IRA balance. In years to follow, you can reduce the original expectancy by 1 year ($\frac{1}{14}$, $\frac{1}{13}$, $\frac{1}{12}$, etc.). This is known as "term certain." Another method available is to recalculate ("annual recalculation" method) the number of years of life expectancy each year. Remember, though, that once you choose a method, you must stay with it.

However, if one spouse dies, only the survivor's life expectancy can be used. When both parties die, the entire balance of the IRA must be paid out within a year to whoever is designated. That lump sum could produce a major tax bill for your beneficiary. By using the "term-certain" method, the beneficiary gets the money in small amounts annually, just as the maker of the IRA would have received.

No matter which method is chosen, you must make a definite decision. If you do not, for example, let the government know whether you wish your IRA money paid out over individual or joint life expectancies by the year you reach age 70½, IRS will make that choice for you through the individual life expectancy method. Also, you will lose your choice again if your IRA does not specify "term-certain." IRS will make the distribution using the "annual recalculation" method.

A change in the law allows you to extend your IRA withdrawal period to cover the combined life expectancy of you and your spouse. This figure will usually be higher than the life expectancy of either husband or wife. For example, as an assumption, a 70-year-old man is expected to live 12 years, a 70-year-old woman, 15 years. However, one or the other might be expected to survive for 18 years. Therefore, the 70-year-old couple can use the 18-year life expectancy figure as the basis of their withdrawals if they wish—and they can recalculate their combined life expectancy each year as well.

## Don't Forget

Are the rules different for individuals who wish to withdraw large sums? Yes. There is a 15 percent excise tax on distributions over $160,000—but they have been suspended for the years 1997–1999. Another reason to act quickly, if this option interests you.

# What Happens If You Die Before You Become Eligible to Use Your IRA Funds?

Whenever you open an IRA, you must designate a beneficiary. Then, in the event of your untimely death, that person must make some key decisions. If your beneficiary is your spouse, he or she may choose any of the following options.

---

## Get Started

1. The spouse can withdraw IRA funds as a lump sum which would be taxable during that year.

2. The spouse can take yearly distributions based on his or her life expectancy.

3. The spouse can use a portion of the money for current needs and roll over the balance.

4. The spouse can convert the IRA into his or her own account. The new owner will have all the rights and obligations of the former owner.

---

Most spouses choose to roll over the money left to them into their own IRA. However, if the beneficiary is not a spouse, he or she has only 5 years to take all the money out of the account and cannot roll the funds into an IRA. Also, if you name as beneficiary your estate, the money in the IRA will be taxed as ordinary income as of the date of your demise.

## How Do IRAs Relate to Revocable Living Trusts?

In the view of most experts, it is not a good idea to make a revocable living trust the beneficiary of an IRA if the owner is over 70 years of age. People use a revocable trust because they may not want a beneficiary to have access to all the money at one time, or they fear the long and costly probate procedures. Some investors want their retirement funds managed by professional after they die, and the revocable trust affords them this feature.

However, the problem arises when the IRA owner (who is over 70½ and has been recalculating the minimum payout each year) dies. Since the revocable trust has no life expectancy, all the money in the IRA is paid into the trust and becomes immediately subject to income tax. If the deceased had named a beneficiary, the beneficiary could withdraw the money based on his or her own life expectancy.

# What Investment Options Are Available for an IRA?

When you invest in an IRA, the law requires that a trustee be named to administer the account. The trustee must file reports with you and with the federal government. Typical IRA trustees include commercial and savings banks, savings and loan institutions, brokerage houses, insurance companies, and other types of investment firms.

As for the type of investment, any of a wide range of choices may be suitable for your IRA, depending on your age and financial status and the degree of risk you wish to take. The only restrictions on IRA investments are these: you may not invest your IRA funds in collectibles, such as postage stamps, coins (except certain U.S. gold and silver coins), antiques, or art; you may not invest your IRA funds in life insurance contracts; and you may not make an investment in which you have a direct interest, as, for example, if you were to buy a home with IRA funds and then rent it from the IRA account.

Here are some of the most popular investment choices for IRA accounts:

*Certificates of deposit:*   An IRA bank account usually takes the form of a certificate of deposit with a minimum term of 18 months. Rates may be fixed in advance or variable. If the rate is variable, find out just how it is set and how often it is adjusted—weekly, monthly, or whatever. In general, the most conservative investment strategy is to invest for the shortest available term.

*Stocks and bonds:*   If you wish, you can deposit your IRA money with a stockbroker, who will act as your trustee. However, you direct the account yourself: you make your own investment decisions and you can buy and sell stocks and bonds, moving your funds from one investment to another, without incurring any taxes on the money.

*Mutual funds:*   You can deposit your IRA money in a mutual fund and so invest not in a few self-selected stocks but in a managed portfolio of many issues put together by a brokerage firm. You may wish to choose a broker who offers a "family of funds" of different types among which you are free to switch your investment from time to time without charge or penalty. Also, remember that there's no need to invest in any of the special tax-exempt mutual funds; your IRA investment is already sheltered from all levels of taxation. Stick to funds which are normally taxable; these usually offer a higher rate of return. Also, look into zero coupon bonds (see Chap. 10) for funding your IRA.

# How Should You Choose Among These Investment Options?

One prime consideration should be how well you have otherwise provided for your retirement. If your IRA is your sole retirement plan, you should invest conservatively; if you have substantial savings outside of the IRA, income which you expect to continue after retirement, or a secure company pension plan, you can afford a bit more risk. Your age is another important factor. Here are some guidelines to use depending on your present age:

*Age 20 to 40:*   When you are young, growth should be your primary goal; a relatively high degree of risk is tolerable. Suggestion: invest your IRA in a diversified portfolio of common stocks or in a mutual fund managed for growth of assets, not income.

*Age 40 to 50:*    Stocks are still an attractive choice. However, if you expect to begin withdrawing your IRA funds when you reach age 59½, redirect some of your funds from growth stocks into current income-generating investments.

*Age 50 to 60:*    At this point, growth is less important, risk less acceptable. Move some, up to half, of your investments out of stocks and into bonds, in order to minimize risk and increase your current flow of income.

*Age 60 and over:*    By now, most of your IRA funds should be in income-producing investments with maturities of 5 years and less. This will provide safety and maximum current interest.

# What About Rollover Distributions to IRAs?

All eligible rollover distributions are subject to a mandatory 20 percent withholding tax. Although this 20 percent withholding would still be considered part of the distribution which is subject to income tax, you can claim a federal tax refund, if the 20 percent withholding results in overwithholding for the year. There are two ways to avoid current taxation on this mandatory 20 percent withholding.

1.  You elect to do a "direct rollover." This means that your distribution is moved directly to another retirement plan or IRA rather than distributed to you. In the case of a direct rollover, the 20 percent withholding would not apply. Under this method, you would need to have your employer or plan coordinator write a check payable to the trustee of your new plan, putting on the memo line of the check the words "Direct Rollover." Once this transfer is made into your IRA, you can take the money out the very next day without the 20 percent withholding. However, you may do so only once a year. If you are under the age of 59½, the entire balance must be put back into an IRA within 60 days or a 10 percent penalty is imposed.

2. You may add your own after-tax funds, up to the amount withheld, to the amount that you actually received in order to roll over an amount equal to your entire taxable distribution. Sounds complicated? Use this as an example. Assume a participant elects to receive a lump-sum distribution of $100,000 from his or her retirement account. Because of the 20 percent withholding rule, the participant would receive only $80,000. However, since he or she is entitled to roll over the entire $100,000, $20,000 of personal funds could be added to bring the total amount of the rollover up to $100,000. The 20 percent withheld at the time of distribution would be refunded when the participant files his or her tax return. If the participant does not choose to add the additional $20,000 personally but instead rolls over only $80,000 of the $100,000 received from the original trustee, he or she must include the $20,000 as taxable income for that year.

If there is a waiting period for you to get into your new employer's plan and you do not want to follow step 1 or 2, you can get the plan coordinator to transfer your funds to a "conduit" IRA. This type of IRA is used as a temporary account for rollovers in order to keep them separate from other IRA funds, since no commingling of funds is acceptable for rollovers. This conduit IRA must be set up at a place where no other IRA of yours exists.

# What Are the Basic Differences Between the Transfer and the Rollover?

Both transfers and rollovers are ways to move retirement funds from one custodian to another. It is the way in which the funds are moved that differs:

A *transfer* means moving IRA funds from one account directly to another, with no distribution of funds to the account owner. Typically, you would make a transfer if you wanted to consolidate sev-

## Don't Forget

Keep the following points in mind when reviewing the 20 percent with-holding:

1. The 20 percent withholding applies only to lump-sum withdrawals and not to periodic withdrawals such as retirees taking a monthly payout.

2. Two types of distributions are not eligible for rollovers and thus are not subject to the 20 percent withholding:

   - Required minimum distribution received after age 70½

   - Payments received in 10 or more annual installments or in a series of equal installments extending over the participant's lifetime

3. It is the participant's responsibility to inform his or her employer or plan sponsor of a desire to transfer.

eral IRAs; if you were to move and wanted your funds managed by an institution close by; or if you weren't happy with your current trustee's service or account management. The IRA places no limits on the number of transfers you make. And, because you never actually receive the funds, you are not required to report these transactions at tax time. You can transfer all or only part of an account, and no tax is withheld from the amounts you transfer.

A *rollover* involves a distribution of retirement funds to the owner, after which the funds are put into another account. Rollovers can be made between IRAs or from a qualified employer retirement plan to an IRA. If you plan to participate in a company retirement plan—for example, a profit-sharing or 401(k) program—you will usually receive all funds in which you are vested if you leave the company for any reason or if the plan is terminated. Depending on your length of service with your employer, this distribution could be sizable. If you choose to keep it, you will pay tax on the distribution, which means a significant portion—depending on your tax situation—will go to the government. But if you roll it over into an IRA, you defer taxation and keep your retirement funds growing until you really need them later, after retirement.

As noted earlier, you can also withdraw funds from one IRA and roll them over into another IRA. And, finally, you can roll over inherited funds from your spouse's IRA or qualified retirement plan.

Whatever the distribution's source, you may roll over all or any portion of the distribution, but the IRS requires that you deposit rollover funds no later than the 60th day after you receive them. Any amount you fail to roll over within this period will bc taxablc as ordinary income (unless, in an IRA-to-IRA rollover, it represents a return of nondeductible IRA contributions.) You may also have to pay a 10 percent penalty for taking a premature distribution.

Neither a transfer nor a rollover affects the amount or the deductibility of your annual contributions to your IRA. They are separate transactions, involving only funds that were previously saved for your retirement.

The IRA is certainly a plan to look into for your retirement, since it can become an excellent vehicle for future income. And on the

## Quick Tips

This important rule governs IRA-to-IRA rollovers: You are permitted to make only one rollover from a given plan in any 12-month period. That is, if you take a distribution from IRA-1 and roll the funds over to IRA-2, you must wait 12 months from the date of the distribution before you can make another rollover from IRA-1. If you make more than one rollover from the same plan within a 12-month period, you may have to pay a 10 percent premature distribution penalty.

topic of retirement plans, remember to plan for the future now because that is where you will be spending the rest of your life.

It's a Wrap

✔ Individual retirement accounts (IRAs) are like long-term savings accounts with tax-deferred benefits.

✔ Thanks to a 1997 rule, stay-at-home spouses and their employed mates can contribute a combined total of up to $4000 in IRAs if they otherwise qualify.

✔ You can make tax-deductible contributions to an IRA if you earn up to $50,000 individually or $80,000 jointly.

✔ Making IRA contributions at the start of the year greatly improves your long-term yield.

✔ You can begin withdrawing from your IRA at age 59½; you must begin doing so at age 70½.

✔ Penalty-free IRA withdrawals are permitted under certain conditions for medical expenses and annuitizing.

✔ The amount you withdraw from IRAs after age 70½ is based on life expectancy.

✔ IRA investors must name a beneficiary, who will have several withdrawal options in the event of the original investor's untimely death.

✔ IRAs are generally invested in CDs, stocks, bonds, and/or mutual funds.

✔ Rollover distributions to IRA are subject to 20 percent withholding tax, but there are ways to avoid this tax.

*Remember to plan for the future now because that is where you will be spending the rest of your life.*

# CHAPTER 24

# The 401(k), the SEP, and the Keogh Plan

*In two days, tomorrow will be yesterday.*

Do I Need to Read This Chapter?

→ Am I clear on the different retirement savings options that may be available to me?

→ If my employer offers a 401(k), am I making the most of it?

→ If I'm self-employed, have I investigated the benefits of SEPs and Keoghs?

A n increasingly popular way of saving for retirement is the *401(k) plan,* named after the tax law provision that makes it possible. The 401(k) is known as the *deferred salary reduction plan* and allows an employee to set aside part of his or her salary into a tax-sheltered account that grows tax-free until after retirement. Don't confuse the 401(k) with a 403(b). A 403(b) is a retirement plan designed for employees of nonprofit organizations (schools, hospitals, etc.), whereas the 401(k) is for employees of private, for-profit businesses. Salary deductions for a 403(b) are treated in the same manner as the funds in the 401(k) account, which is excluded from taxable income, while the interest earned compounds tax-deferred until you withdraw the funds.

# How Does the 401(k) Differ from an Ordinary IRA?

Since you don't have to pay current income tax on the money you deposit in your 401(k) account, the plan is something like an individual retirement account. However, unlike an IRA, a 401(k) plan must be set up by your employer.

## Get Started

To qualify for a 401(k), you must meet all these requirements:

1. A full-time employee

2. Over the age of 21

3. Working for the company at least one year

4. Willing to contribute 20 percent of your gross income or $10,000 (as of 1998), whichever is less. However, if your employer offers matching funds, the maximum is the aggregate of 25 percent of total compensation up to $30,000.

The amount you put into the fund is indexed to increase each year. In recent years this figure has averaged 3 percent annually.

By contrast, an IRA has a limit of $2000 annually. Also, with an IRA you indicate the size of your contribution as a deduction on your federal income tax return. With a 401(k), this is not necessary. Your contribution is deducted from the income reported on your W-2 form and therefore is automatically excluded from federal and state income taxes.

## Quick Tips

While an IRA permits almost any investment vehicle, only a handful of options are allowed with a 401(k): a fixed-interest annuity, a mutual fund investing in stocks, a money market fund, and, perhaps, stock in the company itself. You can opt to put all your contributions into one or another investment vehicle, or you can split your contributions among two or more choices.

# How Does the 401(k) Work?

The 401(k) is in actuality a profit-sharing plan with a cash or deferred arrangement (CODA). This CODA provision permits employees to contribute part of their salary to the 401(k) on a pretax basis, with the amount being deducted from their paychecks. The amount of compensation taken out of salary is not subject to federal, state, or local income tax but is subject to FICA (social security) tax. This money will grow in the account on a tax-deferred basis, as with most other qualified retirement plans.

At the time the 401(k) plan is established by the employer, a specific investment program is set up. The employer usually chooses an investment firm to manage the accounts, and a range of possible investment options is offered. These choices are usually more restricted than they would be with an IRA.

# What About Withdrawal from a 401(k)?

If you leave the company, you can withdraw your 401(k) savings and keep the money if you wish. However, the amount becomes subject to income tax during that year. You can avoid taxation by rolling the money over into an IRA. To do so, you must transfer the money directly from your trustee to the IRA's trustee, making certain that you never take possession of the funds. In this trustee-to-trustee relationship, you will avoid the 20 percent withholding that began in 1993. You are also eligible to withdraw your 401(k) money at any time without having to pay a penalty if you suffer a financial hardship.

Once you reach the age of 59½, the money in your 401(k) account is yours to do with as you please. Of course, it is taxable when you withdraw it. However, your income will probably be lower after you retire, and so might your tax bracket. And the 401(k) account has another major advantage over the IRA when withdrawal time comes. If you withdraw your IRA funds in a lump sum, you must suffer a big tax bite during that year.

However, if you withdraw your 401(k) funds in a lump sum, you can use 5-year forward averaging to spread out and reduce the tax payments. (See Chap. 23.) This means that the withdrawal is taxed as if you'd received only one-fifth of the money each year for a period of 5 years. You may use 10-year forward averaging if you were born before 1936, but the tax rate table is different.

If the owner of the 401(k) dies before withdrawal, the amount of money in the plan is distributed to his or her beneficiaries, and the money is taxed as ordinary income to the beneficiaries. However, if the money is left to a surviving spouse, that spouse may transfer the funds to his or her IRA account.

## How About 401(k) Investments in My Ex-Employer's Stock?

If some of your money is invested in your employer's company stock, rolling over your 401(k) when you leave the firm may not be the best idea. It could be better if you take those shares rather than roll them into an IRA. There are reasons for this procedure.

1. You will owe tax only on the value of your shares at the time they were put into your 401(k) because the transactions will be based on a lower cost basis. For example: the value per share of stock at the time it went into your 401(k) was $10 per share but now, when you are ready to leave, its value jumped to $35 per share. By taking the stock and not rolling it over, you will owe taxes on the $10 figure (your cost basis), not the $35 market value.

2. When you sell the stock you will pay capital gains rather then your ordinary tax rate.

3. Your heirs could receive the gains on these shares tax free. Because you held these shares and have not placed them in an IRA, your heirs' cost basis would be the market value of $35 which would mean they would owe no taxes on your gains. Rolling into an IRA would then have the effect of having your heirs owe ordinary income tax on the value of the shares you left them.

As you can see, the 401(k) plan is a very attractive investment option for you as an employee, especially since the usual employer matching-contribution program in effect doubles your annual savings at no cost to you. And if you can afford to contribute to both a 401(k) account and an IRA, do that, too. You'll benefit right now as well as when you retire.

# How Does the SEP Work?

For a small business (proprietorship, partnership, corporation) the *simplified employee pension,* or *SEP,* is an excellent pension-planning tool, since it can help business owners, including those self-employed, to achieve financial security for their retirement. It was authorized in 1978 by Congress to give small businesses (even self-employed workers without employees) a program of current tax deduction and future pension benefits.

The business sets up an IRA for each employee and contributes, each year, as much as $30,000 or 15 percent (13.043 percent for self-employed) of earnings. These contributions are tax-deductible to the company. Employees may decide how to contribute the funds to their IRAs and can take the IRAs with them when they leave the firm. There is no complex administration, and the start-up and maintenance costs are slight.

## Quick Tips

Are you a deadline kind of person? One of the major features of the SEP is the extra time allowed to initiate it. Many people look for last-minute tax deductions before the April 15 deadline. You can set up an SEP 3½ months into the next year, as compared with the Keogh plan, which requires completion by the last day of the year.

# How Does the Keogh Plan Work?

The Keogh plan is a pension plan designed for the self-employed individual, whether the work is full or part time. In other words, you can work for an employer full time, but if you have any income from self-employment, part of that self-employment income can be contributed to your own Keogh plan.

A Keogh plan account is similar to an IRA in several ways. Your annual contribution to a Keogh account reduces your taxable income, and the sums in your account grow tax-free until you withdraw your investment after reaching the age of 59½; the upper limit on withdrawal is age 70½. At that time, the sums you withdraw are treated as ordinary taxable income. However, your income will probably be lower after retirement, so that the size of your tax bite will be smaller. Early withdrawals prior to age 59½ carry a 10 percent penalty. Therefore, as with an IRA, you should invest in a Keogh account only sums you don't expect to need until retirement. Liquidity is not one of the characteristics of a Keogh account.

## Get Started

For small businesses and their employees, as well as self-employed individuals who work alone, SEPs are attractive retirement vehicles. SEP investors enjoy tax benefits in the present, as well. Before investing, here is what you should know:

1. Employer contributions to the SEP are tax-deductible to the company and are not considered taxable income of the employee. These monies accumulate in the employee's SEP/IRA on a tax-deferred basis.

2. No start-up or annual filing costs are required to be sent to the U.S. Department of Labor. As its name implies, it is a simple plan to administer. The paperwork usually amounts to no more than a one-time completion of a model plan. Unless changes are made in the plan, you do not have to file annually, as you do with a Keogh.

3. All amounts from the SEP are considered ordinary income, with distribution of monies beginning no later than age 70½. Any withdrawal prior to age 59½ may be subject to a 10 percent penalty.

4. All eligible employees over age 21 must be included in the plan.

5. The same percentage that the employer receives must be applied to each employee, including yourself.

6. Lump-sum distributions from the SEP do not qualify for special income averaging, as do Keogh plans.

7. Unlike conventional company pension plans, in which employees usually have to wait a number of years before gaining access to their contributions, the SEP allows employees the right to any contributions the employer makes for their benefit.

# What Are the Differences Between the Keogh and the IRA?

As you will see subsequently, not everyone is eligible for a Keogh account. While the maximum amount you may contribute to an

IRA in any year is $2000, you may invest up to a maximum of $30,000 or 25 percent of your earned income, whichever is less, in a Keogh account under the "money purchase" plan.

## Get Started

1. A "money purchase" Keogh requires a fixed percentage of your income each year.

2. The other type of Keogh is a "profit-sharing" plan. These allow varying contributions each year. This type of Keogh has a tax-deductible limit on contributions of 13.043 percent of your self-employment earnings, up to a maximum of $30,000.

Withdrawals from IRAs and Keoghs are also handled differently. With both, you can withdraw the money either in a lump sum upon retirement or in installments. However, if you withdraw your Keogh investment in a lump sum, you can take advantage of the 5-year forward averaging rule, which allows you to compute your taxable income as if the withdrawal had been spread out over a 5-year period. A 10-year forward averaging period is also available, subject to certain conditions (see Chap. 23). Thus the Keogh plan can produce significantly greater income tax savings at withdrawal time than the IRA.

## Don't Forget

Trying to decide between a Keogh and SEP? In general, SEPs tend to be easier in terms of paperwork. They don't require annual filing, as Keoghs do. On the other hand, Keoghs qualify for special income averaging when you get a lump-sum distribution; SEPs don't.

# How Do You Qualify for a Keogh Plan?

To qualify for a Keogh account, you must be self-employed as the sole proprietor of a business, an unincorporated professional, or a partner in any unincorporated partnership. In addition, if your business has any employees, you are required to include in the plan all those who have worked for you longer than 3 years. You must contribute to their retirement funds the same percentage of their salary that you are contributing to your own. (Naturally, the employer's share of the Keogh investment for employees is treated as a deductible business expense.) The Keogh funds may be invested in almost any kind of instrument favored by the employer, including a certificate of deposit, stocks and bonds, a money market fund, or an insurance account. Collectibles are virtually the only common type of investment not allowed. The employer may choose to manage the Keogh personally or may invest the money in an annuity contract purchased from an insurance company or a mutual fund managed by a broker.

Ever since their introduction, Keoghs have been among the most popular pension plans. In 1984, the contribution limits were raised from $15,000 or 15 percent of earned income to the present $30,000 or 25 percent indexed to inflation. This change has only increased the attractiveness of the Keogh plan. If you're eligible for a Keogh plan account, you should certainly give it serious consideration as an investment option. It is a kind of super IRA which allows the self-employed professional or business proprietor to reduce his or her current taxable income while saving a substantial sum toward retirement. Remember: Judge each day not by the harvest you reap, but by the seeds you plant.

# Do Other Options Exist Besides 401(k)s, SEPs, and Keoghs?

Yes, there are other tax-deductible ways to accumulate money for retirement. In 1996 the government gave the green light to a new plan known as SIMPLE (Savings Incentive Match Plan for Employees), which is available to certain corporations, partnerships, sole proprietors, and tax-exempt or government employers. Two conditions apply: organizations offering the plan cannot have more than 100 employees; and SIMPLE must be the only qualified retirement plan offered.

SIMPLE lives up to its name. It doesn't demand the complicated nondiscrimination tests required by other plans, and the IRS paperwork isn't as complex. However, other factors must be considered.

## Don't Forget

If you're an employer interested in the SIMPLE plan, be aware that you *must* match employee contributions, according to certain formulas. If you're an employee, keep in mind that you and your employer cannot contribute more than $6000 annually to a SIMPLE plan (as of 1997). This total compares unfavorably to the maximums of $9500 allowed in a 401(k) and $30,000 allowed in a SEP-IRA or Keogh. However, a SIMPLE plan may still be better than nothing.

For employees of tax-exempt organizations and schools, tax-sheltered annuities (TSAs) are an option. Under IRS code 403(b), employees can exclude contributions to a TSA from their gross income. Maximum annual contributions are usually limited to the lesser of $10,000 or 16.66 percent of your salary.

Employees should ask their human resources managers for more information on these plans. Employers can get full information on the plans from their business advisors. And on the topic of advice, aspire to inspire before you expire.

✔ Many employers offer the retirement savings plan known as 401(k) and may even provide matching funds. 401(k)s are available to full-time employees who meet certain basic conditions.

✔ Those with 401(k) money invested in their employer's stock should be aware of tax restrictions that will come into play if they leave the company.

✔ Small businesses and self-employed individuals can benefit from simplified employee pension plans (called SEPs or SEP/IRAs) and Keoghs, which allow investors to reduce current taxable income while saving for retirement.

*Aspire to inspire before you expire.*

# CHAPTER 25

# Social Security

*I don't mind being a senior citizen, I just
don't look forward to graduation.*

**Do I Need to Read This Chapter?**

➡ Do I know how social security works?

➡ Am I trying to decide whether to collect social security
at age 62, or later?

➡ Do I understand the payout implications?

➡ Am I aware that I can temporarily "unretire" from social
security after age 62, and thus not be locked into 80
percent benefits for the rest of my life?

➡ Have I checked the accuracy of my social security
records?

➡ Am I a woman who is counting on social security? Am I
alert to all my options?

➡ Am I, or any family members, eligible for nonretirement
social security benefits such as Medicare, disability
income, or survivor's benefits?

S
ome people overlook their social security benefits when calculating their projected retirement income. Other people may count too much on these benefits. Financial planning is a system that must encompass all phases of investments, so know the rules of social security—because for many of us, it has become our most costly investment.

# How Does the System Work?

Both you and your employer contribute a percentage of your wages to social security, up to a designated maximum each year, as well as a percentage to Medicare with no limit. These contributions by both employees and employers are broken down into three separate trust funds:

*OASI—old age and survivors insurance:*   This is a self-contained account separate from other U.S. Treasury revenue which will fully take care of benefit payments to retirees and their survivors. These funds may not be spent for any other purpose.
*DI—disability insurance:*   The same rules apply here as to OASI except that benefit payments go for the disabled.
*HI—health insurance:*   Known also as Medicare, the fund pays all costs of hospital (Part A) but only 20 percent of doctor's fees and other charges (Part B). The balance is funded from general Treasury revenues.

## Get Started

You can qualify for social security retirement benefits in one of two ways. They apply equally to men and women:

1.  As a worker by earning a minimal amount for at least 40 quarters.

2.  As a nonworking spouse by being married to a retired or disabled worker. At retirement (age 65), the spouse will receive half of the benefit of the working spouse.

The working benefit you will receive is based on the 35 highest earning years, so if you began your career at 20 and retired at 65, the lowest 10 years of earnings will not count. This benefit, paid to you monthly, may be increased annually by the cost-of-living adjustment (COLA) based on the Consumer Price Index (CPI).

# What Happens if You Want to Retire Before Age 65?

Many individuals have asked me what I think about retiring before age 65. I have always felt that *it is better to retire too early than too late.* However, you have to understand the social security payout implications.

Consider retirement not as the goal of reaching retirement age, but as entering a retirement zone. At the center of this zone is the standard retirement age, which is 65 (if you were born before 1938) and 65 plus (up to a maximum of 67) if you were born after 1959. At that center point you will be entitled to receive 100 percent of your primary insurance amount (PIA) as it is computed from your record earnings. On the low side of the retirement zone is age 62, which will provide you with early retirement benefits between 70 percent and 80 percent of your PIA. It is 80 percent if your full retirement age is 65 and 70 percent if your full retirement age is 67.

## What Is "Unretirement"?

Take note of this important point. It can make a big difference in your retirement, yet many people aren't aware of it. If you take retirement at age 62, it does not mean that you will be locked into 80 percent of your Social Security benefits for the rest of your life. You are allowed to stop your Social Security benefits and begin them again years later, thus giving you a higher monthly check. This can occur, for example, if during your retirement you take a job that pushes your earnings above the limit which in turn results in a cut in your benefits.

One method to "unretire" is to call the Social Security Administration (SSA) and tell them that you are "unretiring" yourself. In order to do this you will have to furnish the SSA with an estimate of what you will be earning. You will still remain on the benefit roll, but you will not receive a monthly check. At the point you decide to reenter the retirement world, you simply notify SSA of your intentions. When you again begin to receive your monthly check, you may notice a change in the amount you received upon your initial retirement. For each month that your receive Social Security benefits before the age of 65, SSA will reduce your payments by ⅚ of 1 percent but the months or years that you had suspended your benefit check do not count. Your new check, now that you are retired again, would reflect a reduction by only the number of months you actually received your benefit check before "unretiring."

For example, if you retire at 62 and take benefits for one year before you "unretire," when you retire again, your new benefits will be calculated as though you retired only one year early (age 64) which would give you a 6.5 percent (approximate) reduction instead of 20 percent for the rest of your life. Also, any benefits would include an annual cost of living adjustment (COLA) that was made during your suspended time.

## What Happens if You Want to Retire After Age 65?

If you decide to work past age 65, you move to the other side of the zone, known as the *high end*. At this point you will receive a higher monthly social security benefit (more than 100 percent) when you do finally retire. The amount will range from a 3.5 percent increase to an 8 percent increase

### Quick Tips

Another "unretirement" method is available to you. It's much more complicated than the method described previously, but you may wish to consider it. Basically, you can withdraw your application for benefits when you "unretire" which will remove you from the benefit rolls. However, you will have to pay back all the money you received in benefits up to your "unretirement." This must be done in person and requires a new set of applications when you decide to retire again.

depending on your date of birth. At age 70, you will have reached the highest end of the retirement zone, and will not receive any further increase in benefits. However, you do not have to retire to collect your full social security check because you are entitled, at this age, to full benefits, no matter how much you earn.

Also, as far as social security benefits are concerned, it makes no difference what time of the year you retire. Most people in fact retire toward the end of a calendar year simply as a matter of convenience and personal preference. However, the social security law permits you to retire at any time during the year without forfeiting any benefits; payments start any month you choose, provided you meet all the conditions of eligibility.

## Don't Forget

Have you set your retirement date? I recommend applying for social security benefits about three months earlier. This leaves plenty of time to process your claim and handle any questions or problems that may arise.

# How Do You Know You Are Getting Accurate Social Security Benefits?

It would be unthinkable for a person to let years go by without balancing a checkbook; yet that same individual will usually wait until age 65 before making certain that his or her social security account has been accurately credited. By then, if there are errors, it may be too late.

However, there is a way to remedy this situation while you are currently employed. Contact your social security office and ask for the free "Request for Earnings and Benefit Estimate" statement, which will verify your earnings record to date. Merely save your

W-2s (or tax forms, if you are self-employed) and compare the figures. Forty quarters of coverage will entitle you to receive full social security benefits at retirement. By periodically examining your social security account (every 3 years), you will be assured that the income paid from your account will represent all that you have earned.

# What Changes Are Planned for Social Security?

For decades the "normal retirement age" (that's Social Security jargon for the age of eligibility) has been 65. You can, of course, opt to collect Social Security starting at age 62. But your benefits will always be less than if you wait until age 65 to do so, as explained previously.

Beginning in the year 2000, however, this familiar formula will begin to change. Although the changes will affect everyone born after 1938, they won't happen all at once. They'll be phased in.

## Quick Tips

You can access these useful documents on-line through the Social Security Administration's Web site: www.ssa.gov. More than 600 Social Security forms and publications are available there.

Ultimately, by the year 2027, the normal retirement age will be 67 rather than 65. The formula will increase by two months a year for workers reaching age 62 in the years 2000 to 2005, and so on. The best way to determine your own eligibility is to call the national Social Security information number (1-800-772-1213) and ask for the latest edition of the brochure "When You'll Get Your Benefit."

While you're at it, also ask for a "Request for Earnings and Benefit Estimate Statement" (Form SSA-7004). By completing this form and mailing it back, you'll get an idea of how much you can expect in benefits.

**Don't Forget**

A warning: *Don't* rely on Social Security calculations built into retirement planning software. Some programs mistakenly assume that people currently in their 30s and 40s will receive full benefits at age 65. Sorry, baby boomers— that just won't happen. Most of you will have to wait until age 67.

# Are There Special Rules for Women on Social Security?

Because women live longer than men (usually about 7 years), they are more dependent on the government for retirement benefits. Also, women are penalized more than men if they keep working while receiving social security benefits. Thus it is of major importance to understand the role of the female and social security.

The age regulations are the same for everyone. As mentioned previously, you can get full retirement benefits at age 65 if you were born before 1938. The age of full retirement rises slowly until age 67 if you were born in 1960 or later. If you are a widow or a divorced widow, you can begin drawing checks as early as age 62, but at only 80 percent (70 percent when the law of age 67 is fully phased in) of what you would have received at age 65.

**Get Started**

Women who are ready for retirement have the following options:

1. Income based on your own work record
2. Income based on your spouse's work record
3. Income based on your divorced spouse's benefits
4. Income based on divorced widow's benefits
5. Income based on widow's benefits

It is interesting to note that widows and divorced widows who qualify both on their own work records and as widows can enjoy the benefits of both. They can receive reduced benefits at age 62, based on their own work record, and at age 65 they can choose to begin receiving a full widow's benefit. For a detailed discussion on finances and women, see Part V, Chaps. 28 to 30.

# What Are the Family Benefits of a Social Security Plan?

The social security tax that you and your employer pay places you and your family in line for collecting more than just retirement benefits. You may also collect Medicare and disability income. If you become disabled, you get benefits at any age (assuming you have enough quarters of coverage). In order to qualify for disability benefits, you must have earned 20 credits of coverage during the 10-year period ending with the calendar quarter you became disabled. However, if your disability is blindness, or if you become disabled before reaching age 31, more lenient rules apply.

A child (either natural or adopted) may be entitled to benefits upon the death of a parent. To qualify, the child must have been a dependent and (1) be unmarried and either under age 18 or, if a full-time high school student, under age 19, or (2) regardless of age, be disabled before age 22. The child then would receive a monthly benefit equal to 50 percent of the amount the parent would have gotten at age 65.

Thus, you can see that in order to plan for retirement, all areas of income, whether actual or potential, must be considered. And on the topic of planning for retirement, remember that the time to fix the roof is when the sun is shining.

## Don't Forget

Keep in mind that there is a maximum on family benefits. The benefit percentages for family members are the maximum each relative can collect. When more than one family member is collecting benefits based on the insured's earnings record, the actual size of their benefits checks is likely to be smaller. Why? The social security law places a dollar cap on the total monthly benefits paid to a family based on the earnings of one family member.

*It's a Wrap*

✔ Social security is a costly investment—and an involuntary one at that—so it pays to know how it works.

✔ The social security insurance program (SSI) includes old age and survivors insurance, disability insurance, and health insurance known as Medicare.

✔ You can qualify for SSI in either of two ways: by working and earning a minimal amount for at least 40 quarters, or as a nonworking spouse married to a retired or disabled worker.

✔ If you retire at age 62 and begin collecting social security, then decide to "unretire," you can avoid being locked into the 80 percent benefit level for the rest of your life.

✔ By waiting until age 65 or older to collect SSI, you will receive higher benefits.

✔ At age 70 you are entitled to full SSI benefits, no matter how much you earn.

✔ It's advisable to check the accuracy of your social security records every three years.

Women can collect SSI based on their own work record, their spouse's work record, or several other options if divorced or widowed.

✔ People with disabilities are entitled to collect SSI at any age, under certain conditions.

✔ Children may be entitled to SSI benefits upon a parent's death, subject to certain family benefit maximums.

*Remember that the time to fix the roof is when the sun is shining.*

# CHAPTER 26

◆◆◆◆◆◆◆◆◆◆◆◆◆◆◆◆◆◆◆◆◆◆◆◆◆◆◆◆◆◆◆◆◆

# Will It?

◆◆◆◆◆◆◆◆◆◆◆◆◆◆◆◆◆◆◆◆◆◆◆◆◆◆◆◆◆◆◆◆◆

*The only real thing of value we can give our*
*children is what we are, not what we have.*

*Do I Need to Read This Chapter?*

➡ Have I been putting off the making of my will?

➡ Am I aware that 7 out of 10 Americans will die without a will?

➡ Am I confused by all the legalese surrounding wills?

➡ Have I been named an executor of a will? Am I clear on my duties?

➡ Have I taken those duties into account when naming my own executor?

This chapter is essential, because of all the possible threats to your family's assets (inflation, downturn in the market, etc.) only one is definite, and that is your death. I have discussed, in previous chapters, topics ranging from financial planning for young children through financial planning for retirement. Now this chapter completes the life cycle.

By law you have the right to own property, to use it as you wish during your lifetime, and to determine who shall receive it after you die. Everyone makes use of the first two rights, but many give up their third-party right by failing to write a will. Did you know that 7 out of 10 Americans die without a will? This is a shame, because without one you lose control of your estate. This loss affects not only what happens to what you own but also the people who should receive your property after you die. Writing a will is a way of taking care of the people you love in a time period when you will not be there.

# What Is a Will?

## Quick Tips

Be aware that your spoken wishes and/or instructions don't carry any legal weight. In other words, don't expect to lie on your deathbed and issue your will *verbally.* To have a legal basis, you must put your will in writing.

A *will* is simply a set of written instructions as to what should be done with your property after you die. The *testator* (the person whose will it is) and the lawyer will both make important decisions today that will take place in the future and affect other people's lives. A will names those people who will receive your property in the amounts you decide. It also assigns specific shares of your property to each one and describes any particular conditions under which the distribution should occur. Remember, this must be in writing and witnessed.

If you fail to prepare a properly executed will, several unpleasant consequences may follow: your property may not be distributed as you had hoped it would be, your heirs may suffer a greater tax burden and higher administrative costs, and your family and friends may be subject to needless worry and squabbling. Preparing a will is an essential part of meeting your financial responsibilities. An improperly drawn-up or executed will can be rejected by the courts. The decision can render the document invalid, leaving your estate without a will (intestate)—a topic covered at the end of this chapter.

# How Do You Begin to Draw Up a Will?

Let me start by urging that you stay away from prewritten wills or "how to" books encouraging you to draw up your own will. Use an attorney. Your will, and your estate, are too important to fall into the do-it-yourself category.

Before you consider who should receive your possessions at death, you must have some idea of what you own. Start by listing all your assets with their real or estimated value. The total is your gross estate. Because state and federal estate taxes can cut into your gross estate, it's important to know the exact value of your assets. If your taxable estate (equal to your gross estate less debts and expenses) exceeds $625,000, your survivors will face federal estate taxes—which can be steep. No federal tax is due, however, on the first $625,000 of value due (the unified tax credit). This amount will increase in the following stages:

| | | | |
|---|---|---|---|
| 1999 | $650,000 | 2004 | $850,000 |
| 2000–1 | $675,000 | 2005 | $950,000 |
| 2002–3 | $700,000 | 2006 | $1 million |

It should also be noted that no federal estate tax is due on assets left to your spouse or to a charity. The law, however, varies from state to state on the treatment of estate tax.

Because personal and family circumstances change, you should review your will at least once every 5 years to make certain that it still reflects your current wishes and needs.

If only minor changes are needed from time to time, these can be made by means of a written statement (called a *codicil*) attached to the original document. The help of a lawyer is needed for amending a will.

## Get Started

A will doesn't have to be "forever." That is, you can change it. And you should, if one or more of the following events occur:

1. You marry, separate, or divorce

2. Your beneficiary or executor dies

3. You move to another state

4. Federal, state, or estate laws change

5. Family circumstances change

6. Financial matters change

7. You change your mind

As the years go by, we all accumulate assets that are impossible to list in the will. You cannot keep amending the document every time you purchase something of value. Thus you will need a provision in your will, known as a *residuary clause,* that describes how the remainder of your assets not listed in the will should be distributed.

# Who Carries Out the Instructions in a Will?

The instructions you leave in your will are to be carried out by a person you designate as the *executor.* If no one is named in the will as executor (or "personal representative," as in Florida and some other states), the court will appoint an administrator.

As you see, it's necessary to choose wisely when naming an executor, so make certain that the person you have in mind is willing to undertake the job and understands what it entails. I have always recommended that a spouse or adult child, a close friend, or a relative be chosen over a lawyer. The major reason is, of course, cost.

## Get Started

When naming an executor, keep in mind that the job requires attention to detail. It can even be burdensome. So select accordingly. An executor must fulfill this entire list of duties:

1. The executor must obtain the original copy of the will and submit it to probate—that is, request court approval of its validity.

2. The executor may be required to publish a notice of death for a specified period of time.

3. The executor must inventory, appraise, and safeguard all assets of the estate.

4. The executor must open a checking account on behalf of the estate and maintain complete records of all transactions.

5. The executor must apply for all appropriate death benefits, including those available through social security, pension plans, the Veterans Administration, labor unions, and fraternal organizations.

6. The executor must pay all outstanding debts of the deceased.

7. The executor must file and pay local, state, federal income, and estate taxes.

8. The executor must distribute all remaining assets according to the terms of the will.

9. The executor may be required to submit a final accounting to the court.

### Do Spouses Need Separate Wills?

It is just as important for a wife to have a will as for her husband. A married couple often have interlocking or reciprocal wills prepared at the same time. These are separate documents that are carefully interrelated and designed to meet the mutual objectives of both parties. For example, his-and-her wills should specify how the children are to be cared for in the event both parents die at the same time.

And on the topic of marriage, how you own your money is just as important as knowing what you own. Transferring assets from one spouse to another might in some cases be your best financial move. For instance, a joint savings or checking account could be convenient today, but the surviving spouse might need those funds if the account is "frozen" when one of the account holders dies. Also, the law will protect the rights of spouses to receive a minimum share of an estate. In other words, in most states spouses cannot be completely written out of the will unless a prenuptial agreement states so. (See Chap. 29.)

Also, a child who is not mentioned in the will may be entitled to a portion of his or her legal share as if there were no will available. However, this does not preclude a parent from excluding a child if specific mention is made in the will.

# How Can You Be Certain That the Distribution of the Estate Will Be Without Problems?

You can make probate (the settling of the will) easier by following these simple procedures:

1. If you have made previous wills, tell your lawyer to destroy all earlier ones.

2. Choose a successor executor if your original choice cannot serve. Also, list contingent beneficiaries in the event your first choice may die before you or decline the inheritance.

3. In the event you have young children, pick a guardian in case they should become orphans.

4. Devise an order of payment if your estate becomes too small to pay all legacies.

5. Decide in advance whether the executor is to receive the standard compensation or a bequest from you.

6. Keep your will in a safe place (your lawyer's office and a copy at home) but preferably not in a safe deposit box; if the box is sealed upon your death, getting into it may be time-consuming and difficult. If you insist on the safe deposit box, open two of them and put your will in your spouse's safe deposit box and vice versa.

7. When making any bequest, leave a percentage of your estate rather than a fixed dollar amount, because your assets may either grow or shrink over the years. For example, it is better to say that "I leave 10 percent of my estate to XYZ Charity" than to give a specific amount— $50,000, for example. If your estate should be reduced in value for whatever reason by the time you pass on, the $50,000 could be excessive in relation to the needs of those to whom you are leaving the balance of the money. Just remember that you will not be able to bequeath any property you own that is jointly held.

## Quick Tips

**Warning!** As soon as someone named as beneficiary in your will (including your spouse) enters a nursing facility, make certain that the person's name is immediately taken out of your will. Otherwise, upon your death the property left to that beneficiary can be seized in order to pay the nursing home costs.

8. Make certain that your will is properly drafted or it may be interpreted in a manner that you did not wish. For example, if you want to disinherit a child, be sure to specify in your will that you are doing it. If not, the child might later claim to have been overlooked by mistake. Don't use your will to throw your final insult at any individual; find some other means to "get even."

9. In certain situations, it's better to leave property in trusts rather than in outright bequests. A trust is simply an arrangement for transferring your title to your property (your ownership) to

another person or company to hold in trust for you or anyone you designate. Trusts set up under a will are called *testamentary trusts* and become effective upon the death of the person who drew up the will. The trustee holds the property you otherwise would have bequeathed outright, and invests and administers it for the benefit of your stated beneficiaries. Trusts are frequently written into wills to ease the impact of estate taxes (particularly if a great deal of money is involved and to protect the interests of minors until they have matured). There are countless ways of setting up trusts, so great care must be exercised to obtain the best possible legal tax advantages. (See Chap. 27.)

## Is My Will Likely to Be Contested?

Do not concern yourself about having your will contested because more than 99 percent of all will contests are unsuccessful. Remember that very few people are legally able to mount a contest, only those who would have a claim on the estate should the will be overturned. A will can be contested only because of how it was completed, not on the basis of *what it contains.*

The most common claims are based on incompetency of the testator (the one who made the will), fraud or undue influence, or the suspicion that the will was not properly signed. If you want to assure no future challenges, add the "no-contest" clause (*interrorem clause*). It will make any heir a bit hesitant to mount a contest. This clause provides that if an heir should challenge a will, he or she would forfeit all inheritance under the will's conditions.

## Will All My Property Be Passed on Through My Will?

Bear in mind that not all property goes through the courts (probate). Any asset that has a designated beneficiary would pass outside of the will. In fact, a large portion of your estate is likely to pass outside probate court without any effort on your part.

For example, the balance of your employee retirement plan, IRA, or Keogh account, as well as the proceeds of your life insurance policy, will go directly to your designated beneficiaries. Also, any property you own jointly with rights of survivorship will automatically go to the co-owner upon your death.

If you live in one of the community-property states (Arizona, California, Idaho, Louisiana, Nevada, Texas, and Washington), half of all the assets that you acquired during your marriage (except gifts or inheritances) belong to your spouse, with the other half passing under your will.

# What Happens if You Die Without a Will?

If there is no will whatsoever, severe problems can arise. Without a will (*intestate*) you, in essence, have condemned your estate to an unnecessarily prolonged and expensive wait. What happens is that your local court appoints an individual who will administer the distribution of your property in accordance with the laws of your state. However, with a will, it becomes your decision—not that of an outside administrator—as to what will happen to your estate.

States vary in the handling of after-death distributions of property intestate. In some states, the surviving spouse will receive the property if there are no descendants. In other states, parents may be involved in the distribution. In some states, if there are descendants, the spouse will receive one-third of the property, and the children will get equal shares of the balance. If there is only one child, the spouse will receive half. If there are children of a deceased child, they will share in the same manner of their deceased parent. If there is no spouse or child, the mother and father of the deceased will each get one-half of the estate. If there is only one parent, the survivor will get all. If both parents are deceased, brothers or sisters will share equally; and if they are dead, their children will receive the parent's share. If no brothers or sisters exist, the estate will be distributed to more distant relatives in patterns which vary from state to state. If there are no surviving relatives, the estate will go to the state by *escheat.*

Remember that making a will is one of the wisest investments of your life—and after. And on the thought of planning, it is not what happens to you that counts. It is what you do with what happens to you that is important.

It's a Wrap

✔ Financial planning is not complete without making a will, in writing and properly witnessed.

✔ Consult an attorney to prepare a will; don't "do it yourself."

✔ Your survivors must pay federal estate taxes if your taxable estate (equal to your gross estate, minus debts and expenses) exceeds $625,000. However, federal tax is not levied on assets left to a spouse or charity.

✔ The person who carries out the instructions in your will is the executor.

✔ Spouses should have interlocking or reciprocal wills, drawn at the same time.

✔ Allot your estate by percentages, rather than by fixed dollar figures, because your assets may increase or decrease dramatically before you die.

✔ If a beneficiary in your will (including your spouse) enters a nursing home, have your attorney remove his or her name from the will at once. Otherwise, your assets may be seized as payment immediately upon your death.

✔ Assets with a designated beneficiary, such as retirement plans and insurance policies, will pass directly to that person upon your death.

✔ Dying "intestate," or without a will, causes enormous complications that vary by state. Yet 70 percent of Americans will die without a will.

✔ Consider trusts as a way of passing on your property, especially if your estate is large or if children are among your successors. (See the next chapter for a full discussion of trusts.)

***It is not what happens to you that counts. It is what you do with what happens to you that is important.***

# CHAPTER 27

# Trust Me

*This is not the end, nor is it even the beginning of the end. This is just the end of the beginning.*

→ Do I know that trusts can help avoid probate and transfer my assets immediately to my heirs?

→ Am I aware that trusts are an excellent way to protect my wishes in complicated estates involving second marriages and blended families?

→ Do I own real estate in more than one state? If so, do I realize that I should have a living trust to cover it?

→ If I'm interested in trusts, have I also considered their drawbacks?

→ Have I considered other vehicles for estate planning?

→ If I'm trying to shelter assets from nursing-home seizure, am I aware of the role (both good and bad) of irrevocable trusts?

→ Am I clear on the changes in Medicaid rules?

# Are There Alternatives to Having a Will?

A will and a trust are both legal documents that transfer your assets to your designated heirs upon your death. A will names an executor and a trust names a trustee to distribute those assets. But that's where the similarity ends.

## Quick Tips

With all the fancy terms swirling around these highly legal subjects, be careful not to confuse a "living trust" with a living will, which is a document in which you express your wish to give up extraordinary medical treatment if you should become terminally ill. (See Chap. 30.)

One of the major drawbacks of a will is the cost and time to probate it. The process, at a minimum, can take 4 to 8 months, and if you have property in another state, or if any disgruntled relatives contest the will, your heirs might have to wait for years for the settlement. Also, administrative and legal costs during the probate process could run 10 percent or more of the estate. The easiest way to avoid probate and have your assets transferred immediately is to set up a *revocable* or living trust (*intervivos trust*), which transfers your assets to the trust while you are alive.

Since the use of trusts in financial planning is extremely complex, a full discussion of trusts is not the purpose of this chapter. Rather, I have provided a brief description of the many uses of trusts and their impact on financial planning. It is my intent to encourage you to continue to explore with your attorney, and any other person involved in finance, the many aspects of trusts that may meet your specific needs.

# How Do You Create a Revocable Living Trust?

A living trust is created to be effective during the lifetime of the one who creates the trust. It is revocable if the creator states in the trust agreement that he or she has the right during his or her lifetime to terminate (revoke) or change the conditions of the trust at any time and without the permission of anyone else. A living trust may be irrevocable if the creator does not reserve the right to revoke the trust.

When creating the living trust, you must realize that you are required to switch the titles of everything you are placing in the trust from your name to the name of the trust.

## Get Started

In every trust document, there are three principals:

1. The *trustor,* or grantor, who is the person or persons who created the trust and transferred the assets into it.

2. The *trustee,* who is the person or persons charged with the task of managing the assets in the trust. He or she makes all the financial and business decisions concerning the trust assets; trustees have the right to buy, sell, trade, exchange, mortgage, and encumber. In fact, trustees can do virtually anything with trust assets except use them for their own benefit.

3. The *beneficiary,* whose only role is to enjoy the assets.

When you create your trust, you can lawfully become (in most states) all three parties: the trustor, the trustee, and the beneficiary. Under this arrangement, you can act as your own trustee, giving yourself control over your estate while you are alive. You then can appoint a successor trustee if you should become incapacitated or should die. Because the trust is revocable, it can be changed at any time you wish.

# What Are the Major Advantages of the Revocable Living Trust?

In addition to avoiding the costs of probate, a living trust affords many advantages to both the trustor and his or her heirs.

1. A revocable trust can be changed or terminated at any time before the trustor dies.

2. Because the trustor retains the right to get back all property transferred to a revocable trust, those assets are not considered gifts for estate, gift, or income tax purposes. Any income that comes from the assets in the trust will remain taxable to the trustor during his or her lifetime.

3. Unlike a will, a living trust can (in many states) attempt to shield the estate from creditors. With a will, the executor is required to notify the creditors of the death of the maker of the will—by mail and newspaper advertisement—so that they can submit any claims against the estate. No such publicity would take place in a living trust, since no public notification would be needed.

**Quick Tips**

Warning! Many people mistakenly believe that assets transferred to a living trust cannot be accessed by creditors. Generally, no such protection is afforded! Most states have laws that allow creditors to get back what is owed to them from the assets of such trusts.

4. The trust avoids the courts and the general public. For example, when an estate goes through probate, the court freezes its assets for several months and makes notice that interested parties can come forward if they wish to contest the will. However, the assets of the trust are not frozen, and in many cases the trust is dissolved and assets distributed to the beneficiaries long before the disgruntled heir has a chance to act. He or she would then have to sue each beneficiary separately.

5. A living trust provides for the designation of future heirs. For example, if you decide to leave all your worth to your son Tom

and years after your death your son should get divorced (or die), Tom's wife will wind up with most, if not all, of your assets. If she should remarry and begin a new family, your son's children (your grandchildren) could wind up receiving little or none of the inheritance that you left their father, Tom—funds you had assumed would be later used for their benefit. A living trust could keep your assets intact so that they would not be distributed to your son upon your death. This method can be used to ensure your grandchildren the rightful access to your funds regardless of what happens to your son or to his marriage.

The procedure is simple. You name Tom your successor trustee and set up the trust so that he will be able to draw income and a small portion of the principal while he lives. At his death or divorce, or at a certain period of time you designate (when the children reach age 21, 30, 40, or whatever you determine), the trust would be terminated and the assets given to Tom's children (your grandchildren). The wife would have no control in this situation.

Here is another example. Suppose this is your second marriage, and a good one, but you want to leave your assets to your children from your previous marriage. You may think that your wishes would be followed in a will, but that may not be the case. In many states, the law says that you cannot disinherit a spouse. Thus, even though you decided to leave all your property to your children, there could develop a successful challenge in the courts resulting in the possible loss of a portion of your estate against your wishes. With a living trust (in some states), the property in the trust that passes to the children at your death cannot be challenged by a surviving spouse.

6. Although not generally known, anyone owning real estate in more than one state should have a living trust. This is so because the trust will avoid "ancillary probate," a costly, time-consuming judicial process that develops when death occurs to the owner of real estate property in a state other than the one that the deceased owner lived in.

---

**Don't Forget**

Another good vehicle for complicated second-marriage and blended family situations is a Q-TIP trust. (No, it has nothing to do with the little cotton sticks you keep in your medicine cabinet.) Under this trust, your spouse, upon your death, will receive income from your estate for as long as he or she lives. Upon the spouse's demise, the principal of the estate passes to the beneficiary you choose, *not* to the beneficiary of your spouse. Thus you can protect your assets in a second marriage for your children, but still leave income to your beloved new spouse.

---

7. Last, but not least, a living trust can be a source of comfort if you should become incapacitated. If a successor trustee is appointed, a debilitating illness will not cause financial hardship, since your trustee has the authority to pay your bills and handle your investments in a prudent manner. It thus avoids the possibility of having guardianship proceedings, which are costly and difficult to administer. Another simple method to accomplish the same objective is to designate a durable "power of attorney" to someone to make financial and living decisions on your behalf in the event you should become incapacitated.

# What Are the Disadvantages of the Living Trust?

Although you do not have to go through the costly process of probate, the living trust is not without disadvantages.

1. By creating it, you have to place everything you own into the trust. If you hold any assets outside the trust, you may have to go through probate anyway. You can remedy this drawback by placing any "outside assets" into joint ownership with right of survivorship. Bear in mind that jointly held property can duplicate much the same benefits as a living trust, since the property will

pass outside the courts (probate) and will go directly to the surviving joint owner.

2. It will almost always cost more to establish a living trust than a will. Legal fees can be higher and assets must actually be transferred to the trust, which can add additional costs. Also, if you appoint another person as trustee, you will have to pay a fee in accordance with state law (unless the trustee waives the fee).

3. The right to choose your own fiscal year to defer taxes will be lost.

4. The funds in the trust must be used up before the trustor can get any social service benefits (Medicaid, for example).

5. No tax advantage regarding estate taxes is gained by the revocable trust. Nor is there any income tax savings, since all income from the trust passes through to the individual's personal income tax return.

6. You may need to have a simple will regardless of the living trust because you cannot use a trust to name a guardian for your minor children.

7. You will need a will with a "pour-over" clause stating that any property that you forgot to put into your living trust should go there after your death. Those assets will then be subject to probate, but it will not be a lengthy or costly process if your estate is small and if the majority of your assets lie within the confines of the living trust. This extra process may take only a few days to complete. Yet it is crucial to have such a pour-over clause, since there most certainly could be assets that you overlooked while making the living trust.

8. Certain types of assets, such as jewelry and automobiles, are difficult to place in a trust because insurance companies are often reluctant to write a policy for a trust. Also, some assets need not be placed in a trust because they already pass (upon death) to the named beneficiary outside of the probate court. These assets could include IRAs, retirement benefits, life insurance proceeds, and annuities.

**Quick Tips**

Even if you try to cover every eventuality, there are certain circumstances under which a living trust could be rendered inoperative and probate would be required. This situation might arise when:

- Assets are currently subject to litigation (in the event of a lawsuit)
- A tax audit is in progress

# What Other Vehicles Are Available for Estate Planning?

If you were to die tomorrow, the odds are that your heirs would be able to settle your estate without paying an inheritance tax because of changes in federal and state tax codes in the past two decades. The federal exemption was only $60,000 in 1976 but is $625,000 today and will rise to $1,000,000 over a phased-in nine-year period. The federal tax is based on your taxable estate and the taxable portion of any gifts you made during your life. Adding taxable gifts to an estate is a way for the government to discourage people from dodging the federal estate tax by giving away all their property before they die.

**Don't Forget**

What makes a cash gift taxable or not? Here are the magic numbers. You can give up to $10,000 each year to as many people as you wish tax-free, and if your spouse joins in making the gift, $20,000 per recipient tax-free is permitted. Any amount over this annual exclusion is taxable.

If you give more than $10,000 to a couple, you can avoid any IRS hassle if you make out two separate checks. For example, a $20,000 gift to your son and his wife should be written in two checks of $10,000 each, one to your son and one to his wife. If you wish to give a sizable amount at one time, you can do so through self-cancellation installment notes (SCIN), which will cancel out over a period of years. For example, you loan $50,000 to your son, accepting five annual notes of $10,000 each. As agreed, one note is to be paid back to you each year. But at the anniversary of each note, you forgive its payment, thus meeting the requirement of the $10,000 gift limit. However, if you should die during the period that the notes are still outstanding, the value of the notes will remain in your estate and will be considered for estate tax purposes.

## Any Special Guidance for Large Estates?

For those of you who have sizable estates, there is a method of leaving large funds without heavy federal taxation. By bequeathing the estate to your spouse, no tax is incurred. When the surviving spouse dies, tax is then applied to the beneficiaries of the estate over $625,000. However, by creating a bypass trust, you arrange to have up to $1,500,000 passed onto your children tax-free. Here's how it works. In your will you place up to $625,000 in a bypass trust and leave the rest to your spouse. In this way, the lifetime exemption ($625,000) and the unlimited marital deduction that is allowed shield the estate from federal estate taxes. The bypass trust pays income to your spouse and names the children as beneficiaries when the spouse dies. No control can be exercised by the spouse over the bypass trust. When the spouse does pass on, the amount of the trust is not part of his or her estate and so can be passed along (coupled with the spouse's estate up to $625,000) taxfree. Since no one can predict who will die first, both spouses should provide for this trust.

# How Does an Irrevocable Trust Work?

The word *irrevocable* has been bantered around as a way of sheltering assets from nursing-home seizure. All too often I encounter situations in which older people (especially widows) are so concerned about the high cost of nursing facilities that they contemplate placing their assets, through an irrevocable trust, into the hands of their children. Robert Browning wrote "Grow old along with me, the best is yet to be." That statement may not be true for seniors, since the best years may have already passed.

No matter what any poet, orator, or sage may say, old age is still old age. Someone once said that you know you are growing older when everything hurts and what doesn't hurt doesn't work. Older people are of interest to doctors and hospitals, real estate brokers, and travel agents, not always as people, but as sources of income. As your ability to earn money decreases, so too does your stature as a person. Therefore, keep that money for yourself, having the knowledge that you are financially independent.

## Quick Tips

All too often, bitter lessons await parents who deposit their funds into the hands of their children through an irrevocable trust. They quickly learn that the parent-child relationship can reverse itself. The resulting situations can be heart-breaking. In my opinion—based on careful observation—a parent should never have to ask in the future for any money given in the past.

The looming prospect of nursing homes and Medicaid payments only serves to complicate this already thorny matter. You probably know that certain laws have governed Medicaid since 1993. "Medicaid planning," as some call it, is a set of loopholes that allow older people with means to avoid the cost of nursing homes. Through various methods, these people give most of their assets to their heirs, thus making themselves eligible for government assistance. Rulings state that these gifts (set up as irrevocable trusts) must be given away at least 36 months (in some cases up to 60 months if assets are transferred to a trust rather than to a person) before Medicaid takes effect. This time period is known as the "look-back period" and if not properly executed, could yield severe penalties.

## Do Irrevocable Trusts Serve a Purpose for Large Estates?

Aside from the Medicaid situation, the irrevocable trust does serve a purpose in financial planning for a large estate. This type of trust cannot be changed once it is written; thus the name *irrevocable*. As you are aware, estates over $625,000 are levied with estate taxes when the assets of the deceased are distributed to the heirs. These taxes must be paid within 9 months after death. However, the taxes can be reduced by the irrevocable trust if the maker is willing to give away certain assets before he or she dies.

If you leave more than $625,000, almost everything (with few exceptions) above that figure will be subject to federal estate tax. This is the point at which the irrevocable living trust comes into play. Assume, for example, that you have a $300,000 term life insurance policy. This insurance policy means nothing to you now, but at your death it will add $300,000 to your estate. If your present estate is worth $500,000, your heirs will receive less money from your estate simply because the insurance policy proceeds will be counted as part of your assets, putting the total over the $625,000 exemption. To avoid the estate tax on the additional $175,000 ($800,000 − $625,000) you can set up an irrevocable trust that contains only the insurance policy. A trustee is named (other than yourself or your spouse so the asset is not in either of your estates) and that trustee becomes the owner (also perhaps the beneficiary) of the policy. The trustee pays the insurance premium that you gift into the trust. As long as the policy has been placed into the trust at least 3 years before your death, none of the $175,000 benefits will be counted as part of the $625,000 exemption.

It is obvious that any trust should be set up by an estate attorney sensitive to your needs. Interview several lawyers and tell each one as much as you can about your estate. You may lack the legal knowledge, but certainly you can evaluate how comfortable you feel discussing family and financial matters with each attorney. And on the topic of the law, we have about 35 million laws and regulations to enforce the few lines of guidance contained in the Ten Commandments.

✔ Trusts can help you transfer your assets immediately to your heirs, by avoiding probate.

✔ Trusts are especially worth investigating if you want to make sure your estate goes to *your* direct heirs, not those of in-laws or blended families.

✔ Revocable or living trusts are advisable for people who own real estate in more than one state.

✔ Trusts may be a good means of sheltering assets from nursing-home seizure, but consult an attorney specializing in family law or elder law before taking this step.

✔ Irrevocable trusts are most suited to financial planning for a large estate.

*We have about 35 million laws and regulations to enforce the few lines of guidance contained in the Ten Commandments.*

# PART V

Financial
Planning
for Women

# CHAPTER 28

# For Women Only: An Introduction

*With money in your pocket, you are wise and you are beautiful and you sing well, too.*

**Do I Need to Read This Chapter?**

➡ Am I a woman who understands the need to manage my own finances?

➡ Married or single, do I want to make sure I have all my financial bases covered?

# How Does Financial Planning Differ for Women?

Here are statistics that may surprise you. Approximately one half of all marriages will end in divorce. Nearly 80 percent of married women (that's 8 out of 10) will become widows and remain widows for about 15 years. If the husband is under 40 years of age, he is three times more likely to be disabled than to die and after age 55, the chances are he can be disabled for a year or more.

Ready for more grim facts? Today, women constitute 75 percent of the elderly with incomes below poverty levels—yet 80 percent of widows in poverty were not poor before their husbands died. Some of the reasons are not hard to pinpoint. For one thing, with all their progress in the workplace, women still generally earn 30 percent less than men. Less income means less available for saving. Also, because women tend to change jobs more frequently—they miss out on pension benefits, since many employers require at least five years of service before benefits are vested.

At the same time, because of their role as primary caretaker of children and elderly parents, women are out of the workforce an average of 11½ years over a lifetime compared with 16 months for men. This not only results in lower income, but limits chances for promotions that boost salary. And salary is the basis for determining the level of employer and Social Security retirement benefits.

I don't mean to depress you, but I want you to know the facts. Only 28 percent of divorcing women are now entitled to financial support from their ex-spouses (that figure includes child support). Of these women, a third of them never see the money that is due them. Because of this, the average woman's standard of living drops 45 percent in the first year after a divorce, while a man's rises 15 percent. About 50 percent of men over the age of 65 receive a pension. The comparable figure for women is only 22 percent.

The implication is simple and stark: the chances are excellent that at some time in a woman's life, she will be alone and forced to manage her own finances. If you're presently single, you already understand this. If you're married, please read on.

## Don't Forget

Please don't misunderstand the following recommendation. I strongly believe it is essential for a married woman to consider herself financially separate from her husband—all the more so if he supplies most of the family's income and handles most of the financial decisions. You must make a financial plan of your own to provide for the likelihood that eventually you'll be managing your money independently.

## Where to Begin?

To establish your own financial identity, the absolute minimum is to open personal checking and savings accounts and to obtain one or more credit cards in your name only. Why is this necessary? Because a woman whose assets are entirely tied up in joint accounts with her husband, and whose credit cards are all in her husband's name, may face severe financial problems in the future. If you become divorced or widowed, your credit history will be based entirely on your husband's finances, not your own. You may learn, to your dismay, that you lack the financial standing to qualify for your own line of credit. When financial need strikes, this can be a devastating handicap.

Furthermore, any money held in a joint account with your husband may be frozen by the bank or financial institution upon his death, leaving you with no access to funds until after your husband's estate is settled. And in the event of divorce, you may find that all jointly held funds are divided equally, even though you may have contributed more to some accounts.

Next, you should begin to develop an independent retirement plan, one not based on assumptions about your husband's contributions. This may be an uphill struggle. The U.S. retirement system depends largely on social security and private pension plans, both of which are directly tied to the number of years an individual has spent in the workforce. However, the career patterns of women differ greatly from those of men, largely because of the time most women devote to raising their children but also because of other factors, such as the willingness of most women to relocate—and sacrifice their own seniority as employees—when their husbands' careers demand it. As a result of these "liabilities," working women often fail to remain on the job long enough to qualify for their own pension plan.

The point, then, is that married women, whether working outside the home or not, must plan for retirement independently of their husbands. You should develop your own savings and investment plan with a definite goal to be attained by retirement age. You should open your own individual retirement account, invested in financial instruments appropriate for your age and income. And you should become as fully informed about your family's finances as your husband.

# How Do You Choose a Financial Planner?

Once you have developed an overall plan, you may want to "go it on your own." Or you may use a financial professional, one who shares your sense of values and objectives. Financial planners are paid for their work in one of three ways: fee only, commission only, or fee plus commission. When considering an individual as your financial professional, make certain to inquire about his or her education, degrees, and certificates. However, there is an alphabet soup list of experts—each with a special service and a fee schedule that are listed on page 318. In certain cases, an individual may carry more than one title.

## Get Started

Today, more than half of all American women work outside the home, at least part-time. They're savvier about finances than their grandmother and even their mothers were. I applaud this transformation in women's outlooks, and I encourage even more self-education through the following steps:

1. Find a qualified, licensed professional advisor who can help you draw up a financial plan. (See the next section for tips on choosing a financial planner.) With your advisor's assistance, develop a written statement of your personal investment policy, outlining your goals and risk tolerance. Why written? In times of high market volatility, it's tempting to make major changes based on an emotional response to peaks or troughs. Referring back to your own statement of purpose will help you stay the course.

2. Develop a long-term, systematic investment philosophy and a well-allocated portfolio. (*Portfolio* or *asset allocation* refers to the mix of investment classes you utilize, including stocks, bonds, CDs, cash, etc.) With guidance from your chosen professional, set realistic expectations for performance and commit to an *investment discipline* that meets your comfort level. By this I mean monthly investments that you can live with.

3. Make regular, periodic investments in order to take advantage of *dollar cost averaging.* (See page 99.) Remember the adage: buy low, sell high. No one (not even a professional) can accurately and consistently predict market behavior. Since the market naturally rises and falls over time, investing at predetermined points throughout the year means that sometimes you will be buying when investment prices are lower, sometimes higher. Over the lifetime of your investment plan, you will average out these cycles for maximum efficiency of your investment dollar.

*AEP—Accredited Estate Planner:*   Title awarded by the National Association of Estate Planners to professionals who pass an exam and meet educational requirements.

*EA—Enrolled Agent:*   The Internal Revenue Service offers this designation to income tax specialists who have passed an exam and have five years of audit experience with the IRS.

*CFA—Chartered Financial Analyst:*   Awarded by the Association for Investment Management and Research to securities analysts, money managers, and investment advisers who complete a course and pass an exam.

*CFP—Certified Financial Planner:*   Licensed and certified by the Certified Financial Planner Board after meeting educational, examination, and experience requirements.

*CFS—Certified Fund Specialist:*   Awarded by the Institute of Certified Fund Specialists for financial professionals who meet educational and experience requirements and pass an exam.

*ChFC—Chartered Financial Consultant:*   Awarded by the American College in Bryn Mawr, Pennsylvania, to those who have completed a 10-course financial planning curriculum, an exam, and have three years of business experience.

*CLU—Chartered Life Underwriter:*   Also awarded by the American College to insurance and financial services professionals.

*CMFC—Chartered Mutual Fund Consultant:*   Awarded by the National Endowment for Financial Education to professionals in the mutual fund market, such as bank employees and financial planners, who have completed a course sponsored by NEFE and the Investment Company Institute and an exam.

*CPA—Certified Public Accountant:*   Licensed by the state after passing a uniform national examination administered by the American Institute of Certified Public Accountants and completing educational courses.

*CRP—Certified Retirement Planner:*   Requires examination and continuing education, offered by the American Institute of Retirement Planners.

*PFS—Personal Financial Specialist:* Awarded to CPAs by the AICPA after passing an exam and satisfying work experience requirements.

*RIA—Registered Investment Adviser:* Indicates registration with the Securities and Exchange Commission, no examination required. (Stock brokers are exempt from registering as RIAs since they're regulated by the National Association of Securities Dealers. They must pass an NASD exam).

*RFC—Registered Financial Consultant:* Awarded by the International Association of Registered Financial Consultants to professionals meeting educational and experience requirements and who have earned a securities or insurance license or a certification such as CPA, DFA, DFP, CLU.

When you have decided as to the type of financial professional, visit a few. Ask them for information on how other clients' investments have performed under their guidance. And carefully try to assess how well the planners have been able to achieve for their clients the objectives you are seeking. But most important is to ask yourself if you are comfortable with this person handling your financial affairs.

## Quick Tips

As you'll quickly discover, financial planners can charge high fees. However, as with most purchases, you get what you pay for. Think about how you select a physician, a school for your children, a home for your family. With your future quality of life hanging in the balance, forego the "bargain" and choose the best qualified person you can—one whose personal style is comfortable for you. What happens with money in your life is as intimate as sex—and as central to your well-being. So choose an advisor you trust and like.

# Should Women Have Their Own Wills?

Every woman should have her own will and keep it up to date. It could even be argued that a wife's will is more essential than her husband's since, in most cases, she will outlive him and thus be responsible for not one but two estates—his and hers. This is so even when a wife has few assets of her own. Consider this scenario: a husband dies, leaving all his property to his wife. Shortly afterward, she dies intestate, that is, without a will. All the family's assets would be disposed of according to the laws of intestacy applicable in her state. The results may or may not be in accordance with her wishes.

## What Are the Financial Ramifications of Remarriage?

Second marriages usually bring great happiness. Often, they also bring financial complications, especially for women. As always, it pays to be prepared. Consider these possibilities to protect yourself financially:

1.  A prenuptial agreement (see Chap. 29) can help you by allowing you to keep any assets out of the hands of your new spouse if something should happen to the new marriage (death, divorce, etc.). Newly married couples may feel that this written agreement shows a lack of trust, but in truth it actually helps keep family harmony. I have seen adult children's concerns (the new husband may get all their mother's money) put aside by the use of the prenuptial agreement. To play it safe, hire different lawyers to represent each party in drafting this agreement.

2.  Consider the consequences of remarrying and its effect on social security benefits. If you are a widow under age 60 and are collecting social security benefits based upon your late husband's social security account, remarriage will stop your benefits. However, if you wait until age 60 or later, you will then be able to draw on your new mate's social security account or your late spouse's account, whichever is greater.

3.  If you are over age 55, you are entitled to a one-time capital-gains exclusion (up to $125,000) on the sale of your home (see Chap. 18). Married couples can take this advantage only once even if each owns a home. Therefore, before remarrying, you should consider selling your home and your intended's home so that you will get two exclusions (a total of $250,000) instead of one.

# How Can Assets Be Owned?

In order to plan financially, you must understand the concept of ownership. Joint ownership is the most common method by which married couples take title to their house and other assets. It may also be used by others who wish to share the control of some property. Let's examine the three basic types of joint ownership, each of which has certain special legal and financial characteristics you should know about.

1. *Joint tenancy:* With this type of ownership, both owners have a complete and undivided interest in the property. Neither owner can sell or transfer his or her interest in the property without the consent of the other owner. When one owner dies, the property immediately passes to the surviving owner without having to go to probate (the acceptance of the will of the deceased by an appropriate court). For joint tenancy to be in effect, the names of both owners must appear on the deed or other ownership document.

Both married couples and single people use joint tenancy as a method of guaranteeing ease of transfer of property upon the death of one of the owners.

2. *Tenancy in common:* With this type of ownership, each owner has title to half the property. If one owner dies, his or her share does not automatically pass to the survivor. Instead, it is disposed of in accordance with the will of the deceased. This method is used by friends or relatives who wish to form a joint ownership and share in its benefits while they are alive but want to retain the right to decide individually what happens to their share of the property when they die.

**Quick Tips**

Warning! Joint tenancy cannot substitute for a will. That's because joint tenancy alone may not produce the result you desire. Here's an example: suppose you and your sister buy a summer home together, taking title as joint tenants. You die first, and your sister dies shortly thereafter. Upon your death, your share in the summer home reverts immediately to your sister. Therefore, when she dies, the home goes entirely to her heirs; your own heirs will receive no share in it. This may or may not be what you intended.

3. *Community property:*  In certain states, husband and wife share equally in any property either one accumulates while they are living together. This is so regardless of whose name appears on the deed or ownership papers. Such jointly owned property is called *community property,* and the states where this is a matter of law are called *community-property states* (Arizona, California, Idaho, Louisiana, Nevada, New Mexico, Texas, Washington, and Wisconsin).

There are exceptions under the law to community property: (1) property obtained by either spouse prior to the marriage; (2) property acquired after marriage by gift or inheritance; and (3) property acquired in non-community-property states. Note that the fact that you have moved from a community-property state to a non-community-property state does not automatically exempt you and your spouse from the community-property law. You are still subject to the law for property you obtained while married and a resident of the community property state.

# What of the Emotional Stress That Women Face?

In researching this chapter, I came across some wonderful statements by Judith Stern Peck regarding financial planning for women. Her thoughts and practices provide rich food for thought:

> As I embarked on my own development and moved toward empowerment, I identified a process of seven stages that I call "the seven A's": *awakening, anger, autonomy, anxiety, analysis, acquisition* of knowledge, and *application.*
>
> My *awakening* occurred as I was contemplating my divorce. I suddenly became aware that I would be called upon to negotiate a "business deal," for which I was ill-equipped. I had spent most of my adult years raising my family and pursuing a career in the mental health field. I was ill-informed about money matters.

As the extent of my dependency dawned on me, I could feel the *anger* take over. I was angry at all men in my life—my then-husband, my father, and all those who had perpetuated this myth that men attended to money matters and that they would take care of me. I was angry that such an aura of mystery had been created for me around money, and that there was such a gap in my financial education. I called upon female friends/lawyers to help me. I asked which questions to ask. I attempted my own "speed" course in finance. My reaction to the anger was my determination never to depend on the men in my life so completely for money matters.

My anger propelled me to the next stage—*autonomy*. I knew that I had to gain a sense of independence and control over my life. I realized that I was fighting my own inner contradictions; that is, the desire to have personal power was fighting the desire to be taken care of. I faced this contradiction many times—with lawyers, accountants, and financial advisers.

The fourth stage, *anxiety,* is one that surfaces after the fight for autonomy is won but the feeling of autonomy has not been integrated. This occurs over and over again with women who are experiencing divorce or some other crisis in their lives. Anxiety usually surfaces from the contradictions that revolve around the need to take care of oneself, the desire to be taken care of, and the discomfort due to the lack of skills needed to take care of money matters.

The last two stages of the empowering process are the *acquisition* of knowledge and expertise, and the *application* thereof. These two stages can be experienced through a variety of avenues. The bookstores are filled with self-help books relating to money matters while the news-stands offer a variety of magazines on the subject. Also, there are various courses that are offered in seminar format to enhance knowledge around financial issues. The learning curve becomes increasingly challenged daily, as long as the anxiety is never too overwhelming.

The process of the seven A's is a painful but rewarding one. It requires differentiating the emotional contradictions that we have learned through our family and societal contexts from the practical, rational information and understanding of issues that we can acquire. This process, which enhanced my development and self-definition, has motivated me to help others empower themselves.

# Get Started

1.  *Start early*, and if you didn't start early, start now to invest in your future. The earlier you start, the more tax deferral and compounding of interest can work for you and the greater the chance that your variable investments can grow.

2.  *Save regularly.* The old adage "pay yourself first" applies here. As a rule of thumb, you'll need to save at least 10 percent of your income each year—above what you expect to receive from Social Security and your employer's basic retirement plan—to have enough funds for retirement.

3.  *Don't touch your retirement savings.* Whatever the temptation, don't cash in your retirement accumulations if you change jobs. Even if you put the money back later, it will be very hard—if not impossible—to match what you could have accumulated had you left your funds intact.

4.  *Invest—don't just save—*for retirement. "Safe" savings products, such as money market accounts, may preserve your principal and provide some interest, but their returns have historically barely kept up with inflation. To amass sufficient funds for retirement, you'll need to invest at least some of your accumulations in equities. Although past performance does not guarantee future results, over time equities have historically produced rates of return above inflation and have outperformed interest-earning securities, such as bonds.

5.  *Educate yourself* in financial matters. For general financial information, there's a whole host of newspapers, magazines, newsletters, and books that can help you in your planning. And talk to relatives and friends about their financial plans and experiences.

6.  *Be a role model* for your children and grandchildren. Show them you are an equal partner in managing your family's finances. Take them to your bank and open a savings account for them. Encourage schools to teach economic fundamentals to students of all ages.

# How Can I Ensure a Secure Future?

We all want assurance that our future will be financially secure. Because women live longer and usually earn less than men, their concerns are even more urgent. But regardless of your current situation or age, it's never too early—or too late—to plan for the future. I hope, in summary, that the guidelines listed on page 324 help you on your way.

If you follow your own way and invest for the future, no matter how hard it is for you today, you will gain a sense of security knowing that, maybe for the first time, you have done something for yourself. And on the topic of yourself, since you have to do the things you have to do, be wise enough to do some of the things you want to do.

It's a Wrap

✔ Despite great financial gains made by women in recent decades, they still tend to earn less and suffer greater poverty in old age than men do.

✔ All women, whether they live alone or in a relationship, should plan and be prepared to manage their own finances.

✔ Every woman should have her own will and keep it up to date.

✔ Women who are remarrying should consider a prenuptial agreement (this subject is detailed in the next chapter).

✔ There are three different types of joint ownership; it pays to examine them all before taking title jointly to any home or asset.

***Since you have to do the things you have to do, be wise enough to do some of the things you want to do.***

CHAPTER 29

# Prenuptials and the Marriage Vow

*Courtship is the feast. Marriage is doing the dishes.*

Do I Need to Read This Chapter?

➡ Am I about to marry, especially not for the first time?

➡ Do I have preexisting, separate property to protect? Does my spouse-to-be?

➡ Does the subject of premarital agreements somehow make me uneasy?

➡ Have I thought about all the factors such an agreement should address?

Prenuptial agreements, like estate planning, are no longer exclusively for the rich and famous. The likelihood is great that people marrying today will have preexisting separate property to protect. There is no better method to protect a party's rights, assets, and those financially dependent on each of the parties than by a legally binding contract called a prenuptial agreement. The terms "prenuptial," "premarital," and "antenuptial" are virtually synonymous.

## What Is a Prenuptial Agreement?

In addition to being a contract, a prenuptial agreement is a plan to achieve protection of assets. Those assets acquired prior to the marriage are known as "nonmarital property" and assets acquired during the marriage are known as "marital property." The use and ultimate distribution of assets involves arms-length negotiations between the soon-to-be spouses. While this notion may damper the fires of love ("Love means never having to say 'sign here' "), it is imperative that the parties act openly, in good faith, and take the time to develop a plan in order to satisfy each other's wishes.

The nature of a prenuptial agreement and its inherent legal requirements and characteristics provides each party the freedom to protect his or her nonmarital property from each other. Provisions affecting marital property and other issues arising from the marriage are subject only to notions of fairness and equitable constraints. It cannot be overemphasized that any financial plan should take advantage of the protection available from prenuptial agreements.

**Don't Forget**

A wise person once quipped that a premarital agreement is like putting an asterisk next to the vow "I Do." That is such a true statement—and such a smart practice.

# What Elements Make Up a Prenuptial Agreement?

Like any other legal contract, a prenuptial agreement must satisfy basic legal requirements. The agreement must be in writing, executed by the parties whose signatures are witnessed or notarized and there must be consideration, which is the marriage itself. Indeed, while prenuptial agreements are entered into prior to marriage, the terms and conditions are effective *only* upon marriage. The marriage may be a civil or religious ceremony, so long as it is a valid, recognized ritual effecting a legal union.

All fifty states recognize prenuptial agreements, although the laws of each state are not uniform. There is a Uniform Prenuptial Agreement Act (UPAA), but not every state has adopted its provisions and some of those states that did have made modifications.

In addition to being in writing, executed, and witnessed, a prenuptial agreement must possess characteristics common to all contracts and essentially required in some form by every state law. These four characteristics, which I have identified in the Get Started section, generally test the validity of the agreement when challenged by one party in court. It is important to appreciate, however, that in determining the validity of a prenuptial agreement for whichever reason, generally only the facts and circumstances existing *at the time the agreement was made* are considered by the court.

# What Are the Categories to Be Addressed in a Prenuptial Agreement?

The parties should include any topic important to each of them in their prenuptial agreement. There are available pre-existing forms which contain standard language of a prenuptial agreement but

## Get Started

1. Each party must enter into the prenuptial agreement freely and voluntarily. Courts are sensitive to the personal relationship of the parties, with its attendant frailties and emotional influence. Consequently, courts will not enforce agreements where the circumstances indicate that one party took unfair advantage of the other.

2. The terms of the prenuptial agreement must be fair, considering all facts and circumstances existing at the time the agreement was made. In determining fairness, courts take into account each party's age, health, employment, standard of living, income, assets, family, and so forth.

3. Each party must possess sufficient knowledge of the other party's assets, income, and general financial condition. Full disclosure of financial details is a basic element, and each party should never refrain from requesting that the other party provide tax returns, financial statements, brokerage and mutual fund statements, loan documents, bank statements, employment contracts, compensation arrangements, pension and retirement information, insurance policies, will, trust documents, and prior divorce and separation agreements.

4. Each party must fully understand the legal and practical consequences of the agreement. This rule is related to the rule which prohibits one party from taking unfair advantage of the other. Thus, each party must be afforded the opportunity to consult with *independent* counsel, whether exercised or not. Failure to provide such opportunity could result in a court holding the prenuptial agreement invalid due to unfair advantage.

these standard forms are run-of-the-mill and probably will not deal with specific topics or situations unique to each party.

The prenuptial agreement should contain a blueprint of which assets and income of each spouse are to be used during the marriage and for what purposes. The prenuptial agreement can act like

## Quick Tips

Generally, I am not in favor of "do-it-yourself" books, computer programs, and the like where legal matters are concerned. They are just too important to leave to our own nonprofessional devices, no matter how well-meaning we may be. Still, preexisting forms can provide a starting point. You can modify them in terms of organization and language. Or you can start from scratch.

a business plan in this regard. The agreement can also state how joint assets are to be distributed after the marriage, whether it ends by reason of death of one spouse or divorce. A checklist of important provisions follows.

## 1. Separate Property and Separate Income

Simply identifying each party's separate property is not sufficient. Since one of the major purposes of a prenuptial agreement is to preserve the non-marital assets of each spouse for the children of the first marriage or other family members of each spouse, the prenuptial agreement should be specific in describing each spouse's desires in this regard. Therefore, the prenuptial agreement should state under what circumstances or to what extent, if any, one party has any rights or interest in the nonmarital property of the other.

The prenuptial agreement should state clearly when and how much, if at all, of nonmarital property and/or income from this property is to be used in the marriage and for what purpose. Very often, nonmarital property or income of one spouse identified as nonmarital income is used to satisfy debts incurred after the marriage by one spouse. Generally, the debts incurred by one spouse (the "debtor spouse") can be collected from the other spouse unless the vendor or creditor is notified that one spouse is not responsible for debts of the other. This is true even though the spouse paying the debts does not use or have enjoyment from the items purchased by the debtor spouse.

For example, if one spouse charges purchases on a joint credit card and cannot pay the balances, the nondebtor spouse can be forced, legally, to pay for those purchases using his or her separate property. Worse yet, is where one spouse makes a large purchase on credit, like a boat, and puts it in joint name, but the other spouse is not happy with the purchase. If payments are not made and the value of the boat becomes less than the debt on it, the other spouse may have to use his or her own income or separate property to pay the balance.

Thus, the prenuptial agreement should clearly state how major purchases and joint debt are to be paid for. Spouses who must use separate, nonmarital property to satisfy joint debts or debt of the other spouse should be reimbursed. This can be accomplished in a well thought out prenuptial agreement. Also, the identification of joint funds (wages or other earnings while married) and the use of such funds should be identified.

## 2. Income Tax Returns

A joint debt that always occurs after the marriage is income tax owed on a joint return filed by the married couple, whether federal or state. The total amount of income tax owed on a joint return can be collected from either spouse without regard to which spouse's income or losses produced the amount of tax owed.

As a rule, it is very difficult for a spouse to be relieved of paying joint income taxes, even where the total tax was caused by the other spouse. But there are limited circumstances where a spouse may not be held responsible by the tax authorities for paying joint income taxes. This occurs where a spouse did not know or did not have reason to know that income or losses were omitted or not reported properly on the joint return and where under the circumstances, because of the spouse's ignorance in preparing the joint tax return, it would be unfair to hold that spouse responsible for the total tax.

If a spouse truly does not know about the other's financial affairs, for example, because the other spouse has concealed the information, or the business and financial affairs are too complex for any reasonable person to understand, then the law says it is unfair to hold the unsuspecting spouse responsible for all or a portion of the joint income taxes. The key point is that an "innocent spouse" has to prove his or her status as "innocent" in order to obtain relief from payment.

## Don't Forget

Nonetheless, a so-called "innocent" spouse who signs a joint income tax return cannot simply turn his or her back on the obvious realities of the couple's financial circumstance. What a spouse knows or should have known about the information reported on the tax return is judged by whatever a reasonable person standing in the shoes of the spouse would know or understand.

## 3. Pensions and IRAs

As stated earlier, people use the prenuptial agreement to preserve separate assets for their children of the first marriage or other separate commitments. Pension funds are a classic type of separate asset which a party may want to keep separate from the new spouse. To accomplish and maintain separate asset status for pension funds, prenuptial agreements generally provide that the new spouse waive his or her rights to receive the pension funds of the other spouse. This waiver is necessary because the law mandates that "spouses" be named the primary beneficiary of pension funds. If a spouse is not named a recipient of pension money, the spouse must consent in writing to giving up his or her rights to such money.

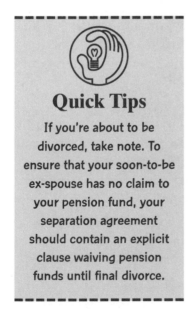

### Quick Tips

If you're about to be divorced, take note. To ensure that your soon-to-be ex-spouse has no claim to your pension fund, your separation agreement should contain an explicit clause waiving pension funds until final divorce.

A person is considered a "spouse" only if he or she is legally married to the other person and the marriage has not been formally ended by a decree of divorce. A legally valid divorce, then, terminates the "spouse" status. A separation agreement alone may not be sufficient.

Prenuptial agreements pose a problem involving the waiver of pension rights because persons entering a prenuptial agreement are *not* "spouses" on the day they sign the agreement. Remember, a prenuptial occurs *before* the marriage even though its terms become effective after the marriage. Since persons signing prenuptial agreements are not married on the day they sign, they are not "spouses." The result is that any waiver of rights to pension funds is not made by a "spouse." As a consequence, any waiver of rights to pension funds contained in a prenuptial agreement is likely not to be valid because it was not signed by a "spouse." The fact that the people signing the prenuptial will become a "spouse" a short time later does not make the waiver valid. In order to validate the waiver right to pension funds that may appear in a prenuptial agreement, it will be necessary for the parties to re-sign the waivers when they become "spouses."

## 4. Other Categories

- A prenuptial agreement can provide for alimony and other maintenance and support, as well as the division of joint or marital property in the event the marriage fails. The prenuptial agreement however cannot deal with child custody issues since this is against public policy.

- The prenuptial agreement cannot eliminate spousal support by one or both parties during the marriage. Similarly, a person cannot be relieved of the obligation to support his or her children. A provision in the prenuptial agreement eliminating or limiting child support is likely not to be enforceable.

- While the prenuptial agreement does not include the parties' wills, it should contain an outline of each party's general intentions of how marital and nonmarital property would be distributed upon death.

The discussion contained in this chapter is only the tip of the iceberg in dealing with prenuptial agreements. Remember, that an attorney should be consulted before drawing up any agreement and that attorney should be separate from the other spouse. And on the topic of marriage, marriage is the only union that cannot be organized because both sides think they are management.

✔ Premarital legal agreements are not just for the rich and famous; they are for everyone who has preexisting, separate property to protect.

✔ While premarital agreements seem "cold and calculating" to some, these agreements usually provide long-term fairness and peace of mind.

✔ Any premarital agreement must meet the conditions of a basic legal contact. That's why it's advisable to draw up such agreements under a lawyer's guidance, rather than trying to do it on your own.

✔ Premarital contracts should address the issues of separate property, separate income, tax returns, pensions, IRAs, alimony, and the division of joint or marital property in case the new marriage fails.

✔ Child custody issues are beyond the scope of premarital contracts.

*Marriage is the only union that cannot be organized, because both sides think they are management.*

# CHAPTER 30

# Unpleasant but Necessary: Health Care Issues for Seniors

*Get everything done before you are.*

**Do I Need to Read This Chapter?**

➡ Have I thought about what will happen to me if I become disabled?

➡ Do I need to provide for my own long-term care?

➡ Am I clear on how to qualify for Medicaid, in the event that I lack long-term care insurance?

➡ Have I considered a prepaid funeral?

➡ Do I understand the life insurance provision known as the accelerated death benefit?

➡ In the event of total incapacity, do I want my life to be artificially prolonged?

➡ Have I drawn up a living will?

Although we do not like to discuss death and disability, at some time these areas must be covered. Especially as a woman, the odds are that you will be alone when a disability may develop. Just walk through any nursing home and see the imbalance in numbers between women and men.

# Is Long-Term Care Insurance Important?

All of us who own a house have homeowners insurance to protect us from the possibility of a fire. Yet, if you are over the age of 65, you have about ten times the chance of going into a nursing home as you do of having your house burn down. We do not, for most of us, think of Long-Term Care Insurance (LTCI) to protect us from the possibility of the tremendous costs of a nursing home stay.

What choice do you have if nursing home care is required? Of course, you could pay for it out of your own pocket, or you could deplete your assets down to the level of meeting state requirements of Medicaid. But that would mean that you would have to give your assets away to meet the 36- to 60-month waiting period. Long-Term Care Insurance is an answer to keeping you independent while protecting the assets you worked your entire life to acquire.

## What Should I Look for in a Long-Term Care Policy?

Recognizing the market for long-term care, many insurance companies are offering some protection, usually pertaining to convalescence in nursing homes or similar health care facilities. Before purchasing such a policy, acquaint yourself with the many terms and concepts they entail:

1. *Type of care*

   - *Skilled care:*  24-hour-a-day care program.
   - *Intermediate care:*  Occasional nursing assistance and rehabilitative care.
   - *Custodial care:*  Helping normal needs (bathing, eating, etc.). Medicare does not cover this.

2. *Elimination period:*   In order to reduce the high cost to you, an elimination period is imposed. This elimination period (from 21 to 365 days) places the cost of daily maintenance on the covered individual for the number of days you choose before the insurance begins to pay. Naturally, the longer the elimination period, the lower the insurance premium, so consider a longer elimination period if you have other assets available to get you through this initial period. Also, make certain that your daily reimbursable rate, once the elimination period is over, is at least two-thirds of the total daily cost of your care.

3. *Guaranteed renewability:*   The policy you choose should have no termination date but should be renewable for life.

4. *Prehospitalization requirement:*   Make certain that the policy does not require that you be hospitalized before being admitted into a nursing home.

5. *Alzheimer's and other disease coverage:*   Certain conditions may not be covered under the policy such as Alzheimer's, which in insurance language is known as an "organically based medical condition."

6. *Inflation adjustment:*   This is a provision that will provide for automatic benefit adjustments to cover any inflationary increases in long-term cost care.

7. *Medical history:*   Be certain you understand about any "pre-existing" medical clauses in the policy.

8. *Facility approval:*   Find out, before you sign up, if the facility you choose is approved by Medicaid so that you can qualify for future benefits.

9. *Tax deduction:*   Just as a sidelight, a portion of the premiums for LTCI is tax deductible if you itemize your tax return. What you do is to add your premium costs to other medical expenses (not reimbursed) and if the total amount exceeds 7.5 percent of your adjusted gross income (AGI) you have a deduction.

## Will Medicaid Cover My Long-Term Care Needs?

People who do not purchase long-term care insurance may eventually qualify for Medicaid, by transferring their funds to other parties. Although I am not in favor of this method of protection, let me explain the procedures. Before August, 1993, people who transferred funds to other parties could be ineligible for Medicaid coverage if their transfer took place less than 30 months prior to entering a nursing home. Now the law increased the time (known as the ineligible or look-back period) to 36 months (and in some cases 60 months) and added a penalty clause, if the transfer was made before the ineligible period was up and the individual filed for Medicaid coverage.

### Quick Tips

Here is some good news for married couples. Although it is true that you must get rid of most of your assets to qualify for Medicaid, you do not have to "go broke" entirely. An at-home spouse can keep up to half of all financial assets with a maximum reaching a bit over $70,000 (varies depending upon your state). You may also keep the house, the car, and personal and household effects not included in the maximum figure.

Let me explain. Each state has an average cost of nursing facility care (about $4000 monthly). The penalty would take the amount of the funds transferred and divide it by the state's average monthly nursing care cost. For example, if an estate of $300,000 is transferred and the individual applies for Medicaid before the ineligible period has been met, the penalty would be computed as $300,000 ÷ $4000 = 75 months. Thus the Medicaid ineligibility period could last for 75 months from the date of the gift. However, if the donor waited until the ineligible period was met before transferring the funds and then afterward applied for Medicaid, he would then qualify for the medical assistance of nursing home care.

Also, if you want to avoid "giving everything away" in order to apply for Medicaid, grant a "Power of Attorney" to your children with instructions for them to enforce the power by paying for your stay out of your funds if you should enter a nursing home, keeping the balance only after you have rightfully qualified for Medicaid.

Bear in mind (depending on the state in which you live in) that there could be a significant difference in the type of care facility and neighborhood you will experience under private-pay versus Medicaid. That one factor alone should make you give a second thought to transferring your assets to your children and living under "artificial poverty," for an event that may never materialize.

---

## Don't Forget

Do you need help in navigating this subject? Many people don't realize it, but thanks to an underpublicized program funded by the Older Americans Act, every state has a public official who can help you through the maze of nursing home complexities. The service is free. Call your state office on aging (listed under the state listings in your phone directory).

---

# What About Prepaid Funerals?

As I have stated before, a female will usually outlive her mate. Thus you will certainly make the funeral arrangements for him, but when you die, who will do this for you?

With today's high cost of funerals, leaving decisions to your grieving family does not make much sense. You could arrange with a funeral home for a preneed plan where you would specify the type of casket and services you would want and then pay for it in installments or one lump sum. There are, however, disadvantages to this arrangement. You may change your mind, you may move, the funeral home may go out of business, or any number of possibilities.

The best method is to plan and pay for your funeral without involving a funeral director or giving up control of your money. Simply write down what you want done and give copies of these instructions to your family or give to whoever you may appoint to enforce your power of attorney.

Moreover, the most sensible method to set aside money for the funeral is to open a Totten trust. In this type of trust, you state that upon your demise, the funds should go to the person designated who is responsible for your funeral. There is no lawyer needed to establish this trust. Because the trust is revocable, you can add or take out money anytime but taxes must be paid on any income from the trust. Although the proceeds will be included in your estate, this trust is not subject to probate so the money can immediately be spent. No specific investment need be used. A simple bank account may be all that is needed.

# What Is the Accelerated Death Benefit?

## Quick Tips

Warning! Despite the advantages of an ADB in certain situations, this option doesn't come easily or inexpensively. There can be additional premium surcharges from 5 to 15 percent or more. Also, certification by a physician must show that the insured is terminally ill and that death should occur no later than one year from the withdrawal of the funds.

The Accelerated Death Benefit, also known as ADB is a provision in a life insurance policy that allows a living person (the insured) to collect from 25 percent to almost the full value of the death benefit of the policy while he or she is still alive tax-free. This situation can occur if the insured is terminally ill and needs money immediately. For the first time in life insurance history, a person does not have to die to make the death benefit available. Each company has its own set of rules, but it is important to know that there now exists this option. What a wonderful idea to be able to have some of that money now so that the insured could close his or her life accomplishing some long held dreams (vacations, gifts, debts paid, etc.) that he or she would never have been able to do were it not for this clause in the policy.

However, ADB defeats the major purpose of life insurance, which is to provide for the surviving beneficiary who must live after the insured passes away. An alternative to the accelerated policy is to borrow against the policy's cash surrender value, if only because that income is not taxable.

# Do You Need a Living Will?

"A living will takes care of you as you die, not afterwards." And that is so important to understand.

I believe that a living will should be drawn up by an attorney. Although prepared forms can be obtained from various organizations and may be acceptable, since the area of living wills is so debatable, I would choose the attorney route for the small additional cost involved. After the will has been completed, I urge you to discuss its contents with your family so that they will understand in absolute terms that it is your intent to have your instructions carried out regardless what they may feel.

A living will should state that you do not wish to have any medical procedure done for you that would artificially prolong your life. "No extraordinary measures" is a phrase commonly used. A while back I came across a letter describing the feelings of an individual regarding "right of choice," and thought it appropriate for my readership:

> *To my family and any other individual responsible for my health and welfare:*
>
> *Realizing that death is a certainty and as much a part of life as being born, if the time comes when I can no longer take part in decisions for my own future, I wish this statement to stand as an expression of my wishes while still of sound mind. I fear the indignities of deterioration, dependence and hopeless pain more than death itself. I therefore ask that medication be mercifully administered to help relieve my suffering. And if there is no reasonable expectation of my recovery, I request that I be allowed to die with dignity and not be kept alive by artificial means or heroic measures.*

## Get Started

In effect, a living will expresses your wishes and enforces your decisions when you are no longer able to do so for yourself. Far from a token gesture, it is a document to be taken seriously and administered with the utmost care. As you contemplate the creation of your living will, take these issues into account:

1. Different states have different requirements for completing and signing a living will.

2. The necessary number of witnesses may vary.

3. Some states specify that witnesses may not be related to you.

4. A notary public may need to attest to the signing of your living will.

5. In some states, living wills are valid for limited periods of time and thus must be updated regularly.

6. Do you live in different states at various times of the year? If so, you must create separate living wills and medical proxy documents for each and every state where you reside—not just the one you claim as your primary residence. This is the only way to be sure your wishes will be honored, regardless of quirks in laws from state to state.

## Will My Living Will Affect My Insurance Policies?

I have been questioned about insurance coverage and the living will. Public policy and state statutes explain that living wills cannot affect an individual's insurance contract. A person's personal decision to have life support systems withheld or withdrawn is not to be considered suicide and thus in no way can invalidate any life insurance policy. But there is much more to say about feelings of choice. I firmly believe that it is each patient's right to decide on his or her life and death. With a person's expectations for life, a person's feeling of pain and a person's expenditure of money, that person is the one who will ultimately pay the price. Therefore, to that person belongs the right to call the tune. But it doesn't always happen that way.

Many adult children or even spouses will not permit the disconnection of a feeding or breathing machine regardless of the wishes of the patient, because most of us do not wish to let go. "Perhaps later," we may say, "after a forthcoming rite of passage (anniversary, graduation, wedding, births of grandchildren, etc.), but not now." We therefore attempt to extend the time by machines and tubes and insane efforts to keep the patient breathing a few more days or weeks. A desperate need born of guilt. All of us must learn to close and say good-bye. Closing does not mean shutting the door and turning away. Closing is the realization that there is our own life after the death of a loved one. It is in the form of memory, and becomes our responsibility to carry that memory while living life to the fullest. Every family member must understand this.

And on the topic of life and death, there is nothing that Nature has made necessary which is more easy than death; we are longer coming into the world than going out of it. There is not any minute of our lives wherein we may not reasonably expect death. What a shame it is over so soon. The more complete one's life is, the less one fears death. . . . People are not afraid of death, per se, but of the incompleteness of their lives.

It's a Wrap

✔ Long-term care insurance can protect your estate from being depleted by long stays in a nursing home or similar facility.

✔ Study the provisions of any long-term care policy very carefully, using the guidelines in this chapter as a starting point.

✔ Medicaid, a type of government health insurance, will pay for long-term care under certain conditions. But be aware of the stringent requirements.

✔ Each state, through its Office of Aging, has a public official who can help guide individuals and families through the maze of long-term care complexities.

✔ The most sensible way to set aside money for your funeral is through a simple and revocable vehicle known as a Totten trust.

✔ Certain life insurance policies offer an Accelerated Death Benefit, allowing you to collect on your policy while you are still alive.

✔ By creating a living will, you can gain control over medical procedures that would artificially prolong your life.

*There is nothing that Nature has made necessary which is more easy than death; we are longer coming into the world than going out of it. There is not any minute of our lives wherein we may not reasonably expect death. What a shame it is over so soon. The more complete one's life is, the less one fears death. . . . People are not afraid of death, per se, but of the incompleteness of their lives.*

# Epilogue

I hope that your reading of the material in this book has given you insight into the financial world and has taken the "utterly confused" status of investing into a more comprehensible realm. Bear in mind:

To look is one thing.
To see what you look at is another.
To understand what you see is a third.
To learn from what you understand is something else.
But to act on what you learn is all that really matters.

And that is the point. You must act now so that you can build a firm financial future for you and your family. Remember that the flowers of all tomorrows are in the seeds of today.

# Index

Accelerated death benefit (ADB) option, 195, 342–343
Actual value, vs. targeted value of investments, 100
Actual yield, on bonds, 31
Adjustable-rate mortgage (ARM), 126
  definition of, 218
  how it works, 218–220
    cap, 219
    index, 219
    interval, 219
Adjustable-rate preferred stock (ARPS), 88
A. M. Best, insurance company ratings service, 11 (chart), 195, 196 (table)
American Association of Retired Persons (AARP), Web site of, for retirement planning, xxii
American Council of Life Insurance, 198
American Municipal Bond Assurance Corporation (AMBAC), 145
America Online, xxi
Annual recalculation method, of withdrawal from IRAs, 255
Annuities:
  classification of, as life insurance, 5–6
  compared with mutual funds, 8

Annuities (*Cont.*):
  distinguishing characteristics of:
    payment return, 7
    premiums, 4–7
    return on investment, 7–8
  evaluation guidelines for, 5
  growth of assets/savings with, 6, 13
  how they work, 4
  insurance company risks associated with:
    credit rating, 10
    dividend payments, 11
    junk-bond holdings, 10–11
    reserves, 11
  repayment options offered with:
    guaranteed-minimum, 9–10
    individual life, 9
    joint-survivor, 9
  tax benefits/consequences of, 12–13
  types of:
    deferred, 7
    fixed-dollar, 7
    guaranteed-minimum, 9–10
    immediate, 7
    individual life, 9
    joint-survivor, 9
    single-premium deferred, 5
    variable, 7–8

Annuitizing, 253
"Appreciation Sharing" clause, 237
Asking price, in bond purchasing, 147
Asset allocation, 317
Assets, joint ownership of:
   community property, 322
   joint tenancy, 321
   tenancy in common, 321

Back-end (rear) load, 73, 194. (*See also* Front-
   end load)
*Beardstown Ladies' Common-Sense Invest-
   ment Guide, The,* 96
Beneficiary, 301
   IRA options concerning, 256–257
Bid/ask differential (*see* Spread)
Bid price, in bond purchasing, 147
Blue-chip stocks, 87
Bondholders, vs. stockholders, 27
Bond market:
   primary, 26
   secondary, 26
Bond mutual funds, 66
Bonds, 26
   callable, 29
   convertible, 30
   corporate, 25–36
   coupon, 27
   debenture, 27
   discounted, 28
   general obligation (GO), 140
   interest rates' inverse relationship to, 28
   junk, 10–11, 34
   municipal, 140–147
      general obligation (GO), 140
      revenue, 140–141
   noncallable, 29
   premium, 28
   registered, 28
   Treasury, 169
   U.S. Savings, 173
      Series EE, 173–182
      Series HH, 182–183
   zero coupon, 106–114
Book value, 97–98
Bullion, 43
Bureau of Public Debt, as source of information for Treasury obligations, 163, 166,
   169, 171, 178

Burial arrangements, as important financial
   record, xix
Bypass trust, 307

Callable bond, 29
Call protection, as investment advantage of
   zero coupon bonds, 29, 108
Cap, of adjustable-rate mortgage, 219
Capital Guaranty (CG), 145
Cash management account (CMA), 122
Cash surrender value, 191–192, 194
Certificates of deposit (CDs), xiv
   comparison of, with other investment
      instruments, 21–23
   guidelines on spreading investments in,
      17
   history/development of, 16
   how they work, 17
   hybrid types of, 22
   justification for purchase of, 18
   primary considerations for planning invest-
      ment in:
      rate of return, 19–21
      term, 18–19
   questions to ask before purchasing, 23
Closing costs, of mortgage financing, 223
CODA (cash or deferred arrangement) provision, of 401(k) plan, 267
Codicil, 290
Collateralized mortgage obligation (CMO),
   131
   basic idea of, 132
   compared to Ginnie Maes, 133, 135–136
   investment safety of, 134–135
   payments, how they work, 132–133
   purchasing of, 134
   risks associated with, 132
   securities backing, 131–132
College tuition, zero coupon bonds as
   investment vehicle of savings for,
   109–110
Common stock, 85–86
   categories of:
      blue-chip stocks, 87
      growth stocks, 87
      income stocks, 87
      speculation stocks, 87
   ownership privileges of, 86–87
   as part of diversified portfolio, xiii

Common stock mutual funds, 64–65
types of:
aggressive growth, 65
global/international, 65
long-term growth, 65
CompuServe, xxi
Computers, use of, in financial
planning/investment, xx–xxiii
Condominium (condo):
advantages of ownership of, 209
definition/nature of, 208–209
disadvantages of ownership of, 209–210
documents needed in ownership of,
210–211
ownership, terms of agreement, 211
as tax-wise investment, 208
Consumer Price Index (CPI), 170, 279
Convertible bond, 30
Cooperative (co-op):
conversions, 215
definition/nature of, 212
investment differences compared with condominium, 212–214
ownership, restrictions/potential liabilities
of, 214
Corporate bonds:
characteristics of, 26–28
factors to be considered in purchase of:
safety, 32–34
yield, 30–32
how they work, 26
and junk bonds, 34
ratings of, 33
sample listing of, 35 (figure)
types of, with respect to:
callability, 29
convertibility, 30
Cost indexes, in assessing relative costs of
similar insurance policies, 192
Cost-of-living adjustment (COLA), 279,
280
Coupon bonds, 27
Coupon rate (*see* Coupon yield)
Coupon yield, on bonds, 31
Credit rating, of insurance companies, 10, 11
(chart), 195, 196 (table)
Credit unions, 16
Current yield, on bonds, 31
"Cutting your losses," xvi

Debentures, 27
Deferred annuity, 7
Deferred salary reduction plan [*see* 401(k)
plan]
Department of Housing and Urban Development (HUD), 120, 234
Diamonds:
comparison with gold, as investment instrument, 45–46
"four C's" characteristics of:
carat, 47
clarity, 47
color, 47
cut, 47
how to purchase, 46
major drawbacks to investment in, 46–47
Discounted bond, 28
Distribution, relationship of, to investment
timing, 76
Diversification:
and investment assessment by age/family
situation, 71
in portfolio planning/management, xiii, xvi
as risk-control investment measure, 60–62
Diversified fund, 61–62
Dividend, 86
Dividend Reinvestment Plans (DRIPs), 76
ownership pros and cons of, 90
Dollar-cost averaging (DCA), 59, 60 (table),
317
in reduction of market risk, 99–100
"Doomsday metal," gold as, 39
Dow Jones Industrial Average (DJIA),
101–102
Down payment, 218
Duration, factor used in bond mutual fund
evaluation, 66

Early withdrawal penalty (EWP):
from annuities, 6
from CDs, 19, 22
from IRAs, 254
Earnings per share, 97
Economic Recovery Tax Act (1981), 197
Effective annual yield, 20
Effective interest rate, of mortgages, 219
Equivalent taxable yield, 143, 144 (table)
formula for determination of, 143
Escheat, 295

Estate planning, vehicles of:
   bypass trust, 307
   cash gifts, 306–307
   irrevocable trusts, 307–310
   revocable living trusts, 300–305
   self-cancellation installment notes (SCIN), 307
Executor:
   as administrator of will, 290
   duties of, 291

401(k) plan, xix
   definition of, 266
   how it differs from ordinary IRA, 266–267
   how it works, 267
   investments, in ex-employer's stock, 268–269
   qualification requirements for, 266
   withdrawal from, 268
   zero coupon bonds as investment choice for, 106
403(b), retirement plan for nonprofit organization employees, 266, 274
Face value, of bonds, 27
Family of (mutual) funds, 52, 59
Fannie Mae reverse mortgage ("Home Keeper"), 235
Fannie Maes:
   how they work, 130–131
   risks of investment in, 131
Federal Home Loan Mortgage Corporation (FHLMC), 123, 130
Federal Housing Administration (FHA), 234, 235
   government-insured mortgages of, 120
Federal National Mortgage Association (FNMA), 123, 130
Federal Reserve banks, 158–160
   locations/phone numbers for, 161 (figure)
Federal Reserve Board, 16, 142
Federal Reserve system, 161 (figure)
Financial Guaranty Insurance Company (FGIC), 145
Financial planners:
   choosing of, 316
   types of, 318–319
Financial planning:
   age guidelines in, xiii
   dealing with financial risk, xiv–xv
   how to begin, x, xii

Financial planning (*Cont.*):
   keeping of financial records/documents in, xix
   overcoming obstacles:
      inflation, xv–xvi
      interest rate risk, xvi
      procrastination, xviii
      taxation, xviii
   use of computers in, xix–xxiii
      on-line financial planning resources, xx–xxi
      resources for retirement planning, xxi
   for women, 314–315
      advised to have own wills, 319–320
      choosing professional financial planner, 316, 318–319
      guidelines for, 324
      joint asset ownership, types of, 321–322
      self-education guidelines, 317
      where to begin, 315–316
Financial records, importance of keeping, xix
Financial Tools, financial planning/investment software, xx
First in–first out (FIFO) rule, 64, 74, 90
Five-year forward averaging, 244–245
Fixed-dollar annuity, 7
Foreclosure, 353
Freddie Macs:
   how they work, 130–131
   risks of investment in, 131
Front-end load, 72. (*See also* Back-end load)
Fund-swapping option, as advantage of mutual fund ownership, 63

Gemological Institute of America (GIA), 46, 47
General obligation (GO) bonds, 140
Ginnie Maes:
   additional factors for consideration of, 126–127
   compared to CMOs, 133
   drawback of investing in, 123
   effect of current interest rates on, 125–126
   how they work, 120–121
   investment safety of, 121
   maturity of, 124
   method of income payment to investors, 121–124
   purchase of, by small investor, 127

Ginnie Maes (*Cont.*):
  as short-term investment instrument, unsuitability of, 124
Goals:
  consideration of, in CD purchase, 18
  importance of, in financial planning, x
  and target dates, interest tables for, xi–xii
Gold:
  characteristics of, as asset/medium of exchange, 38
  as investment instrument, 38–39
  karat, as unit of fineness for, 41
  options for investing in, 41, 42 (table)
    bullion, 43
    certificates, 44
    coins, 43
    stocks, 43–44
  relationship to diamonds, 46–47
  relationship to silver, 44–45
  risks associated with investments in, 40–41
  value of:
    factors involved in, 38
    volatility of, 40
Good till canceled (GTC) order, 84
Government National Mortgage Association (GNMA), 120, 130
Great Depression, 34
Growth stocks, 87
Guaranteed-minimum annuity, 9–10

Health care issues, for seniors:
  Accelerated Death Benefit (ADB), 342–343
  living will, 343–345
  long-term care insurance (LTCI), 338–341
  prepaid funerals, 341–342
Home Equity Conversion Mortgage (HECM), 234–235
Home equity loan, 225–227
  basic types of:
    fixed-rate, 227
    revolving line of credit account, 226
  tax ramifications of refinancing, 227–228
"Home Keeper" (*see* Fannie Mae reverse mortgage)

Immediate annuity, 7
Imputed interest, 109
Income stocks, 87
Index, of adjusted-rate mortgage, 219

Individual life annuity, 9
Individual Retirement Accounts (IRAs), 12, 17
  beneficiary options concerning, 256–257
  definition of, 250
  guidelines for choosing investment options for, 259–260
  how it works/grows, 250–252
  investment options available for, 258
    certificates of deposit, 258–259
    mutual funds, 259
    stocks and bonds, 259
  methods of annual withdrawal from, 255–256
  penalties of early withdrawal from, 254
  relation to revocable living trusts, 257–258
  rollover distribution to:
    adding after-tax funds, 261
    "direct rollover," 261
    lump-sum distribution, 244–246
  Roth, 252
  rules for distribution of, 253–254
  spousal, 251
  tax consequences of, 252
  zero coupon bonds as investment choice for, 106
Inflation:
  impact of, on investment objectives, xv–xvi
  rate, effect on cost of living, xxii (table)
Initial public offering (IPO), 85, 86
Insurance (*see* Life insurance; Long-term care insurance)
Interest rate risk, impact of, on investment objectives, xvi
Interest rates, bonds' inverse relationship to, 28
Internet, xx
Internet Service Provider (ISP), xxi
Interrorem clause ("no-contest" clause), of wills, 294
Interval, of adjustable-rate mortgage, 219
Intervivos trust (*see* Revocable living trust)
Intestacy, 295
Investment clubs, 96
Investment planning, age considerations in, xiii–xiv
Irrevocable trusts:
  in estate planning, 309–310
  how they work, 307–308

Joint-survivor annuity, 9
Junk bonds, holdings of, and strength/rating
    of insurance companies, 10–11

Karat, unit of fineness for gold, 41
Keogh plan, xix
    differences with IRAs, 271–272
    how it works, 270
    qualifications for, 273
    zero coupon bonds as investment choice
        for, 106

Laddering, as method of diversifying bond
        portfolio, 146
Life insurance:
    Accelerated Death Benefit (ADB),
        342–343
    additional policy types/options of, 195, 197
    annuities classified as, 5–6
    arguments against purchasing, for children,
        189
    assessing company solvency, 12
    company ratings, 11 (chart)
        importance of, 194–195, 196 (table)
    evaluating costs of different policies of,
        192
    guidelines for choosing policy, 197–198
    guidelines for purchasing right amount of,
        188
    investment benefits of, 189
    program types of, 190 (table)
        straight (whole) life, 191–192
        term, 190–191
        universal life, 192–194
    purpose of, 188
Life Insurance Guaranty Fund, 12
Limit order, 84
Line of credit, 235
Liquidity:
    as factor in financial planning, xiv
    of zero coupon bonds, 108, 109
Living will, 300, 343–345
    creation of, issues to be taken into account
        in, 344
    effect on insurance policies, 344
Load fund, 72
Long-term care insurance (LTCI):
    importance of, 338
    and Medicaid, 340–341
    policy provisions/terms, 338–339

Managing Your Money, financial
        planning/investment software, xx
Market order, 84
Maturity date, of bonds, 27
Medicaid, and coverage of long-term care
        needs, 340–341
"Medicaid planning," 308
Medicare, 278, 284
Member firm, 83
Microsoft Money, financial planning/invest-
        ment software, xx
Microsoft Network (MSN), xxi
Money market deposit account (MMDA):
    how they work, 52–53
    investment safety considerations of, 55–56
    vs. money market funds, similarities/differ-
        ences, 53–55
Money market funds:
    families of, 52
    how they work, 50–51
    investment safety considerations of, 55–56
    as "parking lot," 50
    small investor access to prevailing interest
        rates of, 50
    types of:
        general, 51
        government-only, 51
        tax-free, 51–52
    vs. bank-issued money market deposit
        accounts, similarities/differences, 53–55
Moody's Investor Services, 135, 145
    bond-rating scale of, 33
    insurance company ratings service of, 11
        (chart), 195, 196 (table)
Mortgage-backed investments (*see* Collateral-
        ized mortgage obligation; Fannie
        Maes; Freddie Macs; Ginnie Maes)
Mortgages:
    basic requirements for, 220
    basic terms relating to:
        effective interest rate, 219
        origination fee, 219
        PITI (principal, interest, taxes, insur-
            ance) total monthly payment, 219
        simple interest rate, 219
    government-insured, 120–121
    and home equity loans, 225
        basic types of, 226–227
        tax ramifications of refinancing, 227–228
    monthly payment schedule, 222 (table)

Mortgages (*Cont.*):
  refinancing of, 220–221
  reverse (RM), 230–239
  tax considerations/benefits in financing of,
    223–225
  types of:
    adjustable-rate (ARM), 218–220
    fixed-rate, 218
Municipal Bond Insurance Association
    (MBIA), 145
Municipal bond mutual funds, 150
  compared to municipal bond unit trusts,
    153, 154 (table), 155
  how they work, 153
  similarity to money market funds, 153,
    155
  as tax-free investment vehicle, 150
Municipal bonds, xiv
  callability of, 140
  finding best bond value, 147
  how they work, 140
  investment advantages of:
    diversity, 142
    high collateral value, 141–142
    marketability, 142
    safety, 141
    tax exemption, 141
  investment disadvantages of, 142–144
  investment risks of, 144–145
  purchasing strategies of, 146–147
  types of:
    general obligation (GO) bonds, 140
    revenue bonds, 140–141
Municipal bond unit trust, 150
  compared to municipal bond mutual funds,
    153, 154 (table), 155
  how it works, 150–152
  shares, 151
  as tax-free investment instrument, 150
  types of, 151
Munis (*see* Municipal bonds)
Mutual funds, xiii
  available information on, 77–78
  computing taxes on, 73
    average price per share, 74
    first in–first out (FIFO), 74, 75
    specific shares, 74, 75
  costs of ownership of:
    load funds, 72
    no-load funds, 72–73

Mutual funds (*Cont.*):
  factors to consider when choosing:
    expenses, 70
    management, 70
    past performance, 70
    personal goals, 71
    risk, 70
  getting started in, 59
  how they work, 58–60
  ownership advantages of, 60–64
  sample listing of, 77 (figure)
  taxable gains on, 75–76
  types of:
    bond funds, 66
    common-stock funds, 64–65

NASDAQ Composite, 103–104
National Association of Investment Clubs
    (NAIC), 96
National Association of Securities Dealers
    Automated Quotations (NASDAQ),
    84
Net asset value (NAV), 64, 75–77
  of municipal bond mutual funds, 153
New York Stock Exchange (NYSE), 83
No-load fund, 72–73
Noncallable bonds, 29
Nondiversified fund, 61–62

Odd-lot order, 84
Opportunity cost, 40
Origination fee, of mortgages, 219
"Over the counter" stocks, 84–85
  sample listing of, 85 (figure)

"Parking lot," money market accounts consid-
    ered as, 50
"Parking lot theory," of CD investment,
    18
Participation certificates (PCs), 130
Par value, 28
Pass-through certificates, 120
Penalties, early withdrawal (EWP):
  from annuities, 6
  from CDs, 19, 22
  from IRAs, 254
"Phantom income," 112
PITI (principal, interest, taxes, insurance),
    total monthly payment of, 219
Points, of mortgage financing, 223–225

Pool factor, 126
Pools, of GNMA's grouped mortgages, 120
Pool speed, 126
Portfolio, diversification in planning/management of, xiii
Power of attorney, 304
Precious metals, investing in, 37–48
Preferred stock, 87–88
Premium bonds, 28
Prenuptial agreement, 292, 320
    categories to be addressed in, 329–331, 334–335
        income tax returns, 332–333
        pensions/IRAs, 333–334
        separate property/separate income, 331–332
    definition/nature of, 328
    elements of, 329
Prepaid funerals, 341–342
Prepayment risk, 135
Pre-refunded premium bonds, 146–147
Price/earnings (P/E) ratio, 95, 97, 98
Primary bond market, 26
Principal, security of, as factor in financial planning, xiii
Private reverse mortgage, 236
Procrastination, impact of, on investment objectives, xviii
Prodigy, xxi
Prospectus, 5, 61

Quicken, financial planning/management software, xx

Rate of return, 97–99
Real estate:
    benefits of, 200–201
    as investment:
        guidelines for purchase of, 202
        REITs as alternative to direct purchase of, 203–206
        rules governing, 201
        tax benefits of selling home, 201
Real estate investment trust (REIT):
    as alternative to direct real estate purchase, 203
    basic categories of:
        equity, 204
        mortgage, 204

Real estate investment trust (REIT) (*Cont.*):
    points to consider before purchase of, 205–206
    pros and cons of, 203–205
Recognition agreement, of co-op ownership, 213
Regional delivery system (RDS), 176
Registered bond, 28
Reinvestment risk, 122
Remarriage, financial ramifications of, 320
"Request for Earnings and Benefit Estimate Statement" (Form SSA-7004), from Social Security Administration, 281–282
Residuary clause, of will, 290
Retirement planning:
    computer software/Web sites available for, xxi–xxiii
    early retirement considerations, 242–243
    and handling lump-sum distributions, 243
        comparison of methods, 245–246
        5-year forward averaging, 244–245
        rollover into IRA, 244, 245
Retire Secure (Price Waterhouse), retirement planning software, xxii
Return on investment (ROI):
    classification of annuities by, 7–8
    as factor in financial planning, xiv
Revenue bonds, 140–141
Reverse mortgage (RM):
    additional information/caveats concerning, 237–238
    beneficial effect of, on retirement, 230
    definition/nature of, 230–231
    determination of payment amount, 233–234
    drawbacks of, 232–233
    eligibility determinants for, 231
    methods of income payment, 235
    payout methods of, 231
    structure of, 232
    types of:
        Fannie Mae, 235
        Home Equity Conversion Mortgage (HECM), 234–235
        private reverse mortgage, 236
        uninsured (fixed-term RM), 236
Revocable living trust:
    creation of, 300–301
    disadvantages of, 304–305

Revocable living trust (*Cont.*):
  major advantages of, 302–304
  relationship of IRAs to, 257
"Rising debt" loans, 232
Risk:
  associated with CMOs, 132
  associated with investment in gold, 40–41
  balanced against security, xv
  as disadvantage of stock investment/owner-
    ship, 89
  as factor to consider in choosing mutual
    fund, 70
  guidelines for handling, xvi
  interest rate, xvi
  of investing in Freddie Macs, 131
  management of, in financial planning,
    xiv–xv
  of municipal bond investment, 144–145
  prepayment, 135
  reinvestment, 122
Risk-reward balance, xvi
Rollover, vs. transfer of IRA funds, 261–264
Round-lot order, 84
Rule of 72, xviii

Savings and loan association, 16
Savings bank, 16
Secondary bond market, 26
"Second to die" policy, 195, 197
Secured bonds, 27
Securities and Exchange Commission (SEC),
  6, 55, 73, 77
Self-cancellation installment notes (SCIN), 307
Series EE bonds, 174
  earned interest on, 176–178
  effect of taxes on, 179–180
  how they work, 174–175
  how to purchase, 175–176
  redemption of, 178–179
  registration options for, 177 (table)
  role of, in planning for college, 180–182
Series HH bonds, 174, 182–183
Silver, as investment instrument, 37, 44–45
Simple interest rate, of mortgages, 219
SIMPLE (Savings Incentive Match Plan for
  Employees), tax-deductible retirement
  plan, 273–274
Simplified employee pension (SEP), xix
  benefits of, 271
  how it works, 269–270

Single master account, of Treasury securities
  holdings, 162
Single-premium deferred annuity (SPDA), 5
Social security:
  changes planned for, 282–283
  determination of accurate benefits from,
    281–282
  family benefits of, 284–285
  how system works, 278–279
  options, for retiring women, 283–284
  qualifying for retirement benefits of, 278
  retiring after age 65, 280–281
  retiring before age 65, 279
  trust funds comprising social security insur-
    ance (SSI) program:
    DI (disability insurance), 278
    HI (health insurance, or Medicare), 278
    OASI (old age and survivors insurance),
      278
  and "unretirement," 279–280
Social Security Administration (SSA), 280
  Web site of, xxii, 282
Speculation, xiii
Speculative stocks, 87
Spread:
  as bid/ask differential, 163
  in municipal bond purchasing, 147
  in municipal bond unit trust
    purchasing/selling, 152
Standard & Poor's (S&P), 135, 145
  bond-rating scale of, 33
  Composite Index (S&P 500), 102–103
  insurance company rating service, 11
    (chart), 12, 195, 196 (table)
  Web site of, for general financial informa-
    tion, xxii
Step-up CD, 22
Stock exchanges:
  organized, 83
  unorganized ("over the counter"),
    84–85
Stockholders, vs. bondholders, 27
Stock market:
  commonsense approaches to, 103
  how investors purchase stocks in, 84–85
  how it works, 82–83
  indicators/indexes, 100–101
    Dow Jones Industrial Average (DJIA),
      101–102
    NASDAQ Composite, 103–104

Stock market, indicators/indexes (*Cont.*):
  Standard & Poor's Composite Index
    (S&P 500), 102–103
  kinds of stocks available:
    common, 85–87
    preferred, 87–88
  learning about investing in, 94–95
  statistical evaluation of stocks in, 97–99
Stock market indexes:
  Dow Jones Industrial Average (DJIA),
    101–102
  NASDAQ Composite, 103–104
  Standard & Poor's Composite Index (S&P
    500), 102–103
Stocks:
  dollar cost averaging (DCA) for risk reduc-
    tion in purchase of, 99–100
  evaluation of, statistics used in:
    book value, 97–98
    earnings per share, 97
    price/earnings (P/E) ratio, 97, 98
    rate of return, 97, 98–99
    yield, 97, 98
  how to purchase, 84
  information from newspaper columns on,
    explained, 95 (figure)
  investment advantages of, 88–89
  investment disadvantages of, 89–90
  over-the-counter (OTC), 84–85, 94
  role of investment clubs in purchase of, 96
  sample listing, 95 (figure)
  types of:
    common, 85–87
    preferred, 87–88
  (*See also* Stock market)
Stop order, xvi, 84
Straight life insurance:
  evaluating costs of different policies, 192
  how it works, 191–192
  superior investment value of, 192
Stripped Treasuries, as safest of zero coupon
    bonds, 113

Targeted value, vs. actual value, of invest-
    ments, 100
Taxable equivalence, decision factor in pur-
    chase of zero coupon bonds, 114
Taxation, impact of, on investment objectives,
    xviii
Taxpayer Relief Act (1997), 201–202

Tax Reform Act (1986), 227
Tax-sheltered annuities (TSAs), 274
Tax status, as factor in financial planning, xiv
Technical and Miscellaneous Revenue Act of
    1988 (TAMRA '88), 180–181
"Tenders," Treasury securities bids,
    159–160
Tenure plan, 235
10-year certain contract, type of guaranteed-
    minimum annuity, 10
Term-certain method, of withdrawal from
    IRAs, 255
Term insurance:
  decreasing term policy, 190
  how it works, 190–191
  level term policy, 190
Term plan, 235
Testator, 288
Third-party guarantee, in municipal bond
    purchase, 145
Total Annual Loan Cost (TALC), of reverse
    mortgages, 233–234
Tranches ("slices"), of CMOs, 132
Transfer, vs. rollover of IRA funds, 261–264
Treasury bills (T-bills):
  how they work, 164
  interest paid on, 167
  at maturity, 168
  nature of, 164
  purchase of, directly from Federal Reserve,
    166–167
  tax consequences of, 167–168
Treasury bonds, 169
Treasury Direct System, 160
  benefits of, 162
  new rules promulgated to overcome prob-
    lems of, 162–163
  obtaining information on, 163
  types of ownership registration through,
    163
  use of direct-deposit payment method in,
    161–162
Treasury Inflation Protection Securities
    (TIPS), 169–171
Treasury notes, 169
  compared to CDs, 22–23
Treasury obligations:
  methods of purchasing, 158
    directly from government, 159–163
    by direct purchase, 159

Treasury obligations, methods of purchasing (*Cont.*):
  through secondary market, 163–164
  obtaining more information concerning, 163, 166, 169, 171
  price closing table for, 165 (figure)
  TIPS (Treasury Inflation Protection Securities), 169–171
  Treasury bills (T-bills), 164–168
  Treasury bonds, 169
  Treasury notes, 169
Trustee, 301
Trustor (grantor), 301
Trust(s):
  as alternative to having will, 300
  bypass, in estate planning, 307
  documents, principals of:
    beneficiary, 301
    trustee, 301
    trustor (grantor), 301
  irrevocable:
    in estate planning, 309–310
    how they work, 307–308
  revocable living:
    creation of, 300–301
    disadvantages of, 304–305
    major advantages of, 302–304
Turnover rate, factor used in stock mutual fund evaluation, 62

Underwriter, 86
Uniform Prenuptial Agreement Act (UPAA), 329
Unit Investment Trust (UIT) (*see* Municipal bond unit trust)
Universal life insurance:
  features/options of, 193–194
  how it works, 192–193
"Unretirement," 279–280
U.S. Savings Bonds:
  how to purchase, 175–176
  Series EE bonds, 174
    earned interest on, 176–178
    effect of taxes on, 179–180
    how they work, 174–175
    redemption of, 178–179
    registration options for, 177 (table)
    role of, in planning for college, 180–182
  Series HH bonds, 174, 182–183
U.S. Treasury Department, 158

Vanguard Retirement Manager (Vanguard Group), retirement planning software, xxi–xxii
Vanishing premium, 193
Variable annuity, 7–8
Variable-rate certificates of deposit, 21
Veterans Administration (VA), government-insured mortgages of, 120

Web sites, for general financial information, xxii
Whole life insurance (*see* Straight life insurance)
Will(s):
  carrying out instructions of, 290–291
  consequences of dying without, 295
  contesting of, 294
  definition/nature of, 288–289
  drawing up of, 289–290
  duties of executor, 291
  events precipitating changes to, 290
  keeping updated, as important financial record, xix
  probate of, guidelines for successful/smooth, 292–294
  property passed through, 294–295
  separate, spouses' need for, 292
  vital importance of, 288
  women should have their own, 319–320
World Wide Web, xxi

Yield, 97, 98
  associated with bonds:
    actual yield, 31
    coupon yield, 31
    current yield, 31
    yield to maturity (YTM), 31–32
  effective annual, 20
  equivalent taxable (ETY), 143, 144 (table)
Yield to call, 108–109
Yield to maturity (YTM), on bonds, 31–32
  example calculation of, 32

Zero coupon bonds:
  disadvantages of, 110–112
    strategies/questions to minimize, 112
  how they work, 106–108
  investment advantages of:
    adaptability, 108, 109

Zero coupon bonds, investment advantages of (*Cont.*):
    call protection, 108
    liquidity, 108, 109
    suitability for tuition savings, 108, 109–110

Zero coupon bonds (*Cont.*):
    personal determination of best type of, 114
    price schedule for, 107 (table)
    vs. zero coupon municipal bonds, 112–113
Zero coupon municipal bonds, 110, 112–113

# About the Author

Joel Lerner is professor and former chairman of the Business Division at Sullivan County Community College, a part of SUNY, where he has taught for over 35 years. He has authored numerous books which have sold over a million copies. He has produced his own TV and radio series, and addresses thousands of people every year on financial management.